Student Solutions Manual to Accompany
LOSS MODELS

Student Solutions Manual to Accompany

LOSS MODELS

From Data to Decisions

Fourth Edition

Stuart A. Klugman
Society of Actuaries

Harry H. Panjer
University of Waterloo

Gordon E. Willmot
University of Waterloo

SOCIETY OF ACTUARIES

A JOHN WILEY & SONS, INC., PUBLICATION

Published by John Wiley & Sons, Inc., Hoboken, New Jersey
Published simultaneously in Canada

For general information on our other products and services or for technical support, please contact our
Customer Care Department within the United States at (800) 762-2974, outside the United States at
(317) 572-3993 or fax (317) 572-4002.

Wiley also publishes its books in a variety of electronic formats. Some content that appears in print may
not be available in electronic formats. For more information about Wiley products, visit our web site at
www.wiley.com.

Library of Congress Cataloging-in-Publication Data is available.

ISBN 978-1-118-31531-6

10 9 8 7 6 5 4 3 2 1

CONTENTS

CHAPTER 1

INTRODUCTION

The solutions presented in this manual reflect the authors' best attempt to provide insights and answers. While we have done our best to be complete and accurate, errors may occur and there may be more elegant solutions. Errata will be posted at the ftp site dedicated to the text and solutions manual:

ftp://ftp.wiley.com/public/sci_tech_med/loss_models/

Should you find errors or would like to provide improved solutions, please send your comments to Stuart Klugman at sklugman@soa.org.

Student Solutions Manual to Accompany Loss Models: From Data to Decisions, Fourth **1** *Edition.* By Stuart A. Klugman, Harry H. Panjer, Gordon E. Willmot
Copyright © 2012 John Wiley & Sons, Inc.

CHAPTER 2

CHAPTER 2 SOLUTIONS

2.1 SECTION 2.2

2.1 $F_5(x) = 1 - S_5(x) = \begin{cases} 0.01x, & 0 \le x < 50, \\ 0.02x - 0.5, & 50 \le x < 75. \end{cases}$

$f_5(x) = F_5'(x) = \begin{cases} 0.01, & 0 < x < 50, \\ 0.02, & 50 \le x < 75. \end{cases}$

$h_5(x) = \dfrac{f_5(x)}{S_5(x)} = \begin{cases} \dfrac{1}{100 - x}, & 0 < x < 50, \\ \dfrac{1}{75 - x}, & 50 \le x < 75. \end{cases}$

2.2 The requested plots follow. The triangular spike at zero in the density function for Model 4 indicates the 0.7 of discrete probability at zero.

Edition. By Stuart A. Klugman, Harry H. Panjer, Gordon E. Willmot

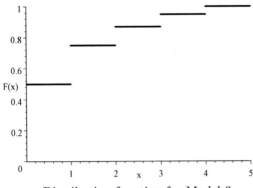

Distribution function for Model 3.

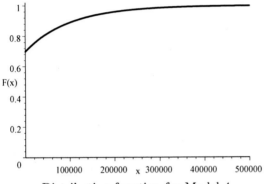

Distribution function for Model 4.

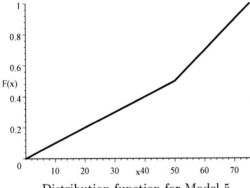

Distribution function for Model 5.

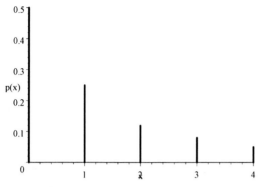

Probability function for Model 3.

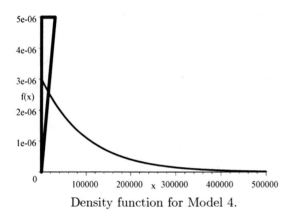

Density function for Model 4.

Density function for Model 5.

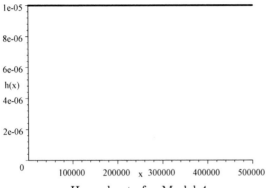

Hazard rate for Model 4.

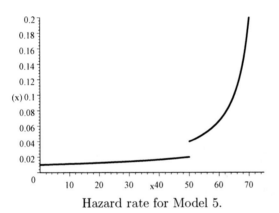

Hazard rate for Model 5.

2.3 $f'(x) = 4(1+x^2)^{-3} - 24x^2(1+x^2)^{-4}$. Setting the derivative equal to zero and multiplying by $(1+x^2)^4$ give the equation $4(1+x^2) - 24x^2 = 0$. This is equivalent to $x^2 = 1/5$. The only positive solution is the mode of $1/\sqrt{5}$.

2.4 The survival function can be recovered as

$$
\begin{aligned}
0.5 &= S(0.4) = e^{-\int_0^{0.4} A + e^{2x}\, dx} \\
&= e^{-Ax - 0.5e^{2x}\big|_0^{0.4}} \\
&= e^{-0.4A - 0.5e^{0.8} + 0.5}.
\end{aligned}
$$

Taking logarithms gives

$$-0.693147 = -0.4A - 1.112770 + 0.5,$$

and thus $A = 0.2009$.

2.5 The ratio is

$$
\begin{aligned}
r &= \frac{\left(\dfrac{10,000}{10,000+d}\right)^2}{\left(\dfrac{20,000}{20,000+d^2}\right)^2} \\
&= \left(\frac{20,000+d^2}{20,000+2d}\right)^2 \\
&= \frac{20,000^2 + 40,000d^2 + d^4}{20,000^2 + 80,000d + 4d^2}.
\end{aligned}
$$

From observation or two applications of L'Hôpital's rule, we see that the limit is infinity.

CHAPTER 3

CHAPTER 3 SOLUTIONS

3.1 SECTION 3.1

3.1
$$\mu_3 = \int_{-\infty}^{\infty} (x - \mu)^3 f(x) dx = \int_{-\infty}^{\infty} (x^3 - 3x^2\mu + 3x\mu^2 - \mu^3) f(x) dx$$
$$= \mu_3' - 3\mu_2'\mu + 2\mu^3,$$

$$\mu_4 = \int_{-\infty}^{\infty} (x - \mu)^4 f(x) dx$$
$$= \int_{-\infty}^{\infty} (x^4 - 4x^3\mu + 6x^2\mu^2 - 4x\mu^3 + \mu^4) f(x) dx$$
$$= \mu_4' - 4\mu_3'\mu + 6\mu_2'\mu^2 - 3\mu^4.$$

3.2 For Model 1, $\sigma^2 = 3{,}333.33 - 50^2 = 833.33$, $\sigma = 28.8675$.
$\mu_3' = \int_0^{100} x^3(0.01) dx = 250{,}000$, $\mu_3 = 0$, $\gamma_1 = 0$.
$\mu_4' = \int_0^{100} x^4(0.01) dx = 20{,}000{,}000$, $\mu_4 = 1{,}250{,}000$, $\gamma_2 = 1.8$.

Student Solutions Manual to Accompany Loss Models: From Data to Decisions, Fourth **9** *Edition.* By Stuart A. Klugman, Harry H. Panjer, Gordon E. Willmot Copyright © 2012 John Wiley & Sons, Inc.

For Model 2, $\sigma^2 = 4,000,000 - 1,000^2 = 3,000,000$, $\sigma = 1,732.05$. μ_3' and μ_4' are both infinite so the skewness and kurtosis are not defined.

For Model 3, $\sigma^2 = 2.25 - .93^2 = 1.3851$, $\sigma = 1.1769$.
$\mu_3' = 0(0.5) + 1(0.25) + 8(0.12) + 27(0.08) + 64(0.05) = 6.57$, $\mu_3 = 1.9012$,
$\gamma_1 = 1.1663$, $\mu_4' = 0(0.5) + 1(0.25) + 16(0.12) + 81(0.08) + 256(0.05) = 21.45$,
$\mu_4 = 6.4416$, $\gamma_2 = 3.3576$.

For Model 4, $\sigma^2 = 6,000,000,000 - 30,000^2 = 5,100,000,000$, $\sigma = 71,414$.
$\mu_3' = 0^3(0.7) + \int_0^\infty x^3(0.000003)e^{-.00001x}dx = 1.8 \times 10^{15}$,
$\mu_3 = 1.314 \times 10^{15}$, $\gamma_1 = 3.6078$.
$\mu_4' = \int_0^\infty x^4(0.000003)e^{-.00001x}dx = 7.2 \times 10^{20}$, $\mu_4 = 5.3397 \times 10^{20}$,
$\gamma_2 = 20.5294$.

For Model 5, $\sigma^2 = 2,395.83 - 43.75^2 = 481.77$, $\sigma = 21.95$.
$\mu_3' = \int_0^{50} x^3(0.01)dx + \int_{50}^{75} x^3(0.02)dx = 142,578.125$, $\mu_3 = -4,394.53$,
$\gamma_1 = -0.4156$.
$\mu_4' = \int_0^{50} x^4(0.01)dx + \int_{50}^{75} x^4(0.02)dx = 8,867,187.5$, $\mu_4 = 439,758.30$,
$\gamma_2 = 1.8947$.

3.3 The standard deviation is the mean times the coefficient of variation, or 4, and so the variance is 16. From (3.3) the second raw moment is $16 + 2^2 = 20$. The third central moment is (using Exercise 3.1) $136 - 3(20)(2) + 2(2)^3 = 32$. The skewness is the third central moment divided by the cube of the standard deviation, or $32/4^3 = 1/2$.

3.4 For a gamma distribution the mean is $\alpha\theta$. The second raw moment is $\alpha(\alpha + 1)\theta^2$, and so the variance is $\alpha\theta^2$. The coefficient of variation is $\sqrt{\alpha\theta^2}/\alpha\theta = \alpha^{-1/2} = 1$. Therefore $\alpha = 1$. The third raw moment is $\alpha(\alpha + 1)(\alpha + 2)\theta^3 = 6\theta^3$. From Exercise 3.1, the third central moment is $6\theta^3 - 3(2\theta^2)\theta + 2\theta^3 = 2\theta^3$ and the skewness is $2\theta^3/(\theta^2)^{3/2} = 2$.

3.5 For Model 1,

$$e(d) = \frac{\int_d^{100}(1 - 0.01x)dx}{1 - 0.01d} = \frac{100 - d}{2}.$$

For Model 2,

$$e(d) = \frac{\int_d^\infty \left(\dfrac{2,000}{x + 2,000}\right)^3 dx}{\left(\dfrac{2,000}{d + 2,000}\right)^3} = \frac{2,000 + d}{2}.$$

For Model 3,

$$
e(d) = \begin{cases}
\dfrac{0.25(1-d) + 0.12(2-d) + 0.08(3-d) + 0.05(4-d)}{0.5} & \\
\quad = 1.86 - d, & 0 \le d < 1, \\[2mm]
\dfrac{0.12(2-d) + 0.08(3-d) + 0.05(4-d)}{0.25} = 2.72 - d, & 1 \le d < 2, \\[2mm]
\dfrac{0.08(3-d) + 0.05(4-d)}{0.13} = 3.3846 - d, & 2 \le d < 3, \\[2mm]
\dfrac{0.05(4-d)}{0.05} = 4 - d, & 3 \le d < 4.
\end{cases}
$$

For Model 4,

$$
e(d) = \frac{\int_d^\infty 0.3 e^{-0.00001x}\,dx}{0.3 e^{-0.00001d}} = 100{,}000.
$$

The functions are straight lines for Models 1, 2, and 4. Model 1 has negative slope, Model 2 has positive slope, and Model 4 is horizontal.

3.6 For a uniform distribution on the interval from 0 to w, the density function is $f(x) = 1/w$. The mean residual life is

$$
\begin{aligned}
e(d) &= \frac{\int_d^w (x-d) w^{-1}\,dx}{\int_d^w w^{-1}\,dx} \\[2mm]
&= \frac{\left.\dfrac{(x-d)^2}{2w}\right|_d^w}{\dfrac{w-d}{w}} \\[2mm]
&= \frac{(w-d)^2}{2(w-d)} \\[2mm]
&= \frac{w-d}{2}.
\end{aligned}
$$

The equation becomes

$$
\frac{w - 30}{2} = \frac{100 - 30}{2} + 4,
$$

with a solution of $w = 108$.

3.7 From the definition,

$$
e(\lambda) = \frac{\int_\lambda^\infty (x - \lambda)\lambda^{-1} e^{-x/\lambda}\,dx}{\int_\lambda^\infty \lambda^{-1} e^{-x/\lambda}\,dx} = \lambda.
$$

3.8
$$E(X) = \int_0^\infty xf(x)dx = \int_0^d xf(x)dx + \int_d^\infty df(x)dx + \int_d^\infty (x-d)f(x)dx$$
$$= \int_0^d xf(x)dx + d[1 - F(d)] + e(d)S(d) = E[X \wedge d] + e(d)S(d).$$

3.9 For Model 1, from (3.8),
$$E[X \wedge u] = \int_0^u x(0.01)dx + u(1 - 0.01u) = u(1 - 0.005u)$$

and from (3.10),
$$E[X \wedge u] = 50 - \frac{100 - u}{2}(1 - 0.01u) = u(1 - 0.005u).$$

From (3.9),
$$E[X \wedge u] = -\int_{-\infty}^0 0\,dx + \int_0^u 1 - 0.01x\,dx = u - \frac{0.01u^2}{2} = u(1 - 0.005u).$$

For Model 2, from (3.8),
$$E[X \wedge u] = \int_0^u x\frac{3(2{,}000)^3}{(x + 2{,}000)^4}\,dx + u\frac{2{,}000^3}{(2{,}000 + u)^3} = 1000\left[1 - \frac{4{,}000{,}000}{(2{,}000 + u)^2}\right],$$

and from (3.10),
$$E[X \wedge u] = 1{,}000 - \frac{2{,}000 + u}{2}\left(\frac{2{,}000}{2{,}000 + u}\right)^3 = 1{,}000\left[1 - \frac{4{,}000{,}000}{(2{,}000 + u)^2}\right].$$

From (3.9),
$$E[X \wedge u] = \int_0^u \left(\frac{2{,}000}{2{,}000 + x}\right)^3 dx = \frac{-2{,}000^3}{2(2{,}000 + x)^2}\Big|_0^u$$
$$= 1{,}000\left[1 - \frac{4{,}000{,}000}{(2{,}000 + u)^2}\right].$$

For Model 3, from (3.8),
$$E[X \wedge u] = \begin{cases} 0(0.5) + u(0.5) = 0.5u, & 0 \le u < 1, \\[2mm] 0(0.5) + 1(0.25) + u(0.25) = 0.25 + 0.25u, & 1 \le u < 2, \\[2mm] \begin{aligned} &0(0.5) + 1(0.25) + 2(0.12) + u(0.13) \\ &= 0.49 + 0.13u, \end{aligned} & 2 \le u < 3, \\[4mm] \begin{aligned} &0(0.5) + 1(0.25) + 2(0.12) + 3(0.08) + u(0.05) \\ &= 0.73 + 0.05u, \end{aligned} & 3 \le u < 4, \end{cases}$$

and from (3.10),

$$
E[X \wedge u] = \begin{cases}
0.93 - (1.86 - u)(0.5) = 0.5u, & 0 \le u < 1, \\
0.93 - (2.72 - u)(0.25) = 0.25 + 0.25u, & 1 \le u < 2, \\
0.93 - (3.3846 - u)(0.13) = 0.49 + 0.13u, & 2 \le u < 3, \\
0.93 - (4 - u)0(.05) = 0.73 + 0.05u, & 3 \le u < 4.
\end{cases}
$$

For Model 4, from (3.8),

$$
\begin{aligned}
E[X \wedge u] &= \int_0^u x(0.000003)e^{-0.00001x}\,dx + u(0.3)e^{-0.00001u} \\
&= 30{,}000[1 - e^{-0.00001u}],
\end{aligned}
$$

and from (3.10),

$$
E[X \wedge u] = 30{,}000 - 100{,}000(0.3e^{-0.00001u}) = 30{,}000[1 - e^{-0.00001u}].
$$

3.10 For a discrete distribution (which all empirical distributions are), the mean residual life function is

$$
e(d) = \frac{\sum_{x_j > d}(x_j - d)p(x_j)}{\sum_{x_j > d} p(x_j)}.
$$

When d is equal to a possible value of X, the function cannot be continuous because there is jump in the denominator but not in the numerator. For an exponential distribution, argue as in Exercise 3.7 to see that it is constant. For the Pareto distribution,

$$
\begin{aligned}
e(d) &= \frac{E(X) - E(X \wedge d)}{S(d)} \\
&= \frac{\frac{\theta}{\alpha-1} - \frac{\theta}{\alpha-1}\left[1 - \left(\frac{\theta}{\theta+d}\right)^{\alpha-1}\right]}{\left(\frac{\theta}{\theta+d}\right)^{\alpha}} \\
&= \frac{\theta}{\alpha-1}\frac{\theta+d}{\theta} = \frac{\theta+d}{\alpha-1},
\end{aligned}
$$

which is increasing in d. Only the second statement is true.

3.11 Applying the formula from the solution to Exercise 3.10 gives

$$
\frac{10{,}000 + 10{,}000}{0.5 - 1} = -40{,}000,
$$

which cannot be correct. Recall that the numerator of the mean residual life is $E(X) - E(X \wedge d)$. However, when $\alpha \leq 1$, the expected value is infinite and so is the mean residual life.

3.12 The right truncated variable is defined as $Y = X$ given that $X \leq u$. When $X > u$, this variable is not defined. The kth moment is

$$E(Y^k) = \frac{\int_0^u x^k f(x)dx}{F(u)} = \frac{\sum_{x_i \leq u} x_i^k p(x_i)}{F(u)}.$$

3.13 This is a single parameter Pareto distribution with parameters $\alpha = 2.5$ and $\theta = 1$. The moments are $\mu_1 = 2.5/1.5 = 5/3$ and $\mu_2 = 2.5/.5 - (5/3)^2 = 20/9$. The coefficient of variation is $\sqrt{20/9}/(5/3) = 0.89443$.

3.14 $\mu = 0.05(100) + 0.2(200) + 0.5(300) + 0.2(400) + 0.05(500) = 300$.
$\sigma^2 = 0.05(-200)^2 + 0.2(-100)^2 + 0.5(0)^2 + 0.2(100)^2 + 0.05(200)^2 = 8,000$.
$\mu_3 = 0.05(-200)^3 + 0.2(-100)^3 + 0.5(0)^3 + 0.2(100)^3 + 0.05(200)^3 = 0$.
$\mu_4 = 0.05(-200)^4 + 0.2(-100)^4 + 0.5(0)^4 + 0.2(100)^4 + 0.05(200)^4 = 200,000,000$.
Skewness is $\gamma_1 = \mu_3/\sigma^3 = 0$. Kurtosis is $\gamma_2 = \mu_4/\sigma^4 = 200,000,000/8,000^2 = 3.125$.

3.15 The Pareto mean residual life function is

$$e_X(d) = \frac{\int_d^\infty \theta^\alpha (x+\theta)^{-\alpha} dx}{\theta^\alpha (x+d)^{-\alpha}} = (d+\theta)/(\alpha - 1),$$

and so $e_X(2\theta)/e_X(\theta) = (2\theta + \theta)/(\theta + \theta) = 1.5$.

3.16 Sample mean: $0.2(400) + 0.7(800) + 0.1(1,600) = 800$. Sample variance: $0.2(-400)^2 + 0.7(0)^2 + 0.1(800)^2 = 96,000$. Sample third central moment: $0.2(-400)^3 + 0.7(0)^3 + 0.1(800)^3 = 38,400,000$. Skewness coefficient: $38,400,000/96,000^{1.5} = 1.29$.

3.2   SECTION 3.2

3.17 The pdf is $f(x) = 2x^{-3}$, $x \geq 1$. The mean is $\int_1^\infty 2x^{-2}dx = 2$. The median is the solution to $.5 = F(x) = 1 - x^{-2}$, which is 1.4142. The mode is the value where the *pdf* is highest. Because the pdf is strictly decreasing, the mode is at its smallest value, 1.

3.18 For Model 2, solve $p = 1 - \left(\frac{2,000}{2,000+\pi_p}\right)^3$ and so $\pi_p = 2,000[(1-p)^{-1/3} - 1]$ and the requested percentiles are 519.84 and 1419.95.

For Model 4, the distribution function jumps from 0 to 0.7 at zero and so $\pi_{0.5} = 0$. For percentile above 70, solve $p = 1 - 0.3e^{-0.00001\pi_p}$, and so $\pi_p = -100{,}000 \ln[(1-p)/0.3]$ and $\pi_{0.8} = 40{,}546.51$.

For Model 5, the distribution function has two specifications. From $x = 0$ to $x = 50$ it rises from 0.0 to 0.5, and so for percentiles at 50 or below, the equation to solve is $p = 0.01\pi_p$ for $\pi_p = 100p$. For $50 < x \leq 75$, the distribution function rises from 0.5 to 1.0, and so for percentiles from 50 to 100 the equation to solve is $p = 0.02\pi_p - 0.5$ for $\pi_p = 50p + 25$. The requested percentiles are 50 and 65.

3.19 The two percentiles imply

$$0.1 = 1 - \left(\frac{\theta}{\theta + \theta - k}\right)^\alpha,$$

$$0.9 = 1 - \left(\frac{\theta}{\theta + 50 - 3k}\right)^\alpha.$$

Rearranging the equations and taking their ratio yield

$$\frac{0.9}{0.1} = \left(\frac{6\theta - 3k}{2\theta - k}\right)^\alpha = 3^\alpha.$$

Taking logarithms of both sides gives $\ln 9 = \alpha \ln 3$ for $\alpha = \ln 9 / \ln 3 = 2$.

3.20 The two percentiles imply

$$0.25 = 1 - e^{-(1{,}000/\theta)^\tau},$$

$$0.75 = 1 - e^{-(100{,}000/\theta)^\tau}.$$

Subtracting and then taking logarithms of both sides give

$$\ln 0.75 = -(1{,}000/\theta)^\tau,$$

$$\ln 0.25 = -(100{,}000/\theta)^\tau.$$

Dividing the second equation by the first gives

$$\frac{\ln 0.25}{\ln 0.75} = 100^\tau.$$

Finally, taking logarithms of both sides gives $\tau \ln 100 = \ln[\ln 0.25 / \ln 0.75]$ for $\tau = 0.3415$.

3.3   SECTION 3.3

3.21 The sum has a gamma distribution with parameters $\alpha = 16$ and $\theta = 250$. Then, $\Pr(S_{16} > 6{,}000) = 1 - \Gamma(16; 6{,}000/250) = 1 - \Gamma(16; 24)$. From the

Central Limit Theorem, the sum has an approximate normal distribution with mean $\alpha\theta = 4{,}000$ and variance $\alpha\theta^2 = 1{,}000{,}000$ for a standard deviation of 1000. The probability of exceeding 6,000 is $1 - \Phi[(6{,}000 - 4{,}000)/1{,}000] = 1 - \Phi(2) = 0.0228$.

3.22 A single claim has mean $8{,}000/(5/3) = 4{,}800$ and variance

$$2(8{,}000)^2/[(5/3)(2/3)] - 4{,}800^2 = 92{,}160{,}000.$$

The sum of 100 claims has mean 480,000 and variance 9,216,000,000, which is a standard deviation of 96,000. The probability of exceeding 600,000 is approximately

$$1 - \Phi[(600{,}000 - 480{,}000)/96{,}000] = 1 - \Phi(1.25) = 0.106.$$

3.23 The mean of the gamma distribution is $5(1{,}000) = 5{,}000$ and the variance is $5(1{,}000)^2 = 5{,}000{,}000$. For 100 independent claims, the mean is 500,000 and the variance is 500,000,000 for a standard deviation of 22,360.68. The probability of total claims exceeding 525,000 is

$$1 - \Phi[(525{,}000 - 500{,}000)/22{,}360.68] = 1 - \Phi(1.118) = 0.13178.$$

3.24 The sum of 2,500 contracts has an approximate normal distribution with mean $2{,}500(1{,}300) = 3{,}250{,}000$ and standard deviation $\sqrt{2{,}500}(400) = 20{,}000$. The answer is $\Pr(X > 3{,}282{,}500) \doteq \Pr[Z > (3{,}282{,}500 - 3{,}250{,}000)/20{,}000] = \Pr(Z > 1.625) = 0.052$.

3.4 SECTION 3.4

3.25 While the Weibull distribution has all positive moments, for the inverse Weibull moments exist only for $k < \tau$. Thus by this criterion, the inverse Weibull distribution has a heavier tail. With regard to the ratio of density functions, it is (with the inverse Weibull in the numerator and marking its parameters with asterisks)

$$\frac{\tau^*\theta^{*\tau^*}x^{-\tau^*-1}e^{-(\theta^*/x)^{\tau^*}}}{\tau\theta^{-\tau}x^{\tau-1}e^{-(x/\theta)^\tau}} \propto x^{-\tau-\tau^*}e^{-(\theta^*/x)^{\tau^*}+(x/\theta)^\tau}.$$

The logarithm is
$$(x/\theta)^\tau - (\theta^*/x)^{\tau^*} - (\tau + \tau^*)\ln x.$$

The middle term goes to zero, so the issue is the limit of $(x/\theta)^\tau - (\tau+\tau^*)\ln x$, which is clearly infinite. With regard to the hazard rate, for the Weibull distribution we have

$$h(x) = \frac{\tau x^{\tau-1}\theta^{-\tau}e^{-(x/\theta)^\tau}}{e^{-(x/\theta)^\tau}} = \tau x^{\tau-1}\theta^{-\tau},$$

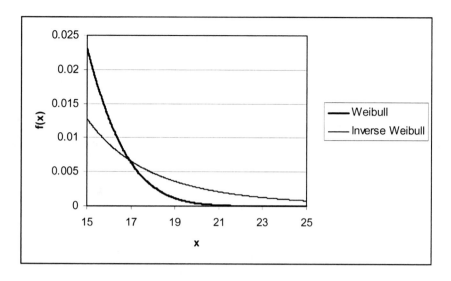

Figure 3.1   Tails of a Weibull and inverse Weibull distribution.

which is clearly increasing when $\tau > 1$, constant when $\tau = 1$, and decreasing when $\tau < 1$. For the inverse Weibull,

$$h(x) = \frac{\tau x^{-\tau-1}\theta^\tau e^{-(\theta/x)^\tau}}{1 - e^{-(\theta/x)^\tau}} \propto \frac{1}{x^{\tau+1}[e^{(\theta/x)^\tau} - 1]}.$$

The derivative of the denominator is

$$(\tau + 1)x^\tau [e^{(\theta/x)^\tau} - 1] + x^{\tau+1}e^{(\theta/x)^\tau}\theta^\tau(-\tau)x^{-\tau-1},$$

and the limiting value of this expression is $\theta^\tau > 0$. Therefore, in the limit, the denominator is increasing and thus the hazard rate is decreasing.

Figure 3.1 displays a portion of the density function for Weibull ($\tau = 3$, $\theta = 10$) and inverse Weibull ($\tau = 4.4744$, $\theta = 7.4934$) distributions with the same mean and variance. The heavier tail of the inverse Weibull distribution is clear.

3.26 Means:

$$\begin{aligned}
\text{Gamma} &: \quad 0.2(500) = 100. \\
\text{Lognormal} &: \quad \exp(3.70929 + 1.33856^2/2) = 99.9999. \\
\text{Pareto} &: \quad 150/(2.5 - 1) = 100.
\end{aligned}$$

Second moments:

$$\begin{aligned}
\text{Gamma} &: \quad 500^2(0.2)(1.2) = 60{,}000. \\
\text{Lognormal} &: \quad \exp[2(3.70929) + 2(1.33856)^2] = 59{,}999.88. \\
\text{Pareto} &: \quad 150^2(2)/[1.5(0.5)] = 60{,}000.
\end{aligned}$$

Density functions:

Gamma : $0.62851x^{-0.8}e^{-0.002x}$.

Lognormal : $(2\pi)^{-1/2}(1.338566x)^{-1}\exp\left[-\dfrac{1}{2}\left(\dfrac{\ln x - 3.70929}{1.338566}\right)^2\right]$.

Pareto : $688{,}919(x+150)^{-3.5}$.

The gamma and lognormal densities are equal when $x = 2{,}221$ while the lognormal and Pareto densities are equal when $x = 9{,}678$. Numerical evaluation indicates that the ordering is as expected.

3.27 For the Pareto distribution

$$
\begin{aligned}
e(x) &= \int_0^\infty \frac{S(y+x)}{S(x)}\,dy = \int_0^\infty \frac{\left(\frac{\theta}{\theta+y+x}\right)^\alpha}{\left(\frac{\theta}{\theta+x}\right)^\alpha}\,dy \\
&= (\theta+x)^\alpha \int_0^\infty (\theta+y+x)^{-\alpha}\,dy \\
&= (\theta+x)^\alpha \left.\frac{(\theta+y+x)^{-\alpha+1}}{-\alpha+1}\right|_0^\infty \\
&= (\theta+x)^\alpha \frac{(\theta+x)^{-\alpha+1}}{\alpha-1} = \frac{\theta+x}{\alpha-1}.
\end{aligned}
$$

Thus $e(x)$ is clearly increasing and $e(x) \geq 0$, indicating a heavy tail. The square of the coefficient of variation is

$$
\frac{\frac{2\theta^2}{(\alpha-1)(\alpha-2)} - \frac{\theta^2}{(\alpha-1)^2}}{\frac{\theta^2}{(\alpha-1)^2}} = \frac{2(\alpha-1)}{\alpha-2} - 1,
$$

which is greater than 1, also indicating a heavy tail.

3.28
$$
\begin{aligned}
M_Y(t) &= \int_0^\infty e^{ty}\frac{S_X(y)}{E(X)}\,dy = \left.\frac{e^{ty}}{t}\frac{S_X(y)}{E(X)}\right|_0^\infty + \int_0^\infty \frac{e^{ty}}{t}\frac{f_X(y)}{E(X)}\,dy \\
&= -\frac{1}{tE(X)} + \frac{M_X(t)}{tE(X)} = \frac{M_X(t)-1}{tE(X)}.
\end{aligned}
$$

This result assumes $\lim_{y\to\infty} e^{ty}S_X(y) = 0$. An application of L'Hôpital's rule shows that this is the same limit as $(-t^{-1})\lim_{y\to\infty} e^{ty}f_X(y)$. This limit must be zero, otherwise the integral defining $M_X(t)$ will not converge.

3.29 (a)
$$
\begin{aligned}
S(x) &= \int_x^\infty (1+2t^2)e^{-2t}\,dt \\
&= -(1+t+t^2)e^{-2t}\big|_x^\infty \\
&= (1+x+x^2)e^{-2x}, \quad x \geq 0.
\end{aligned}
$$

(b)
$$h(x) = -\frac{d}{dx}\ln S(x) = \frac{d}{dx}(2x) - \frac{d}{dx}\ln(1 + x + x^2)$$
$$= 2 - \frac{1 + 2x}{1 + x + x^2}.$$

(c) For $y \geq 0$,

$$\int_y^\infty S(t)dt = \int_y^\infty (1 + t + t^2)e^{-2t}dt$$
$$= -(1 + t + \tfrac{1}{2}t^2)e^{-2t}|_y^\infty = (1 + y + \tfrac{1}{2}y^2)e^{-2y}.$$

Thus,

$$S_e(x) = \frac{\int_x^\infty S(t)dt}{\int_0^\infty S(t)dt} = \left(1 + x + \tfrac{1}{2}x^2\right)e^{-2x}, \quad x \geq 0.$$

(d)

$$e(x) = \frac{\int_x^\infty S(t)dt}{S(x)} = \frac{1 + x + \tfrac{1}{2}x^2}{1 + x + x^2} \text{ from (a) and (c).}$$

(e) Using (b),

$$\lim_{x\to\infty} h(x) = \lim_{x\to\infty}\left(2 - \frac{1 + 2x}{1 + x + x^2}\right) = 2,$$
$$\lim_{x\to\infty} e(x) = \frac{1}{\lim\limits_{x\to\infty} h(x)} = \frac{1}{2}.$$

(f) Using (d), we have

$$e(x) = 1 - \frac{\tfrac{1}{2}x^2}{1 + x + x^2},$$

and so

$$e'(x) = -\frac{x}{1 + x + x^2} + \frac{\tfrac{1}{2}x^2(1 + 2x)}{(1 + x + x^2)^2} = \frac{-x(1 + x + x^2) + \tfrac{1}{2}x^2 + x^3}{(1 + x + x^2)^2}$$
$$= -\frac{x + \tfrac{1}{2}x^2}{(1 + x + x^2)^2} \leq 0.$$

Also, from (b) and (e), $h(0) = 1, h(\tfrac{1}{2}) = \tfrac{6}{7}$, and $h(\infty) = 2$.

3.30 (a) Integration by parts yields

$$\int_x^\infty (y - x)f(y)dy = \int_x^\infty S(y)dy,$$

and hence $S_e(x) = \int_x^\infty f_e(y)dy = \frac{1}{E(X)}\int_x^\infty S(y)dy$, from which the result follows.

(b) It follows from (a) that

$$E(X)S_e(x) = \int_x^\infty yf(y)dy - x\int_x^\infty f(y)dy = \int_x^\infty yf(y)dy - xS(x),$$

which gives the result by addition of $xS(x)$ to both sides.

(c) Because $e(x) = E(X)S_e(x)/S(x)$, from (b)

$$\int_x^\infty yf(y)dy = S(x)\left[x + \frac{E(X)S_e(x)}{S(x)}\right] = S(x)[x + e(x)],$$

and the first result follows by division of both sides by $x+e(x)$. The inequality then follows from $E(X) = \int_0^\infty yf(y)dy \geq \int_x^\infty yf(y)dy$.

(d) Because $e(0) = E(X)$, the result follows from the inequality in (c) with $e(x)$ replaced by $E(X)$ in the denominator.

(e) As in (c), it follows from (b) that

$$\int_x^\infty yf(y)dy = S_e(x)\left\{E(X) + \frac{xS(x)}{S_e(x)}\right\} = S_e(x)\left\{E(X) + \frac{xE(X)}{e(x)}\right\},$$

that is,

$$\int_x^\infty yf(y)dy = E(X)S_e(x)\left\{\frac{e(x)+x}{e(x)}\right\},$$

from which the first result follows by solving for $S_e(x)$. The inequality then follows from the first result since $E(X) = \int_0^\infty yf(y)dy \geq \int_x^\infty yf(y)dy$.

3.5 SECTION 3.5

3.31 Denote the risk measures by $\rho(X) = \mu_X + k\sigma_X$, $\rho(Y) = \mu_Y + k\sigma_Y$, and $\rho(X+Y) = \mu_{X+Y} + k\sigma_{X+Y}$. Note that $\mu_{X+Y} = \mu_X + \mu_Y$ and

$$\begin{aligned}\sigma_{X+Y}^2 &= \sigma_X^2 + \sigma_Y^2 + 2\rho\sigma_X\sigma_Y \\ &\leq \sigma_X^2 + \sigma_Y^2 + 2\sigma_X\sigma_Y = (\sigma_X + \sigma_Y)^2,\end{aligned}$$

where ρ here is the correlation coefficient, not the risk measure, and must be less than or equal to one. Therefore, $\sigma_{X+Y} \leq \sigma_X + \sigma_Y$. Thus,

$$\rho(X+Y) \leq \mu_X + \mu_Y + k(\sigma_X + \sigma_Y) = \rho(X) + \rho(Y),$$

which establishes subadditivity.

Because $\mu_{cX} = c\mu_X$ and $\sigma_{cX} = c\sigma_X$, $\rho(cX) = c\mu_X + kc\sigma_X = c\rho(X)$, which establishes positive homogeneity.

Because $\mu_{X+c} = \mu_X + c$ and $\sigma_{X+c} = \sigma_X$, $\rho(X+c) = \mu_X + c + k\sigma_X = \rho(X) + c$, which establishes translation invariance.

For the example given, note that $X \leq Y$ for all possible pairs of outcomes. Also, $\mu_X = 3$, $\mu_Y = 4$, $\sigma_X = \sqrt{3}$, $\sigma_Y = 0$. With $k = 1$, $\rho(X) = 3 + \sqrt{3} = 4.732$, which is greater than $\rho(Y) = 4 + 0 = 4$, violating monotonicity.

3.32 The cdf is $F(x) = 1 - \exp(-x/\theta)$, and so the percentile solves $p = 1 - \exp(-\pi_p/\theta)$ and the solution is $\mathrm{VaR}_p(X) = \pi_p = -\theta \ln(1-p)$. Because the exponential distribution is memoryless, $e(\pi_p) = \theta$ and so $\mathrm{TVaR}_p(X) = \mathrm{VaR}_p(X) + e(\pi_p) = \pi_p + \theta$.

3.33 The cdf is $F(x) = 1 - [\theta/(\theta + x)]^\alpha$ and so the percentile solves $p = 1 - [\theta/(\theta + \pi_p)]^\alpha$ and the solution is $\mathrm{VaR}_p(X) = \pi_p = \theta[(1-p)^{-1/\alpha} - 1]$. From (3.13) and Appendix A,

$$
\begin{aligned}
\mathrm{TVaR}_p(X) &= \pi_p + \frac{E(X) - E(X \wedge \pi_p)}{1 - F(\pi_p)} \\[2mm]
&= \pi_p + \frac{\frac{\theta}{\alpha-1} - \frac{\theta}{\alpha-1}\left[1 - \left(\frac{\theta}{\theta+\pi_p}\right)^{\alpha-1}\right]}{1 - p} \\[2mm]
&= \pi_p + \frac{\frac{\theta}{\alpha-1}\left(\frac{\theta}{\theta+\pi_p}\right)^{\alpha-1}}{1 - p}.
\end{aligned}
$$

Substitute $1 - p$ for $[\theta/(\theta + \pi_p)]^\alpha$ to obtain

$$
\mathrm{TVaR}_p(X) = \pi_p + \frac{\theta}{\alpha - 1}\left(\frac{\theta}{\theta + \pi_p}\right)^{-1} = \pi_p + \frac{\theta + \pi_p}{\alpha - 1}.
$$

3.34 First, obtain

$$
\Phi^{-1}(0.90) = 1.28155, \ \Phi^{-1}(0.99) = 2.32635, \ \text{and} \ \Phi^{-1}(0.999) = 3.09023.
$$

Using $\pi_p = \mu + \sigma\Phi^{-1}(p)$, the results for the normal distribution are obtained.
For the Pareto distribution, using $\theta = 150$ and $\alpha = 2.5$ and the formulas in Example 3.17,

$$
\mathrm{VaR}_p(X) = 120\left[(1 - p)^{-1/2.2} - 1\right]
$$

will yield the results.
For the Weibull(50, 0.5) distribution and the formulas in Appendix A,

$$
p = 1 - \exp\left[-\left(\frac{\pi_p}{50}\right)^{0.5}\right]
$$

from which

$$
\mathrm{VaR}_p(X) = \pi_p = 50\left\{[-\ln(1 - p)]^2\right\},
$$

which gives the results.

3.35 From Exercise 3.34, $\text{VaR}_{0.999}(X) = \pi_{0.999} = 2{,}385.85$. The mean is $E(X) = \theta\Gamma(1 + 1/\tau) = 50\Gamma(3) = 100$. From Appendix A,

$$
\begin{aligned}
E(X \wedge \pi_{0.999}) &= \theta\Gamma(1 + 1/\tau)\Gamma\left[1 + 1/\tau; \left(\frac{\pi_{0.999}}{\theta}\right)^{\tau}\right] \\
&\quad + \pi_{0.999}\exp\left[-\left(\frac{\pi_{0.999}}{\theta}\right)^{\tau}\right] \\
&= 50\Gamma(3)\Gamma(3; 6.9078) + 2{,}385.85\exp(-6.9078) \\
&= 100\Gamma(3; 6.9078) + 2{,}385.85\exp(-6.9078).
\end{aligned}
$$

The value of $\Gamma(3; 6.9078)$ can be obtained using the Excel function GAMMADIST(6.90775, 3, 1, TRUE). It is 0.968234.

Therefore, $E(X \wedge \pi_{0.999}) = 99.209$. From these results using (3.13),

$$
\text{TVaR}_{0.999}(X) = 2{,}385.85 + 1{,}000(100 - 99.209) = 3{,}176.63.
$$

(The answer is sensitive to the number of decimal places retained.)

3.36 For the exponential distribution,

$$
\text{VaR}_{0.95}(X) = 500\left[-\ln(0.05)\right] = 1{,}497.866.
$$

Therefore $\text{TVaR}_{0.95}(X) = 1{,}997.866$.

From Example 3.19, for the Pareto distribution,

$$
\begin{aligned}
\text{VaR}_{0.95}(X) &= 1{,}000\left[(0.05)^{-1/3} - 1\right] = 1{,}714.4176 \\
E(X \wedge \pi_{0.95}) &= 500\left[1 - \left(\frac{1{,}000}{2{,}714.4176}\right)^{2}\right] = 432.140 \\
\text{TVaR}_{0.95}(X) &= 1{,}714.2 + \frac{500 - 432.140}{0.05} = 3{,}071.63.
\end{aligned}
$$

3.37 For $x > x_0$,

$$
\begin{aligned}
\frac{d}{dx}E(X|X > x) &= \frac{d}{dx}\left[\frac{\int_x^\infty yf(y)dy}{S(x)}\right] \\
&= -\frac{xf(x)}{S(x)} - \frac{\int_x^\infty yf(y)dy}{[S(x)]^2}[-f(x)] \\
&= h(x)\left[\frac{\int_x^\infty yf(y)dy}{S(x)} - x\right] \\
&= h(x)\frac{\int_x^\infty (y - x)f(y)dy}{S(x)} = h(x)e(x).
\end{aligned}
$$

Because $h(x) \geq 0$ and $e(x) \geq 0$, the derivative must be nonnegative.

CHAPTER 4

CHAPTER 4 SOLUTIONS

4.1 SECTION 4.2

4.1 Arguing as in the examples,

$$
\begin{aligned}
F_Y(y) &= \Pr(X \le y/c) \\
&= \Phi\left[\frac{\ln(y/c) - \mu}{\sigma}\right] \\
&= \Phi\left[\frac{\ln y - (\ln c + \mu)}{\sigma}\right],
\end{aligned}
$$

which indicates that Y has the lognormal distribution with parameters $\mu + \ln c$ and σ. Because no parameter was multiplied by c, there is no scale parameter. To introduce a scale parameter, define the lognormal distribution function as $F(x) = \Phi\left(\frac{\ln x - \ln \nu}{\sigma}\right)$. Note that the new parameter ν is simply e^{μ}. Then, arguing as before,

$$
\begin{aligned}
F_Y(y) &= \Pr(X \le y/c) \\
&= \Phi\left[\frac{\ln(y/c) - \ln\nu}{\sigma}\right] \\
&= \Phi\left[\frac{\ln y - (\ln c + \ln\nu)}{\sigma}\right] \\
&= \Phi\left[\frac{\ln y - \ln c\nu}{\sigma}\right]
\end{aligned}
$$

demonstrating that ν is a scale parameter.

4.2 The following is not the only possible set of answers to this question. Model 1 is a uniform distribution on the interval 0 to 100 with parameters 0 and 100. It is also a beta distribution with parameters $a = 1$, $b = 1$, and $\theta = 100$. Model 2 is a Pareto distribution with parameters $\alpha = 3$ and $\theta = 2000$. Model 3 would not normally be considered a parametric distribution. However, we could define a parametric discrete distribution with arbitrary probabilities at $0, 1, 2, 3$, and 4 being the parameters. Conventional usage would not accept this as a parametric distribution. Similarly, Model 4 is not a standard parametric distribution, but we could define one as having arbitrary probability p at zero and an exponential distribution elsewhere. Model 5 could be from a parametric distribution with uniform probability from a to b and a different uniform probability from b to c.

4.3 For this year,

$$
\Pr(X > d) = 1 - F(d) = \left(\frac{\theta}{\theta + d}\right)^2.
$$

For next year, because θ is a scale parameter, claims will have a Pareto distribution with parameters $\alpha = 2$ and 1.06θ. That makes the probability $\left(\frac{1.06\theta}{1.06\theta + d}\right)^2$. Then

$$
\begin{aligned}
r &= \lim_{d\to\infty}\left[\frac{1.06(\theta + d)}{1.06\theta + d}\right]^2 \\
&= \lim_{d\to\infty}\frac{1.1236\theta^2 + 2.2472\theta d + 1.1236d^2}{1.1236\theta^2 + 2.12\theta d + d^2} \\
&= \lim_{d\to\infty}\frac{2.2472\theta + 2.2472d}{2.12\theta + 2d} \\
&= \lim_{d\to\infty}\frac{2.2472}{2} = 1.1236.
\end{aligned}
$$

4.4 The mth moment of a k-point mixture distribution is

$$
\begin{aligned}
\mathrm{E}(Y^m) &= \int y^m [a_1 f_{X_1}(y) + \cdots + a_k f_{X_k}(y)] dy \\
&= a_1 \mathrm{E}(Y_1^m) + \cdots + a_k \mathrm{E}(Y_k^m).
\end{aligned}
$$

For this problem, the first moment is

$$
a \frac{\theta_1}{\alpha - 1} + (1 - a) \frac{\theta_2}{\alpha + 1} \text{ if } \alpha > 1.
$$

Similarly, the second moment is

$$
a \frac{2\theta_1^2}{(\alpha - 1)(\alpha - 2)} + (1 - a) \frac{2\theta_2^2}{(\alpha + 1)\alpha} \text{ if } \alpha > 2.
$$

4.5 Using the results from Exercise 4.4, $\mathrm{E}(X) = \sum_{i=1}^{K} a_i \mu_i'$, and for the gamma distribution this becomes $\sum_{i=1}^{K} a_i \alpha_i \theta_i$. Similarly, for the second moment we have $\mathrm{E}(X^2) = \sum_{i=1}^{K} a_i \mu_2'$, which, for the gamma distribution, becomes $\sum_{i=1}^{K} a_i \alpha_i (\alpha_i + 1) \theta_i^2$.

4.6 Parametric distribution families: It would be difficult to consider Model 1 as being from a parametric family (although the uniform distribution could be considered as a special case of the beta distribution). Model 2 is a Pareto distribution and as such is a member of the transformed beta family. As a stretch, Model 3 could be considered a member of a family that places probability (the parameters) on a given number of non-negative integers. Model 4 could be a member of the "exponential plus family," where the plus means the possibility of discrete probability at zero. Creating a family for Model 5 seems difficult.

Variable-component mixture distributions: Only Model 5 seems to be a good candidate. It is a mixture of uniform distributions in which the component uniform distributions are on adjoining intervals.

4.7 For this mixture distribution,

$$
\begin{aligned}
F(5{,}000) &= 0.75\Phi\left(\frac{5{,}000 - 3{,}000}{1{,}000}\right) + 0.25\Phi\left(\frac{5{,}000 - 4{,}000}{1{,}000}\right) \\
&= 0.75\Phi(2) + 0.25\Phi(1) \\
&= 0.75(0.9772) + 0.25(0.8413) = 0.9432.
\end{aligned}
$$

The probability of exceeding 5,000 is $1 - 0.9432 = 0.0568$.

4.8 The distribution function of Z is

$$
\begin{aligned}
F(z) &= 0.5\left[1 - \frac{1}{1 + (z/\sqrt{1{,}000})^2}\right] + 0.5\left[1 - \frac{1}{1 + z/1{,}000}\right] \\
&= 1 - 0.5\frac{1{,}000}{1{,}000 + z^2} - 0.5\frac{1{,}000}{1000 + z} \\
&= 1 - \frac{0.5(1{,}000^2 + 1{,}000z + 1{,}000^2 + 1{,}000z^2)}{(1{,}000 + z^2)(1{,}000 + z)}.
\end{aligned}
$$

The median is the solution to $0.5 = F(m)$ or

$$
\begin{aligned}
(1{,}000 + m^2)(1{,}000 + m) &= 2(1{,}000)^2 + 1{,}000m + 1{,}000m^2 \\
1{,}000^2 + 1{,}000m^2 + 1{,}000m + m^3 &= 2(1{,}000)^2 + 1{,}000m + 1{,}000m^2 \\
m^3 &= 1{,}000^2 \\
m &= 100.
\end{aligned}
$$

The distribution function of W is

$$
\begin{aligned}
F_W(w) &= \Pr(W \le w) = \Pr(1.1Z \le w) = \Pr(Z \le w/1.1) = F_Z(w/1.1) \\
&= 0.5\left[1 - \frac{1}{1 + (w/1.1\sqrt{1{,}000})^2}\right] + 0.5\left[1 - \frac{1}{1 + z/1{,}100}\right].
\end{aligned}
$$

This is a 50/50 mixture of a Burr distribution with parameters $\alpha = 1$, $\gamma = 2$, and $\theta = 1.1\sqrt{1{,}000}$ and a Pareto distribution with parameters $\alpha = 1$ and $\theta = 1{,}100$.

4.9 Right censoring creates a mixed distribution with discrete probability at the censoring point. Therefore, Z is matched with (c). X is similar to Model 5, which has a continuous distribution function but the density function has a jump at 2. Therefore, X is matched with (b). The sum of two continuous random variables will be continuous as well, in this case over the interval from 0 to 5. Therefore, Y is matched with (a).

4.10 The density function is the sum of five functions. They are (where it is understood that the function is zero where not defined)

$$
\begin{aligned}
f_1(x) &= 0.03125,\ 1 \le x \le 5, \\
f_2(x) &= 0.03125,\ 3 \le x \le 7, \\
f_3(x) &= 0.09375,\ 4 \le x \le 8, \\
f_4(x) &= 0.06250,\ 5 \le x \le 9, \\
f_5(x) &= 0.03125,\ 8 \le x \le 12.
\end{aligned}
$$

Adding the functions yields

$$f(x) = \begin{cases} 0.03125, & 1 \le x < 3, \\ 0.06250, & 3 \le x < 4, \\ 0.15625, & 4 \le x < 5, \\ 0.18750, & 5 \le x < 7, \\ 0.15625, & 7 \le x < 8, \\ 0.09375, & 8 \le x < 9, \\ 0.03125, & 9 \le x < 12. \end{cases}$$

This is a mixture of seven uniform distributions, each being uniform over the indicated interval. The weight for mixing is the value of the density function multiplied by the width of the interval.

4.11

$$\begin{aligned} F_Y(y) &= \Phi\left[\frac{y/c - \mu}{\mu}\left(\frac{\theta c}{y}\right)^{1/2}\right] + \exp\left(\frac{2\theta}{\mu}\right)\Phi\left[-\frac{y/c + \mu}{\mu}\left(\frac{\theta c}{y}\right)^{1/2}\right] \\ &= \Phi\left[\frac{y - c\mu}{c\mu}\left(\frac{\theta c}{y}\right)^{1/2}\right] + \exp\left(\frac{2c\theta}{c\mu}\right)\Phi\left[-\frac{y + c\mu}{c\mu}\left(\frac{\theta c}{y}\right)^{1/2}\right], \end{aligned}$$

and so Y is inverse Gaussian with parameters $c\mu$ and $c\theta$. Because it is still inverse Gaussian, it is a scale family. Because both μ and θ change, there is no scale parameter.

4.12 $F_Y(y) = F_X(y/c) = 1 - \exp[-(y/c\theta)^\tau]$, which is a Weibull distribution with parameters τ and $c\theta$.

CHAPTER 5

CHAPTER 5 SOLUTIONS

5.1 SECTION 5.2

5.1 $F_Y(y) = 1 - (1 + y/\theta)^{-\alpha} = 1 - \left(\frac{\theta}{\theta+y}\right)^\alpha$. This is the cdf of the Pareto distribution. The pdf is $f_Y(y) = dF_Y(y)/dy = \frac{\alpha\theta^\alpha}{(\theta+y)^{\alpha+1}}$.

5.2 After three years, values are inflated by 1.331. Let X be the 1995 variable and $Y = 1.331X$ be the 1998 variable. We want

$$\Pr(Y > 500) = \Pr(X > 500/1.331) = \Pr(X > 376).$$

From the given information we have $\Pr(X > 350) = 0.55$ and $\Pr(X > 400) = 0.50$. Therefore, the desired probability must be between these two values.

5.3 Inverse:

$$F_Y(y) = 1 - \left[1 - \left(\frac{\theta}{\theta + y^{-1}}\right)^\alpha\right] = \left(\frac{y}{y + \theta^{-1}}\right)^\alpha.$$

Student Solutions Manual to Accompany Loss Models: From Data to Decisions, Fourth 29
Edition. By Stuart A. Klugman, Harry H. Panjer, Gordon E. Willmot
Copyright © 2012 John Wiley & Sons, Inc.

This is the inverse Pareto distribution with $\tau = \alpha$ and $\theta = 1/\theta$. Transformed: $F_Y(y) = 1 - \left(\frac{\theta}{\theta + y^\tau}\right)^\alpha$. This is the Burr distribution with $\alpha = \alpha$, $\gamma = \tau$, and $\theta = \theta^{1/\tau}$. Inverse transformed:

$$F_Y(y) = 1 - \left[1 - \left(\frac{\theta}{\theta + y^{-\tau}}\right)^\alpha\right] = \left[\frac{y^\tau}{y^\tau + (\theta^{-1/\tau})^\tau}\right]^\alpha.$$

This is the inverse Burr distribution with $\tau = \alpha$, $\gamma = \tau$, and $\theta = \theta^{-1/\tau}$.

5.4
$$F_Y(y) = 1 - \frac{(y^{-1}/\theta)^\gamma}{1 + (y^{-1}/\theta)^\gamma} = \frac{1}{1 + (y^{-1}/\theta)^\gamma} = \frac{(y\theta)^\gamma}{1 + (y\theta)^\gamma}.$$

This is the loglogistic distribution with γ unchanged and $\theta = 1/\theta$.

5.5
$$F_Z(z) = \Phi\left[\frac{\ln(z/\theta) - \mu}{\sigma}\right] = \Phi\left[\frac{\ln z - \ln \theta - \mu}{\sigma}\right],$$

which is the cdf of another lognormal distribution with $\mu = \ln \theta + \mu$ and $\sigma = \sigma$.

5.6 The distribution function of Y is

$$
\begin{aligned}
F_Y(y) &= \Pr(Y \le y) = \Pr[\ln(1 + X/\theta) \le y] \\
&= \Pr(1 + X/\theta \le e^y) \\
&= \Pr[X \le \theta(e^y - 1)] \\
&= 1 - \left[\frac{\theta}{\theta + \theta(e^y - 1)}\right]^\alpha \\
&= 1 - \left(\frac{1}{e^y}\right)^\alpha = 1 - e^{-\alpha y}.
\end{aligned}
$$

This is the distribution function of an exponential random variable with parameter $1/\alpha$.

5.7 $X|\Theta = \theta$ has pdf

$$f_{X|\Theta}(x|\theta) = \frac{\tau\,[(x/\theta)^\tau]^\alpha \exp[-(x/\theta)^\tau]}{x\Gamma(\alpha)},$$

and Θ has pdf

$$f_\Theta(\theta) = \frac{\tau\,[(\delta/\theta)^\tau]^\beta \exp[-(\delta/\theta)^\tau]}{\theta\Gamma(\beta)}.$$

The mixture distribution has pdf

$$
\begin{aligned}
f(x) &= \int_0^\infty \frac{\tau\,[(x/\theta)^\tau]^\alpha \exp[-(x/\theta)^\tau]}{x\Gamma(\alpha)} \frac{\tau\,[(\delta/\theta)^\tau]^\beta \exp[-(\delta/\theta)^\tau]}{\theta\Gamma(\beta)}\,d\theta \\
&= \frac{\tau^2 x^{\tau\alpha} \delta^{\tau\beta}}{x\Gamma(\alpha)\Gamma(\beta)} \int_0^\infty \theta^{-\tau\alpha-\tau\beta-1} \exp[-\theta^{-\tau}(x^\tau+\delta^\tau)]\,d\theta \\
&= \frac{\tau^2 x^{\tau\alpha}\delta^{\tau\beta}}{x\Gamma(\alpha)\Gamma(\beta)} \frac{\Gamma(\alpha+\beta)}{\tau(x^\tau+\delta^\tau)^{\alpha+\beta}} = \frac{\Gamma(\alpha+\beta)\tau x^{\tau\alpha-1}\delta^{\tau\beta}}{\Gamma(\alpha)\Gamma(\beta)(x^\tau+\delta^\tau)^{\alpha+\beta}},
\end{aligned}
$$

which is a transformed beta pdf with $\gamma = \tau$, $\tau = \alpha$, $\alpha = \beta$, and $\theta = \delta$.

5.8 The requested gamma distribution has $\alpha\theta = 1$ and $\alpha\theta^2 = 2$ for $\alpha = 0.5$ and $\theta = 2$. Then

$$
\begin{aligned}
\Pr(N=1) &= \int_0^\infty \frac{e^{-\lambda}\lambda^1}{1!} \frac{\lambda^{-0.5}e^{-0.5\lambda}}{2^{0.5}\Gamma(0.5)}\,d\lambda \\
&= \frac{1}{\Gamma(0.5)\sqrt{2}} \int_0^\infty \lambda^{0.5} e^{-1.5\lambda}\,d\lambda \\
&= \frac{1}{1.5\Gamma(0.5)\sqrt{3}} \int_0^\infty y^{0.5} e^{-y}\,dy \\
&= \frac{\Gamma(1.5)}{1.5\Gamma(0.5)\sqrt{3}} \\
&= \frac{0.5}{1.5\sqrt{3}} = 0.19245.
\end{aligned}
$$

Line 3 follows from the substitution $y = 1.5\lambda$. Line 5 follows from the gamma function identity $\Gamma(1.5) = 0.5\Gamma(0.5)$. N has a negative binomial distribution, and its parameters can be determined by matching moments. In particular, we have $\mathrm{E}(N) = \mathrm{E}[\mathrm{E}(N|\Lambda)] = \mathrm{E}(\Lambda) = 1$ and $\mathrm{Var}(N) = \mathrm{E}[\mathrm{Var}(N|\Lambda)] + \mathrm{Var}[\mathrm{E}(N|\Lambda)] = \mathrm{E}(\Lambda) + \mathrm{Var}(\Lambda) = 1 + 2 = 3$.

5.9 The hazard rate for an exponential distribution is $h(x) = f(x)/S(x) = \theta^{-1}$. Here θ is the parameter of the exponential distribution, not the value from the exercise. But this means that the θ in the exercise is the reciprocal of the exponential parameter, and thus the density function is to be written $F(x) = 1 - e^{-\theta x}$. The unconditional distribution function is

$$
\begin{aligned}
F_X(x) &= \int_1^{11} (1 - e^{-\theta x})0.1\,d\theta \\
&= 0.1(\theta + x^{-1}e^{-\theta x})\Big|_1^{11} \\
&= 1 + \frac{1}{10x}(e^{-11x} - e^{-x}).
\end{aligned}
$$

Then, $S_X(0.5) = 1 - F_X(0.5) = -\frac{1}{10(0.5)}(e^{-5.5} - e^{-0.5}) = 0.1205.$

5.10 We have

$$
\begin{aligned}
\Pr(N \geq 2) &= 1 - F_N(1) \\
&= 1 - \int_0^5 (e^{-\lambda} + \lambda e^{-\lambda})0.2\,d\lambda \\
&= 1 - [-(1+\lambda)e^{-\lambda} - e^{-\lambda}]0.2\big|_0^5 \\
&= 1 + 1.2e^{-5} + 0.2e^{-5} - 0.2 - 0.2 \\
&= 0.6094.
\end{aligned}
$$

5.11 With probability p, $p_2 = 0.5^2 = 0.25$. With probability $1 - p$, $p_2 = \binom{4}{2}(0.5)^4 = 0.375$. Mixed probability is $0.25p + 0.375(1-p) = 0.375 - 0.125p$.

5.12 It follows from (5.3) that

$$f_X(x) = -S'(x) = -M'_\Lambda[-A(x)][-a(x)] = a(x)M'_\Lambda[-A(x)].$$

Then

$$h_X(x) = \frac{f_X(x)}{S_X(x)} = \frac{a(x)M'_\Lambda[-A(x)]}{M_\Lambda[-A(x)]}.$$

5.13 It follows from Example 5.7 with $\alpha = 1$ that $S_X(x) = (1+\theta x^\gamma)^{-1}$, which is a loglogistic distribution with the usual (i.e., in Appendix A) parameter θ replaced by $\theta^{-1/\gamma}$.

5.14 (a) Clearly, $a(x) > 0$, and we have

$$A(x) = \int_0^x a(t)dt = \frac{\theta}{2}\int_0^x (1+\theta t)^{-\frac{1}{2}}dt = \sqrt{1+\theta t}\big|_0^x = \sqrt{1+\theta x} - 1.$$

Because $A(\infty) = \infty$, it follows that $h_{X|\Lambda}(x|\lambda) = \lambda a(x)$ satisfies $h_{X|\Lambda}(x|\lambda) > 0$ and $\int_0^\infty h_{X|\Lambda}(x|\lambda)dx = \infty$.

(b) Using (a), we find that

$$S_{X|\Lambda}(x|\lambda) = e^{-\lambda(\sqrt{1+\theta x}-1)}.$$

It is useful to note that this conditional survival function may itself be shown to be an exponential mixture with inverse Gaussian frailty.

(c) It follows from Example 3.7 that $M_\Lambda(t) = (1-t)^{-2\alpha}$ and thus from (5.3) that X has a Pareto distribution with survival function $S_X(x) = M_\Lambda(1 - \sqrt{1+\theta x}) = (1+\theta x)^{-\alpha}$.

(d) The survival function $S_X(x) = (1 + \theta x)^{-\alpha}$ is also of the form given by (5.3) with mixed exponential survival function $S_{X|\Lambda}(x|\lambda) = e^{-\lambda x}$ and gamma frailty with moment generating function $M_\Lambda(t) = (1 - \theta t)^{-\alpha}$, as in Example 3.7.

5.15 Write $F_X(x) = 1 - M_\Lambda[-A(x)]$, and thus

$$S_1(x) = \frac{1 - M_\Lambda[-A(x)]}{E(\Lambda)A(x)} = M_1[-A(x)],$$

where

$$M_1(t) = \frac{M_\Lambda(t) - 1}{tE(\Lambda)}$$

is the moment generating function of the equilibrium distribution of Λ, as is clear from Exercise 3.28. Therefore, $S_1(x)$ is again of the form given by (5.3), but with the distribution of Λ now given by the equilibrium pdf $\Pr(\Lambda > \lambda)/E(\Lambda)$.

5.16 (a)

$$M_{\Lambda_s}(t) = \int_{\text{all } \lambda} e^{t\lambda} f_{\Lambda_s}(\lambda) d\lambda = \frac{1}{M_\Lambda(-s)} \int_{\text{all } \lambda} e^{(t-s)\lambda} f_{\Lambda_s}(\lambda) d\lambda$$

$$= \frac{M_\Lambda(t-s)}{M_\Lambda(-s)},$$

with the integral replaced by a sum if Λ is discrete.

(b) $M'_{\Lambda_s}(t) = \dfrac{M'_\Lambda(t-s)}{M_\Lambda(-s)}$ and thus $E(\Lambda_s) = M'_{\Lambda_s}(0) = \dfrac{M'_\Lambda(-s)}{M_\Lambda(-s)}.$

Also, $M''_{\Lambda_s}(t) = \dfrac{M''_\Lambda(t-s)}{M_\Lambda(-s)}$, implying that $E(\Lambda_s^2) = M''_{\Lambda_s}(0) = \dfrac{M''_\Lambda(-s)}{M_\Lambda(-s)}.$

Now,

$$c'_\Lambda(t) = \frac{M'_\Lambda(t)}{M_\Lambda(t)}, \text{ and replacement of } t \text{ by } -s \text{ yields}$$

$$c'_\Lambda(-s) = E(\Lambda_s). \text{ Similarly,}$$

$$c''_\Lambda(t) = \frac{M''_\Lambda(t)}{M_\Lambda(t)} - \left[\frac{M'_\Lambda(t)}{M_\Lambda(t)}\right]^2, \text{ and so}$$

$$c''_\Lambda(-s) = \frac{M''_\Lambda(-s)}{M_\Lambda(-s)} - \left[\frac{M'_\Lambda(-s)}{M_\Lambda(-s)}\right]^2 = E(\Lambda_s^2) - [E(\Lambda_s)]^2 = \text{Var}(\Lambda_s).$$

(c)

$$h_X(x) = -\frac{d}{dx}\ln S_X(x) = -\frac{d}{dx}\ln M_\Lambda[-A(x)] = -\frac{d}{dx}c_\Lambda[-A(x)]$$

$$= a(x)c'_\Lambda[-A(x)].$$

(d)

$$
\begin{aligned}
h'_X(x) &= a'(x)c'_\Lambda[-A(x)] + a(x)\frac{d}{dx}c'_\Lambda[-A(x)] \\
&= a'(x)c'_\Lambda[-A(x)] - [a(x)]^2 c''_\Lambda[-A(x)].
\end{aligned}
$$

(e) Using (b) and (d), we have

$$
h'_X(x) = a'(x)\mathrm{E}[\Lambda_{A(x)}] - [a(x)]^2\,\mathrm{Var}[\Lambda_{A(x)}] \le 0
$$

if $a'(x) \le 0$ because $\mathrm{E}[\Lambda_{A(x)}] \ge 0$ and $\mathrm{Var}[\Lambda_{A(x)}] \ge 0$. But $\frac{d}{dx}h_{X|\Lambda}(x|\lambda) = \lambda a'(x)$, and thus $a'(x) \le 0$ when $\frac{d}{dx}h_{X|\Lambda}(x|\lambda) \le 0$.

5.17 Using the first definition of a spliced model, we have

$$
f_X(x) = \begin{cases} \tau, & 0 < x < 1{,}000 \\ \gamma e^{-x/\theta}, & x > 1{,}000, \end{cases}
$$

where the coefficient τ is a_1 multiplied by the uniform density of 0.001 and the coefficient γ is a_2 multiplied by the scaled exponential coefficient. To ensure continuity we must have $\tau = \gamma e^{-1{,}000/\theta}$. Finally, to ensure that the density integrates to 1, we have

$$
\begin{aligned}
1 &= \int_0^{1{,}000} \gamma e^{-1{,}000/\theta}\,dx + \int_{1{,}000}^\infty \gamma e^{-x/\theta}\,dx \\
&= 1{,}000\gamma e^{-1{,}000/\theta} + \gamma\theta e^{-1{,}000/\theta},
\end{aligned}
$$

which implies $\gamma = [(1{,}000+\theta)e^{-1{,}000/\theta}]^{-1}$. The final density, a one-parameter distribution, is

$$
f_X(x) = \begin{cases} \dfrac{1}{1{,}000 + \theta}, & 0 < x \le 1{,}000, \\[2ex] \dfrac{e^{-x/\theta}}{(1{,}000 + \theta)e^{-1{,}000/\theta}}, & x \ge 1{,}000. \end{cases}
$$

Figure 5.1 presents this density function for the value $\theta = 1{,}000$.

5.18 $f_Y(y) = \exp(-|(\ln y)/\theta|)/2\theta y$. For $x \le 0$, $F_X(x) = \frac{1}{2\theta}\int_{-\infty}^x e^{t/\theta}dt = \frac{1}{2}e^{t/\theta}\big|_{-\infty}^x = \frac{1}{2}e^{x/\theta}$. For $x > 0$ it is $\frac{1}{2} + \frac{1}{2\theta}\int_0^x e^{-t/\theta}dt = 1 - \frac{1}{2}e^{-x/\theta}$. With exponentiation the two descriptions are $F_Y(y) = \frac{1}{2}e^{\ln y/\theta}$, $0 < y \le 1$, and $F_Y(y) = 1 - \frac{1}{2}e^{-\ln y/\theta}$, $y \ge 1$.

5.19 $F(x) = \int_1^x 3t^{-4}dt = 1 - x^{-3}$. $Y = 1.1X$. $F_Y(y) = 1 - (x/1.1)^{-3}$. $\Pr(Y > 2.2) = 1 - F_Y(2.2) = (2.2/1.1)^{-3} = 0.125$.

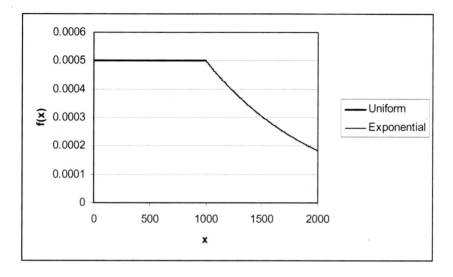

Figure 5.1   Continuous spliced density function.

5.20 (a) $\Pr(X^{-1} \le x) = \Pr(X \ge 1/x) = \Pr(X > 1/x)$, and the pdf is, therefore,

$$
\begin{aligned}
f_{1/X}(x) &= \frac{d}{dx} \Pr\left(X > \frac{1}{x}\right) \\
&= \frac{1}{x^2} f\left(\frac{1}{x}\right) \\
&= \sqrt{\frac{\theta x^3}{2\pi}} \exp\left[-\frac{\theta x}{2}\left(\frac{1 - \mu x}{\mu x}\right)^2\right]\left(\frac{1}{x^2}\right) \\
&= \sqrt{\frac{\theta}{2\pi x}} \exp\left[-\frac{\theta}{2x}\left(x - \frac{1}{\mu}\right)^2\right], \quad x > 0.
\end{aligned}
$$

(b) The inverse Gaussian pdf may be expressed as

$$
f(x) = \sqrt{\frac{\theta}{2\pi}} e^{\theta/\mu} x^{-1.5} \exp\left(-\frac{\theta x}{2\mu^2} - \frac{\theta}{2x}\right).
$$

Thus, $\int_0^\infty f(x)dx = 1$ may be expressed as

$$
\int_0^\infty x^{-1.5} \exp\left(-\frac{\theta x}{2\mu^2} - \frac{\theta}{2x}\right) dx = \sqrt{\frac{2\pi}{\theta}} e^{-\theta/\mu},
$$

valid for $\theta > 0$ and $\mu > 0$. Then

$$e^{t_1 x + t_2 x^{-1}} f(x) = \sqrt{\frac{\theta}{2\pi}} e^{\theta/\mu} x^{-1.5} \exp\left[-\left(\frac{\theta}{2\mu^2} - t_1\right) x - \left(\frac{\theta}{2} - t_2\right) \frac{1}{x}\right]$$

$$= \sqrt{\frac{\theta}{2\pi}} e^{\theta/\mu} x^{-1.5} \exp\left(-\frac{\theta_* x}{2\mu_*^2} - \frac{\theta_*}{2x}\right),$$

where $\theta_* = \theta - 2t_2$ and $\mu_* = \mu\sqrt{\frac{\theta - 2t_2}{\theta - 2\mu^2 t_1}}$. Therefore, if $\theta_* > 0$ and $\mu_* > 0$,

$$M(t_1, t_2) = \int_0^\infty e^{t_1 x + t_2 x^{-1}} f(x)\, dx$$

$$= \sqrt{\frac{\theta}{2\pi}} e^{\theta/\mu} \int_0^\infty x^{-1.5} \exp\left(-\frac{\theta_* x}{2\mu_*^2} - \frac{\theta_*}{2x}\right) dx$$

$$= \sqrt{\frac{\theta}{2\pi}} e^{\theta/\mu} \sqrt{\frac{2\pi}{\theta_*}} e^{-\theta_*/\mu_*}$$

$$= \sqrt{\frac{\theta}{\theta - 2t_2}} \exp\left[\frac{\theta}{\mu} - \frac{\theta - 2t_2}{\mu}\sqrt{\frac{\theta - 2\mu^2 t_1}{\theta - 2t_2}}\right]$$

$$= \sqrt{\frac{\theta}{\theta - 2t_2}} \exp\left[\frac{\theta - \sqrt{(\theta - 2t_2)(\theta - 2\mu^2 t_1)}}{\mu}\right].$$

(c)
$$M_X(t) = M(t, 0)$$

$$= \exp\left(\frac{\theta - \sqrt{\theta(\theta - 2\mu^2 t)}}{\mu}\right) = \exp\left[\frac{\theta}{\mu}\left(1 - \sqrt{1 - \frac{2\mu^2}{\theta} t}\right)\right].$$

(d)
$$M_{1/X}(t) = M(0, t)$$

$$= \sqrt{\frac{\theta}{\theta - 2t}} \exp\left(\frac{\theta - \sqrt{\theta(\theta - 2t)}}{\mu}\right)$$

$$= \sqrt{\frac{\theta}{\theta - 2t}} \exp\left[\frac{\theta}{\mu}\left(1 - \sqrt{1 - \frac{2t}{\theta}}\right)\right]$$

$$= \left(1 - \frac{2}{\theta} t\right)^{-1/2} \exp\left[\frac{\theta_1}{\mu_1}\left(1 - \sqrt{1 - \frac{2\mu_1^2}{\theta_1} t}\right)\right],$$

where $\theta_1 = \theta/\mu^2$ and $\mu_1 = 1/\mu$. Thus $M_{1/X}(t) = M_{Z_1}(t) M_{Z_2}(t)$ with $M_{Z_1}(t) = \left(1 - \frac{2}{\theta} t\right)^{-1/2}$ the mgf of a gamma distribution with $\alpha = 1/2$ and θ replaced by $2/\theta$ (in the notation of Example 3.7). Also, $M_{Z_2}(t)$ is the mgf of an inverse Gaussian distribution with θ replaced by $\theta_1 = \theta/\mu^2$ and μ by $\mu_1 = 1/\mu$, as is clear from (c).

(e)

$$M_Z(t) = \mathrm{E}\left\{\exp\left[\frac{t}{X}\left(\frac{X-\mu}{\mu}\right)^2\right]\right\} = \mathrm{E}\left[\exp\left(\frac{t}{\mu^2}X - \frac{2t}{\mu} + \frac{t}{X}\right)\right],$$

and, therefore,

$$
\begin{aligned}
M_Z(t) &= e^{-\frac{2t}{\mu}} M\left(\frac{t}{\mu^2}, t\right) \\
&= e^{-\frac{2t}{\mu}} \sqrt{\frac{\theta}{\theta - 2t}} \exp\left[\frac{\theta - \sqrt{(\theta - 2t)^2}}{\mu}\right] \\
&= \sqrt{\frac{\theta}{\theta - 2t}} \exp\left[-\frac{2t}{\mu} + \frac{\theta - (\theta - 2t)}{\mu}\right] \\
&= \left(1 - \frac{2}{\theta}t\right)^{-1/2},
\end{aligned}
$$

the same gamma mgf discussed in (d).

(f) First rewrite the mgf as

$$M_X(t) = \exp\left[\frac{\theta}{\mu} - (2\theta)^{\frac{1}{2}}\left(\frac{\theta}{2\mu^2} - t\right)^{\frac{1}{2}}\right].$$

Then,

$$
\begin{aligned}
M_X'(t) &= -(2\theta)^{\frac{1}{2}}\left(\frac{1}{2}\right)\left(\frac{\theta}{2\mu^2} - t\right)^{-\frac{1}{2}}(-1)M_X(t) \\
&= \left(\frac{1}{2}\right)^{\frac{1}{2}}\theta^{\frac{1}{2}}\left(\frac{\theta}{2\mu^2} - t\right)^{-\frac{1}{2}}M_X(t).
\end{aligned}
$$

Similarly,

$$
\begin{aligned}
M_X''(t) &= \left(\frac{1}{2}\right)^{\frac{3}{2}}\theta^{\frac{1}{2}}\left(\frac{\theta}{2\mu^2} - t\right)^{-\frac{3}{2}}M_X(t) \\
&\quad + \left(\frac{1}{2}\right)^{\frac{1}{2}}\theta^{\frac{1}{2}}\left(\frac{\theta}{2\mu^2} - t\right)^{-\frac{1}{2}}M_X'(t) \\
&= M_X(t)\left[\left(\frac{1}{2}\right)^{\frac{3}{2}}\theta^{\frac{1}{2}}\left(\frac{\theta}{2\mu^2} - t\right)^{-\frac{3}{2}} + \left(\frac{1}{2}\right)\theta\left(\frac{\theta}{2\mu^2} - t\right)^{-1}\right],
\end{aligned}
$$

and the result holds for $k = 1, 2$. Assuming that it holds for $k \geq 2$, differentiating again yields

$$M_X^{(k+1)}(t) = M_X'(t) \sum_{n=0}^{k-1} \frac{(k+n-1)!}{(k-n-1)!n!} \left(\frac{1}{2}\right)^{\frac{k+3n}{2}} \theta^{\frac{k-n}{2}} \left(\frac{\theta}{2\mu^2} - t\right)^{-\frac{k+n}{2}}$$

$$+ M_X(t) \sum_{n=0}^{k-1} \frac{(k+n-1)!}{(k-n-1)!n!} \left(\frac{1}{2}\right)^{\frac{k+3n}{2}} \theta^{\frac{k-n}{2}} \left(\frac{k+n}{2}\right) \left(\frac{\theta}{2\mu^2} - t\right)^{-\frac{k+n}{2}-1}$$

$$= M_X(t) \sum_{n=0}^{k-1} \frac{(k+n-1)!}{(k-n-1)!n!} \left(\frac{1}{2}\right)^{\frac{k+1+3n}{2}} \theta^{\frac{k+1-n}{2}} \left(\frac{\theta}{2\mu^2} - t\right)^{-\frac{k+1+n}{2}}$$

$$+ M_X(t) \sum_{n=0}^{k-1} \frac{(k+n)!}{(k-n-1)!n!} \left(\frac{1}{2}\right)^{\frac{k+2+3n}{2}} \theta^{\frac{k-n}{2}} \left(\frac{\theta}{2\mu^2} - t\right)^{-\frac{k+2+n}{2}} .$$

Now, change the index of summation in the second sum to obtain

$$M_X^{(k+1)}(t)$$

$$= M_X(t) \sum_{n=0}^{k-1} \frac{(k+n-1)!}{(k-n-1)!n!} \left(\frac{1}{2}\right)^{\frac{k+1+3n}{2}} \theta^{\frac{k+1-n}{2}} \left(\frac{\theta}{2\mu^2} - t\right)^{-\frac{k+1+n}{2}}$$

$$+ M_X(t) \sum_{n=1}^{k} \frac{(k+n-1)!}{(k-n)!(n-1)!} \left(\frac{1}{2}\right)^{\frac{k+3n-1}{2}} \theta^{\frac{k+1-n}{2}} \left(\frac{\theta}{2\mu^2} - t\right)^{-\frac{k+1+n}{2}} .$$

Separate out the two terms when $n = 0$ and $n = k$ and combine the others to obtain

$$M_X^{(k+1)}(t) = M_X(t)\left[\left(\frac{1}{2}\right)^{\frac{k+1}{2}}\theta^{\frac{k+1}{2}}\left(\frac{\theta}{2\mu^2}-t\right)^{-\frac{k+1}{2}}\right.$$

$$\left.+\frac{(2k-1)!}{(k-1)!}\left(\frac{1}{2}\right)^{2k-\frac{1}{2}}\theta^{\frac{1}{2}}\left(\frac{\theta}{2\mu^2}-t\right)^{-\frac{2k+1}{2}}\right]$$

$$+M_X(t)\sum_{n=1}^{k-1}\frac{(k+n-1)!}{(k-n)!n!}\left(\frac{1}{2}\right)^{\frac{k+1+3n}{2}}\theta^{\frac{k+1-n}{2}}$$

$$\times\left(\frac{\theta}{2\mu^2}-t\right)^{-\frac{k+1+n}{2}}[(k-n)+2n]$$

$$= M_X(t)\left[\left(\frac{1}{2}\right)^{\frac{k+1}{2}}\theta^{\frac{k+1}{2}}\left(\frac{\theta}{2\mu^2}-t\right)^{-\frac{k+1}{2}}\right.$$

$$\left.+\frac{(2k)!}{k!}\left(\frac{1}{2}\right)^{2k+\frac{1}{2}}\theta^{\frac{1}{2}}\left(\frac{\theta}{2\mu^2}-t\right)^{-\frac{2k+1}{2}}\right]$$

$$+ M_X(t)\sum_{n=1}^{k-1}\frac{(k+n)!}{(k-n)!n!}\left(\frac{1}{2}\right)^{\frac{k+1+3n}{2}}\theta^{\frac{k+1-n}{2}}\left(\frac{\theta}{2\mu^2}-t\right)^{-\frac{k+1+n}{2}}$$

$$= M_X(t)\sum_{n=0}^{k}\frac{(k+n)!}{(k-n)!n!}\left(\frac{1}{2}\right)^{\frac{k+1+3n}{2}}\theta^{\frac{k+1-n}{2}}\left(\frac{\theta}{2\mu^2}-t\right)^{-\frac{k+1+n}{2}},$$

and the kth derivative of $M_X(t)$ is as given by induction on n. Then,

$$\left(\frac{1}{2}\right)^{\frac{k+3n}{2}}\theta^{\frac{k-n}{2}}\left(\frac{\theta}{2\mu^2}-0\right)^{-\frac{k+n}{2}} = \left(\frac{1}{2}\right)^{\frac{k+3n-k-n}{2}}\theta^{\frac{k-n-k-n}{2}}\mu^{k+n}$$

$$= \frac{\mu^{k+n}}{(2\theta)^n},$$

and the result follows from

$$E(X^k) = M_X^{(k)}(0).$$

(g) Clearly,

$$K_{\frac{1}{2}}\left(\frac{\theta}{\mu}\right) = K_{-\frac{1}{2}}\left(\frac{\theta}{\mu}\right) = \sqrt{\frac{\pi\mu}{2\theta}}e^{-\frac{\theta}{\mu}},$$

which implies from (f) that, for $m = 1, 2, ...$, the moment result may be stated as

$$\int_0^\infty x^m f(x)dx = \sqrt{\frac{2\theta}{\pi\mu}}\mu^m e^{\frac{\theta}{\mu}}K_{m-\frac{1}{2}}\left(\frac{\theta}{\mu}\right) = \frac{\mu^m K_{m-\frac{1}{2}}\left(\frac{\theta}{\mu}\right)}{K_{\frac{1}{2}}\left(\frac{\theta}{\mu}\right)},$$

which is also obviously true when $m = 0$. But,

$$f(x) = \sqrt{\frac{\theta}{2\pi}} x^{-\frac{3}{2}} e^{-\frac{\theta}{2\mu^2 x}(x^2 - 2\mu x + \mu^2)} = \sqrt{\frac{\theta}{2\pi}} e^{\frac{\theta}{\mu}} \left[x^{-\frac{3}{2}} e^{-\frac{\theta}{2\mu^2} x - \frac{\theta}{2x}} \right],$$

and thus

$$\sqrt{\frac{\theta}{2\pi}} e^{\frac{\theta}{\mu}} \int_0^\infty x^{m-\frac{3}{2}} e^{-\frac{\theta}{2\mu^2 x} - \frac{\theta}{2x}} dx = \sqrt{\frac{2\theta}{\pi\mu}} \mu^m e^{\frac{\theta}{\mu}} K_{m-\frac{1}{2}} \left(\frac{\theta}{\mu} \right),$$

or, equivalently,

$$\int_0^\infty x^{m-\frac{3}{2}} e^{-\frac{\theta}{2\mu^2 x} - \frac{\theta}{2x}} dx = 2\mu^{m-\frac{1}{2}} K_{m-\frac{1}{2}} \left(\frac{\theta}{\mu} \right).$$

Let $\alpha = \theta/(2\mu^2)$, implying that $\mu = \sqrt{\theta/(2\alpha)}$, and also that $\theta/\mu = 2\mu\alpha = \sqrt{2\alpha\theta}$.

5.2   SECTION 5.3

5.21 Let $\tau = \alpha/\theta$, and then in the Pareto distribution substitute $\tau\theta$ for α. The limiting distribution function is

$$\lim_{\theta \to \infty} 1 - \left(\frac{\theta}{x + \theta} \right)^{\tau\theta} = 1 - \lim_{\theta \to \infty} \left(\frac{\theta}{x + \theta} \right)^{\tau\theta}.$$

The limit of the logarithm is

$$
\begin{aligned}
\lim_{\theta \to \infty} \tau\theta[\ln\theta - \ln(x + \theta)] &= \tau \lim_{\theta \to \infty} \frac{\ln\theta - \ln(x + \theta)}{\theta^{-1}} \\
&= \tau \lim_{\theta \to \infty} \frac{\theta^{-1} - (x + \theta)^{-1}}{-\theta^{-2}} \\
&= -\tau \lim_{\theta \to \infty} \frac{x\theta}{x + \theta} = -\tau x.
\end{aligned}
$$

The second line and the final limit use L'Hôpital's rule. The limit of the distribution function is then $1 - \exp(-\tau x)$, an exponential distribution.

5.22 The generalized Pareto distribution is the transformed beta distribution with $\gamma = 1$. The limiting distribution is then transformed gamma with $\tau = 1$, which is a gamma distribution. The gamma parameters are $\alpha = \tau$ and $\theta = \xi$.

5.23 Hold α constant and let $\theta\tau^{1/\gamma} \to \xi$. Then let $\theta = \xi\tau^{-1/\gamma}$. Then

$$
\begin{aligned}
f(x) &= \frac{\Gamma(\alpha+\tau)\gamma x^{\gamma\tau-1}}{\Gamma(\alpha)\Gamma(\tau)\theta^{\gamma\tau}(1+x^\gamma\theta^{-\gamma})^{\alpha+\tau}} \\[2mm]
&= \frac{e^{-\alpha-\tau}(\alpha+\tau)^{\alpha+\tau-1}(2\pi)^{1/2}\gamma x^{\gamma\tau-1}}{\Gamma(\alpha)e^{-\tau}\tau^{\tau-1}(2\pi)^{1/2}\xi^{\gamma\tau}\tau^{-\tau}(1+x^\gamma\xi^{-\gamma}\tau)^{\alpha+\tau}} \\[2mm]
&= \frac{e^{-\alpha}\left(1+\frac{\alpha}{\tau}\right)^{\alpha+\tau-1}\gamma x^{-\gamma\alpha-1}}{\Gamma(\alpha)\tau^{-\alpha-\tau}\xi^{\gamma(\tau+\alpha)}\xi^{-\gamma\alpha}x^{-\gamma(\tau+\alpha)}(1+x^\gamma\xi^{-\gamma}\tau)^{\alpha+\tau}} \\[2mm]
&= \frac{e^{-\alpha}\left(1+\frac{\alpha}{\tau}\right)^{\alpha+\tau-1}\gamma x^{-\gamma\alpha-1}}{\Gamma(\alpha)\xi^{-\gamma\alpha}\left[1+\frac{(\xi/x)^\gamma}{\tau}\right]^{\alpha+\tau}} \\[2mm]
&\to \frac{\gamma\xi^{\gamma\alpha}}{\Gamma(\alpha)x^{\gamma\alpha+1}e^{(\xi/x)^\gamma}}.
\end{aligned}
$$

5.3 SECTION 5.4

5.24 From Example 5.12, $r(\theta) = -1/\theta$ and $q(\theta) = \theta^\alpha$. Then, $r'(\theta) = 1/\theta^2$ and $q'(\theta) = \alpha\theta^{\alpha-1}$. From (5.9),

$$
\mu(\theta) = \frac{q'(\theta)}{r'(\theta)q(\theta)} = \frac{\alpha\theta^{\alpha-1}}{\theta^{-2}\theta^\alpha} = \alpha\theta.
$$

With $\mu'(\theta) = \alpha$ and (5.10),

$$
\text{Var}(X) = \frac{\mu'(\theta)}{r'(\theta)} = \frac{\alpha}{\theta^{-2}} = \alpha\theta^2.
$$

5.25 For the mean,

$$
\begin{aligned}
\ln f(x;\theta) &= \ln p(m,x) + mr(\theta)x - m\ln q(\theta), \\[2mm]
\frac{\partial \ln f(x;\theta)}{\partial\theta} &= \frac{\partial f(x;\theta)}{\partial\theta}\frac{1}{f(x;\theta)} = \left[mr'(\theta)x - \frac{mq'(\theta)}{q(\theta)}\right], \\[2mm]
\frac{\partial f(x;\theta)}{\partial\theta} &= \left[mr'(\theta)x - \frac{mq'(\theta)}{q(\theta)}\right]f(x;\theta),
\end{aligned}
$$

$$
\begin{aligned}
0 = \int \frac{\partial f(x;\theta)}{\partial\theta}dx &= mr'(\theta)\int xf(x;\theta)dx - \frac{mq'(\theta)}{q(\theta)}\int f(x;\theta)dx \\[2mm]
&= mr'(\theta)\text{E}(X) - \frac{mq'(\theta)}{q(\theta)}, \\[2mm]
\text{E}(X) &= q'(\theta)/[r'(\theta)q(\theta)] = \mu(\theta).
\end{aligned}
$$

For the variance,

$$\frac{\partial f(x;\theta)}{\partial \theta} = mr'(\theta)[x - \mu(\theta)]f(x;\theta),$$

$$\frac{\partial^2 f(x;\theta)}{\partial \theta^2} = mr''(\theta)[x - \mu(\theta)]f(x;\theta) - mr'(\theta)\mu'(\theta)f(x;\theta)$$
$$+ m[r'(\theta)]^2[x - \mu(\theta)]^2 f(x;\theta),$$

$$0 = \int \frac{\partial^2 f(x;\theta)}{\partial \theta^2} dx = 0 - mr'(\theta)\mu'(\theta)(1) + m^2[r'(\theta)]^2 E\{[X - \mu(\theta)]^2\}$$
$$= -mr'(\theta)\mu'(\theta) + m^2[r'(\theta)]^2 \text{Var}(X),$$

$$\text{Var}(X) = \mu'(\theta)/[mr'(\theta)].$$

5.26 (a) We prove the result by induction on m. Assume that X_j has a continuous distribution (if X_j is discrete, simply replace the integrals by sums in what follows). If $m = 1$, then $S = X$, and the result holds with $p(x) = p_1(x)$. If true for m with $p(x) = p_m^*(x)$, then for $m + 1$, S has pdf (by the convolution formula) of the form

$$\int_0^s \frac{p_m^*(s - x)e^{r(\theta)(s-x)}}{\prod_{j=1}^m q_j(\theta)} \frac{p_{m+1}(x)e^{r(\theta)x}}{q_{m+1}(\theta)} dx$$
$$= \frac{e^{r(\theta)s}\left[\int_0^s p_m^*(s - x)p_{m+1}(x)dx\right]}{\prod_{j=1}^{m+1} q_j(\theta)},$$

which is of the desired form with $p_{m+1}^*(s) = \int_0^s p_m^*(s - x)p_{m+1}(x)dx$. It is instructive to note that $p(x)$ is clearly the convolution of the functions $p_1(x), p_2(x), \ldots, p_m(x)$.

(b) By (a), S has pf of the form

$$f(s;\theta) = \frac{p_m^*(s)e^{r(\theta)s}}{[q(\theta)]^m}.$$

If X_j has a continuous distribution and S has pdf $f(s;\theta)$, then that of $\bar{X}$ is

$$f_1(\bar{x};\theta) = mf(m\bar{x};\theta) = \frac{mp_m^*(m\bar{x})e^{mr(\theta)\bar{x}}}{[q(\theta)]^m}$$

of the desired form with $p(m, x) = mp_m^*(mx)$. If X_j is discrete, the pf of $\bar{X}$ is clearly of the desired form with $p(m, x) = p_m^*(mx)$.

CHAPTER 6

CHAPTER 6 SOLUTIONS

6.1 SECTION 6.1

6.1
$$
\begin{aligned}
P_N(z) &= \sum_{k=0}^{\infty} p_k z^k = \sum_{k=0}^{\infty} p_k e^{k \ln z} = M_N(\ln z) \\
P_N'(z) &= z^{-1} M_N'(\ln z) \\
P_N'(1) &= M_N'(0) = \mathrm{E}(N) \\
P_N''(z) &= -z^{-2} M_N'(\ln z) + z^{-2} M_N''(\ln z) \\
P_N''(1) &= -\mathrm{E}(N) + \mathrm{E}(N^2) = \mathrm{E}[N(N-1)].
\end{aligned}
$$

6.2 SECTION 6.5

6.2 For Exercise 14.3, the values at $k = 1, 2, 3$ are 0.1000, 0.0994, and 0.1333, which are nearly constant. The Poisson distribution is recommended. For Exercise 14.5, the values at $k = 1, 2, 3, 4$ are 0.1405, 0.2149, 0.6923, and 1.3333, which is increasing. The geometric/negative binomial is recommended (although the pattern looks more quadratic than linear).

Student Solutions Manual to Accompany Loss Models: From Data to Decisions, Fourth **43** *Edition*. By Stuart A. Klugman, Harry H. Panjer, Gordon E. Willmot

6.3 For the Poisson, $\lambda > 0$ and so it must be $a = 0$ and $b > 0$. For the binomial, m must be a positive integer and $0 < q < 1$. This requires $a < 0$ and $b > 0$ provided $-b/a$ is an integer ≥ 2. For the negative binomial, both r and β must be positive so $a > 0$ and b can be anything provided $b/a > -1$.

The pair $a = -1$ and $b = 1.5$ cannot work because the binomial is the only possibility but $-b/a = 1.5$, which is not an integer. For proof, let p_0 be arbitrary. Then $p_1 = (-1 + 1.5/1)p = 0.5p$ and $p_2 = (-1 + 1.5/2)(0.5p) = -0.125p < 0$.

6.3   SECTION 6.6

6.4
$$p_k = p_{k-1}\left[\frac{\beta}{1+\beta} + \frac{r-1}{k}\frac{\beta}{1+\beta}\right] = p_{k-1}\frac{\beta}{1+\beta}\frac{k+r-1}{k}$$
$$= p_{k-2}\left(\frac{\beta}{1+\beta}\right)^2\frac{k+r-1}{k}\frac{k+r-2}{k-1}$$
$$= p_1\left(\frac{\beta}{1+\beta}\right)^{k-1}\frac{k+r-1}{k}\frac{k+r-2}{k-1}\cdots\frac{r+1}{2}.$$

The factors will be positive (and thus p_k will be positive) provided $p_1 > 0$, $\beta > 0$, $r > -1$, and $r \neq 0$.

To see that the probabilities sum to a finite amount,
$$\sum_{k=1}^{\infty}p_k = p_1\sum_{k=1}^{\infty}\left(\frac{\beta}{1+\beta}\right)^{k-1}\frac{k+r-1}{k}\frac{k+r-2}{k-1}\cdots\frac{r+1}{2}$$
$$= p_1\frac{1}{r}\sum_{k=1}^{\infty}\left(\frac{\beta}{1+\beta}\right)^{k-1}\binom{k+r-1}{k}$$
$$= p_1\frac{(1+\beta)^{r+1}}{r\beta}\sum_{k=1}^{\infty}\left(\frac{1}{1+\beta}\right)^r\left(\frac{\beta}{1+\beta}\right)^k\binom{k+r-1}{k}.$$

The terms of the summand are the pf of the negative binomial distribution and so must sum to a number less than one (p_0 is missing), and so the original sum must converge.

6.5 From the previous solution (with $r = 0$),
$$1 = \sum_{k=1}^{\infty}p_k = p_1\sum_{k=1}^{\infty}\left(\frac{\beta}{1+\beta}\right)^{k-1}\frac{k-1}{k}\frac{k-2}{k-1}\cdots\frac{1}{2}$$
$$= p_1\sum_{k=1}^{\infty}\left(\frac{\beta}{1+\beta}\right)^{k-1}\frac{1}{k}$$
$$= p_1\frac{1+\beta}{\beta}\left[-\ln\left(1-\frac{\beta}{1+\beta}\right)\right]$$

using the Taylor series expansion for $\ln(1-x)$. Thus

$$p_1 = \frac{\beta}{(1+\beta)\ln(1+\beta)}$$

and

$$p_k = \left(\frac{\beta}{1+\beta}\right)^k \frac{1}{k\ln(1+\beta)}.$$

6.6

$$
\begin{aligned}
P(z) &= \frac{1}{\ln(1+\beta)}\sum_{k=1}^{\infty}\left(\frac{\beta}{1+\beta}\right)^k\frac{1}{k}z^k \\
&= \frac{1}{\ln(1+\beta)}\left[-\ln\left(1-\frac{z\beta}{1+\beta}\right)\right] \\
&= \frac{\ln\left(\frac{1+\beta}{1+\beta-z\beta}\right)}{\ln(1+\beta)} \\
&= 1 - \frac{\ln[1-\beta(z-1)]}{\ln(1+\beta)}.
\end{aligned}
$$

6.7 The pgf goes to $1-(1-z)^{-r}$ as $\beta \to \infty$. The derivative with respect to z is $-r(1-z)^{-r-1}$. The expected value is this derivative evaluated at $z=1$, which is infinite due to the negative exponent.

CHAPTER 7

CHAPTER 7 SOLUTIONS

7.1 SECTION 7.1

7.1 Poisson: $P(z) = e^{\lambda(z-1)}$, $B(z) = e^z$, $\theta = \lambda$.
  Negative binomial: $P(z) = [1 - \beta(z-1)]^{-r}$, $B(z) = (1-z)^{-r}$, $\theta = \beta$.
  Binomial: $P(z) = [1 + q(z-1)]^m$, $B(z) = (1+z)^m$, $\theta = q$.

7.2 The geometric–geometric distribution has pgf

$$
\begin{aligned}
P_{GG}(z) &= (1 - \beta_1\{[1 - \beta_2(z-1)]^{-1} - 1\})^{-1} \\
&= \frac{1 - \beta_2(z-1)}{1 - \beta_2(1 + \beta_1)(z-1)}.
\end{aligned}
$$

The Bernoulli–geometric distribution has pgf

$$
\begin{aligned}
P_{BG}(z) &= 1 + q\{[1 - \beta(z-1)]^{-1} - 1\} \\
&= \frac{1 - \beta(1 - q)(z-1)}{1 - \beta(z-1)}.
\end{aligned}
$$

Student Solutions Manual to Accompany Loss Models: From Data to Decisions, Fourth **47**
Edition. By Stuart A. Klugman, Harry H. Panjer, Gordon E. Willmot
Copyright © 2012 John Wiley & Sons, Inc.

The ZM geometric distribution has pgf

$$
\begin{aligned}
P_{ZMG}(z) &= p_0 + (1 - p_0)\frac{[1 - \beta^*(z - 1)]^{-1} - (1 + \beta^*)^{-1}}{1 - (1 + \beta^*)^{-1}} \\
&= \frac{1 - (p_0\beta^* + p_0 - 1)(z - 1)}{1 - \beta^*(z - 1)}.
\end{aligned}
$$

In $P_{BG}(z)$, replace $1 - q$ with $(1 + \beta_1)^{-1}$ and replace β with $\beta_2(1 + \beta_1)$ to see that it matches $P_{GG}(z)$. It is clear that the new parameters will stay within the allowed ranges.

In $P_{GG}(z)$, replace q with $(1 - p_0)(1 + \beta^*)/\beta^*$ and replace β with β^*. Some algebra leads to $P_{ZMG}(z)$.

7.3 The binomial–geometric distribution has pgf

$$
\begin{aligned}
P_{BG}(z) &= \left\{ 1 + q\left[\frac{1}{1 - \beta(z - 1)} - 1 \right] \right\}^m \\
&= \left[\frac{1 - \beta(1 - q)(z - 1)}{1 - \beta(z - 1)} \right]^m.
\end{aligned}
$$

The negative binomial–geometric distribution has pgf

$$
\begin{aligned}
P_{NBG}(z) &= \left\{ 1 - \beta_1\left[\frac{1}{1 - \beta_2(z - 1)} - 1 \right] \right\}^{-r} \\
&= \left[\frac{1 - \beta_2(1 + \beta_1)(z - 1)}{1 - \beta_2(z - 1)} \right]^{-r} \\
&= \left[\frac{1 - \beta_2(z - 1)}{1 - \beta_2(1 + \beta_1)(z - 1)} \right]^{r}.
\end{aligned}
$$

In the binomial–geometric pgf, replace m with r, $\beta(1 - q)$ with β_2, and β with $(1 + \beta_1)\beta_2$ to obtain $P_{NBG}(z)$.

7.2   SECTION 7.2

7.4
$$
\begin{aligned}
P_S(z) &= \prod_{i=1}^{n} P_{S_i}(z) = \prod_{i=1}^{n} \exp\{\lambda_i[P_2(z) - 1]\} \\
&= \exp\left\{ \left(\sum_{i=1}^{n} \lambda_i \right)[P_2(z) - 1] \right\}.
\end{aligned}
$$

This is a compound distribution. The primary distribution is Poisson with parameter $\sum_{i=1}^{n} \lambda_i$. The secondary distribution has pgf $P_2(z)$.

7.5 $P(z) = \sum_{k=0}^{\infty} z^k p_k$, $P^{(1)}(z) = \sum_{k=0}^{\infty} k z^{k-1} p_k$,

$$
\begin{aligned}
P^{(j)}(z) &= \sum_{k=0}^{\infty} k(k-1)\cdots(k-j+1)z^{k-j}p_k, P^{(j)}(1) \\
&= \sum_{k=0}^{\infty} k(k-1)\cdots(k-j+1)p_k \\
&= \mathrm{E}[N(N-1)\cdots(N-j+1).
\end{aligned}
$$

$$
\begin{aligned}
P(z) &= \exp\{\lambda[P_2(z) - 1]\}, \\
P^{(1)}(z) &= \lambda P(z)P_2^{(1)}(z), \\
\mu &= P^{(1)}(1) = \lambda P(1)m_1' = \lambda m_1'.
\end{aligned}
$$

$$
\begin{aligned}
P^{(2)}(z) &= \lambda^2 P(z)\left[P_2^{(1)}\right]^2 + \lambda P(z)P_2^{(2)}(z), \\
\mu_2' - \mu &= P^{(2)}(1) = \lambda^2(m_1')^2 + \lambda(m_2' - m_1').
\end{aligned}
$$

Then $\mu_2' = \lambda^2(m_1')^2 + \lambda m_2'$ and $\mu_2 = \mu_2' - \mu^2 = \lambda m_2'$.

$$
\begin{aligned}
P^{(3)}(z) &= \lambda^3 P(z)\left[P_2^{(1)}\right]^3 + 3\lambda^2 P(z)P_2^{(1)}(z)P_2^{(2)}(z) + \lambda P(z)P_2^{(3)}(z), \\
\mu_3' - 3\mu_2' + 2\mu &= \lambda^3(m_1')^3 + 3\lambda^2 m_1'(m_2' - m_1') + \lambda(m_3' - 3m_2' + 2m_1').
\end{aligned}
$$

Then,

$$
\begin{aligned}
\mu_3 &= \mu_3' - 3\mu_2'\mu + 2\mu^3 \\
&= (\mu_3' - 3\mu_2' + 2\mu) + 3\mu_2' - 2\mu - 3\mu_2'\mu + 2\mu^3 \\
&= \lambda^3(m_1')^3 + 3\lambda^2 m_1'(m_2' - m_1') + \lambda(m_3' - 3m_2' + 2m_1') \\
&\quad + 3[\lambda^2(m_1')^2 + \lambda m_2'] - 2\lambda m_1' - 3\lambda m_1'[\lambda^2(m_1')^2 + \lambda m_2'] + 2\lambda^3(m_1')^3 \\
&= \lambda^3[(m_1')^3 - 3(m_1')^3 + 2(m_1')^3] \\
&\quad + \lambda^2[3m_1'm_2' - 3(m_1')^2 + 3(m_1')^2 - 3m_1'm_2'] \\
&\quad + \lambda[m_3' - 3m_2' + 2m_1' + 3m_2' - 2m_1'] \\
&= \lambda m_3'.
\end{aligned}
$$

7.6 For the binomial distribution, $m_1' = mq$ and $m_2' = mq(1-q) + m^2q^2$. For the third central moment, $P^{(3)}(z) = m(m-1)(m-2)[1+q(z-1)]^{m-3}q^3$ and $P^{(3)}(1) = m(m-1)(m-2)q^3$. Then, $m_3' = m(m-1)(m-2)q^3 + 3mq - 3mq^2 + 3m^2q^2 - 2mq$.

$$\mu = \lambda m_1' = \lambda mq.$$
$$\sigma^2 = \lambda m_2' = \lambda(mq - mq^2 + m^2q^2) = \lambda mq(1 - q + mq) = \mu[1 + q(m - 1)].$$

$$
\begin{aligned}
\mu_3 &= \lambda m_3' = \lambda mq(m^2q^2 - 3mq^2 + 2q^2 + 3 - 3q + 3m - 2) \\
&= \lambda mq(3)(1 - q + mq) - \lambda mq(2) + \lambda mq(m^2q^2 - 3mq^2 + 2q^2) \\
&= 3\sigma^2 - 2\mu + \lambda mq(m^2q^2 - 3mq^2 + 2q^2) \\
&= 3\sigma^2 - 2\mu + \lambda mq(m - 1)(m - 2)q^2.
\end{aligned}
$$

Now,

$$\frac{m - 2}{m - 1}\frac{(\sigma^2 - \mu)^2}{\mu} = \frac{m - 2}{m - 1}\frac{\mu^2[q(m - 1)]^2}{\mu} = (m - 2)(m - 1)\lambda mq^3$$

and the relationship is shown.

7.3   SECTION 7.3

7.7 For the compound distribution, the pgf is $P(z) = P_{NB}[P_P(z)]$ which is exactly the same as for the mixed distribution because mixing distribution goes on the outside.

7.8
$$P_N(z) = \prod_{i=1}^{n} P_{N_i}(z) = \prod_{i=1}^{n} P_i[e^{\lambda(z-1)}].$$

Then N is mixed Poisson. The mixing distribution has pgf $P(z) = \prod_{i=1}^{n} P_i(z)$.

7.9 Because Θ has a scale parameter, we can write $\Theta = cX$, where X has density (probability, if discrete) function $f_X(x)$. Then, for the mixed distribution (with formulas for the continuous case)

$$
\begin{aligned}
p_k &= \int \frac{e^{-\lambda\theta}(\lambda\theta)^k}{k!} f_\Theta(\theta)d\theta \\
&= \frac{\lambda^k}{k!} \int e^{-\lambda\theta}\theta^k f_X(\theta/c)c^{-1}d\theta \\
&= \frac{\lambda^k}{k!} \int e^{-\lambda cx}c^k x^k f_X(x)dx.
\end{aligned}
$$

The parameter λ appears only as the product λc. Therefore, the mixed distribution does not depend on λ as a change in c will lead to the same distribution.

7.10
$$p_k = \int_0^\infty \frac{e^{-\theta}\theta^k}{k!}\frac{\alpha^2}{\alpha+1}(\theta+1)e^{-\alpha\theta}d\theta$$

$$= \frac{\alpha^2}{k!(\alpha+1)}\int_0^\infty \theta^k(\theta+1)e^{-(\alpha+1)\theta}d\theta$$

$$= \frac{\alpha^2}{k!(\alpha+1)}\int_0^\infty \beta^k(\alpha+1)^{-k-1}\left(\frac{\beta}{\alpha+1}+1\right)e^{-\beta}d\beta$$

$$= \frac{\alpha^2}{k!(\alpha+1)^{k+2}}\left[\frac{\Gamma(k+2)}{\alpha+1}+\Gamma(k+1)\right]$$

$$= \frac{\alpha^2[(k+1)/(\alpha+1)+1]}{(\alpha+1)^{k+2}}.$$

The pgf of the mixing distribution is

$$P(z) = \int_0^\infty z^\theta \frac{\alpha^2}{\alpha+1}(\theta+1)e^{-\alpha\theta}d\theta$$

$$= \frac{\alpha^2}{\alpha+1}\int_0^\infty (\theta+1)e^{-(\alpha-\ln z)\theta}d\theta$$

$$= \frac{\alpha^2}{\alpha+1}\left[-\frac{\theta+1}{\alpha-\ln z}e^{-(\alpha-\ln z)\theta}-\frac{\theta+1}{(\alpha-\ln z)^2}e^{-(\alpha-\ln z)\theta}\right]\Big|_0^\infty$$

$$= \frac{\alpha^2}{\alpha+1}\left[\frac{1}{\alpha-\ln z}+\frac{1}{(\alpha-\ln z)^2}\right],$$

and so the pgf of the mixed distribution [obtained by replacing $\ln z$ with $\lambda(z-1)$] is

$$P(z) = \frac{\alpha^2}{\alpha+1}\left\{\frac{1}{\alpha-\lambda(z-1)}+\frac{1}{[\alpha-\lambda(z-1)]^2}\right\}$$

$$= \frac{\alpha}{\alpha+1}\frac{\alpha}{\alpha-\lambda(z-1)}+\frac{1}{\alpha+1}\left[\frac{\alpha}{\alpha-\lambda(z-1)}\right]^2,$$

which is a two-point mixture of negative binomial variables with identical values of β. Each is also a Poisson–logarithmic distribution with identical logarithmic secondary distributions. The equivalent distribution has a logarithmic secondary distribution with $\beta = \lambda/\alpha$ and a primary distribution that is a mixture of Poissons. The first Poisson has $\lambda = \ln(1+\lambda/\alpha)$ and the second Poisson has $\lambda = 2\ln(1+\lambda/\alpha)$. To see that this is correct, note that the pgf is

$$P(z) = \frac{\alpha}{\alpha+1}\exp\left\{\ln\left(1+\frac{\lambda}{\alpha}\right)\frac{\ln[1-\lambda(z-1)/\alpha]}{\ln(1+\lambda/\alpha)}\right\}$$

$$+\frac{1}{\alpha+1}\exp\left\{2\ln\left(1+\frac{\lambda}{\alpha}\right)\frac{\ln[1-\lambda(z-1)/\alpha]}{\ln(1+\lambda/\alpha)}\right\}$$

$$= \frac{\alpha}{\alpha+1}\ln\left[1-\frac{\lambda(z-1)}{\alpha}\right]+\frac{1}{\alpha+1}\left[1-\frac{\lambda(z-1)}{\alpha}\right]^2.$$

7.4 SECTION 7.5

7.11 (a) $p_0 = e^{-4} = 0.01832$. $a = 0, b = 4$ and then $p_1 = 4p_0 = 0.07326$ and $p_2 = (4/2)p_1 = 0.14653$.

(b) $p_0 = 5^{-1} = 0.2$. $a = 4/5 = 0.8, b = 0$ and then $p_1 = (4/5)p_0 = 0.16$ and $p_2 = (4/5)p_1 = 0.128$.

(c) $p_0 = (1+2)^{-2} = 0.11111$. $a = 2/3, b = (2-1)(2/3) = 2/3$ and then $p_1 = (2/3 + 2/3)p_0 = 0.14815$ and $p_2 = (2/3 + 2/6)p_1 = 0.14815$.

(d) $p_0 = (1-0.5)^8 = 0.00391$. $a = -0.5/(1-0.5) = -1, b = (8+1)(1) = 9$ and then $p_1 = (-1+9)p_0 = 0.3125$ and $p_2 = (-1+9/2)p_1 = 0.10938$.

(e) $p_0 = 0$, $p_1 = 4/\ln(5) = 0.49707$. $a = 4/5 = 0.8, b = -0.8$ and then $p_2 = (0.8 - 0.8/2)p_1 = 0.14472$.

(f) $p_0 = 0$, $p_1 = \frac{-0.5(4)}{5^{0.5} - 5} = 0.72361$. $a = 4/5 = 0.8, b = (-0.5 - 1)(0.8) = -1.2$ and then $p_2 = (0.8 - 1.2/2)p_1 = 0.14472$.

(g) The secondary probabilities were found in part (f). Then $g_0 = e^{-2} = 0.13534$, $g_1 = \frac{2}{1}(1)(0.72361)(0.13534) = 0.19587$, and

$$g_2 = \frac{2}{2}[1(0.723671)(0.19587) + 2(0.14472)(0.13534)] = 0.18091.$$

(h) $p_0^M = 0.5$ is given. $p_1^T = 1/5 = 0.2$ and then $p_1^M = (1-0.5)0.2 = 0.1$. From part (b), $a = 0.8, b = 0$ and then $p_2^M = (0.8)p_1^M = 0.08$.

(i) The secondary Poisson distribution has $f_0 = e^{-1} = 0.36788$, $f_1 = 0.36788$, and $f_2 = 0.18394$. Then, $g_0 = e^{-4(1-0.36788)} = 0.07978$. From the recursive formula, $g_1 = \frac{4}{1}(1)(0.36788)(0.07978) = 0.11740$, and $g_2 = \frac{4}{2}[1(0.36788)(0.11740) + 2(0.18394)(0.07978)] = 0.14508$.

(j) For the secondary ETNB distribution, $f_0 = 0$, $f_1 = \frac{2(0.5)}{1.5^3 - 1.5} = 0.53333$. With $a = b = 1/3$, $f_2 = (1/3 + 1/6)f_1 = 0.26667$. Then, $g_0 = e^{-4} = 0.01832$, $g_1 = \frac{4}{1}(1)(0.53333)(0.01832) = 0.03908$, and

$$g_2 = \frac{4}{2}[1(0.53333)(0.03908) + 2(0.26667)(0.01832)] = 0.06123.$$

(k) With $f_0 = 0.5$ (given) the other probabilities from part (j) must be multiplied by 0.5 to produce $f_1 = 0.26667$ and $f_2 = 0.13333$. Then, $g_0 =$

$e^{-4(1-0.5)} = 0.01832$, $g_1 = \frac{8}{1}(1)(0.26667)(0.01832) = 0.03908$, and

$$g_2 = \frac{8}{2}[1(0.26667)(0.03908) + 2(0.13333)(0.01832)] = 0.06123.$$

7.12 $p_k/p_{k-1} = \left(\frac{k-1}{k}\right)^{\rho+1} \neq a + b/k$ for any choices of a, b, and ρ, and for all k.

CHAPTER 8

CHAPTER 8 SOLUTIONS

8.1 SECTION 8.2

8.1 For the excess loss variable,

$$f_Y(y) = \frac{0.000003e^{-0.00001(y+5,000)}}{0.3e^{-0.00001(5,000)}} = 0.00001e^{-0.00001y}, \; F_Y(y) = 1 - e^{-0.00001y}.$$

For the left censored and shifted variable,

$$f_Y(y) = \begin{cases} 1 - 0.3e^{-0.05} = 0.71463, & y = 0, \\ 0.000003e^{-0.00001(y+5,000)}, & y > 0, \end{cases}$$

$$F_Y(y) = \begin{cases} 0.71463, & y = 0, \\ 1 - 0.3e^{-0.00001(y+5,000)}, & y > 0, \end{cases}$$

and it is interesting to note that the excess loss variable has an exponential distribution.

Student Solutions Manual to Accompany Loss Models: From Data to Decisions, Fourth **55** Edition. By Stuart A. Klugman, Harry H. Panjer, Gordon E. Willmot
Copyright © 2012 John Wiley & Sons, Inc.

8.2 For the per-payment variable,

$$f_Y(y) = \frac{0.000003e^{-0.00001y}}{0.3e^{-0.00001(5,000)}} = 0.00001e^{-0.00001(y-5,000)},$$

$$F_Y(y) = 1 - e^{-0.00001(y-5,000)}, \; y > 5000.$$

For the per-loss variable,

$$f_Y(y) = \begin{cases} 1 - 0.3e^{-0.05} = 0.71463, & y = 0, \\ 0.000003e^{-0.00001y}, & y > 5,000, \end{cases}$$

$$F_Y(y) = \begin{cases} 0.71463, & 0 \le y \le 5,000, \\ 1 - 0.3e^{-0.00001y}, & y > 5,000. \end{cases}$$

8.3 From Example 3.1 $E(X) = 30,000$ and from Exercise 3.9,

$$E(X \wedge 5,000) = 30,000[1 - e^{-0.00001(5,000)}] = 1463.12.$$

Also $F(5,000) = 1 - 0.3e^{-0.00001(5,000)} = 0.71463$, and so for an ordinary deductible the expected cost per loss is 28,536.88 and per payment is 100,000. For the franchise deductible, the expected costs are $28,536.88 + 5,000(0.28537) = 29,963.73$ per loss and $100,000 + 5,000 = 105,000$ per payment.

8.4 For risk 1,

$$E(X) - E(X \wedge d) = \frac{\theta}{\alpha - 1} - \frac{\theta}{\alpha - 1}\left[1 - \left(\frac{\theta}{\theta + k}\right)^{\alpha - 1}\right]$$

$$= \frac{\theta^\alpha}{(\alpha - 1)(\theta + k)^{\alpha - 1}}.$$

The ratio is then

$$\frac{\theta^{0.8\alpha}}{(0.8\alpha - 1)(\theta + k)^{0.8\alpha - 1}} \bigg/ \frac{\theta^\alpha}{(\alpha - 1)(\theta + k)^{\alpha - 1}} = \frac{(\theta + k)^{0.2\alpha}(\alpha - 1)}{\theta^{0.2\alpha}(0.8\alpha - 1)}.$$

As k goes to infinity, the limit is infinity.

8.5 The expected cost per payment with the 10,000 deductible is

$$\frac{E(X) - E(X \wedge 10,000)}{1 - F(10,000)} = \frac{20,000 - 6,000}{1 - 0.60} = 35,000.$$

At the old deductible, 40% of losses become payments. The new deductible must have 20% of losses become payments and so the new deductible is 22,500. The expected cost per payment is

$$\frac{E(X) - E(X \wedge 22,500)}{1 - F(22,500)} = \frac{20,000 - 9,500}{1 - 0.80} = 52,500.$$

The increase is $17,500/35,000 = 50\%$.

8.2   SECTION 8.3

8.6 From Exercise 8.3, the loss elimination ratio is

$$(30,000 - 28,536.88)/30,000 = 0.0488.$$

8.7 With inflation at 10% we need

$$E(X \wedge 5,000/1.1) = 30,000[1 - e^{-0.00001(5,000/1.1)}] = 1333.11.$$

After inflation, the expected cost per loss is $1.1(30,000 - 1333.11) = 31,533.58$ an increase of 10.50%. For the per payment calculation we need $F(5,000/1.1) = 1 - 0.3e^{-0.00001(5,000/1.1)} = 0.71333$ for an expected cost of 110,000, an increase of exactly 10%.

8.8 $E(X) = \exp(7 + 2^2/2) = \exp(9) = 8103.08.$ The limited expected value is

$$
\begin{aligned}
E(X \wedge 2,000) &= e^9 \Phi\left(\frac{\ln 2,000 - 7 - 2^2}{2}\right) + 2,000\left[1 - \Phi\left(\frac{\ln 2,000 - 7}{2}\right)\right] \\
&= 8,103.08\Phi(-1.7) + 2,000[1 - \Phi(0.3)] \\
&= 8,103.08(0.0446) + 2,000(0.3821) = 1,125.60.
\end{aligned}
$$

The loss elimination ratio is $1,125.60/8,103.08 = 0.139.$ With 20% inflation, the probability of exceeding the deductible is

$$
\begin{aligned}
\Pr(1.2X > 2,000) &= \Pr(X > 2,000/1.2) \\
&= 1 - \Phi\left(\frac{\ln(2,000/1.2) - 7}{2}\right) \\
&= 1 - \Phi(0.2093) \\
&= 0.4171,
\end{aligned}
$$

and, therefore, 4.171 losses can be expected to produce payments.

8.9 The loss elimination ratio prior to inflation is

$$
\begin{aligned}
\frac{E(X \wedge 2k)}{E(X)} &= \frac{\frac{k}{2-1}\left[1 - \left(\frac{k}{2k+k}\right)^{2-1}\right]}{\frac{k}{2-1}} \\
&= \frac{2k}{2k+k} = \frac{2}{3}.
\end{aligned}
$$

Because θ is a scale parameter, inflation of 100% will double it to equal $2k$. Repeating the preceding gives the new loss elimination ratio of

$$1 - \left(\frac{2k}{2k + 2k}\right) = \frac{1}{2}.$$

8.10 The original loss elimination ratio is

$$\frac{E(X \wedge 500)}{E(X)} = \frac{1,000(1 - e^{-500/1,000})}{1,000} = 0.39347.$$

Doubling it produces the equation

$$0.78694 = \frac{1,000(1 - e^{-d/1,000})}{1,000} = 1 - e^{-d/1,000}.$$

The solution is $d = 1,546$.

8.11 For the current year the expected cost per payment is

$$\frac{E(X) - E(X \wedge 15,000)}{1 - F(15,000)} = \frac{20,000 - 7,700}{1 - 0.70} = 41,000.$$

After 50% inflation it is

$$\frac{1.5[E(X) - E(X \wedge 15,000/1.5)]}{1 - F(15,000/1.5)} = \frac{1.5[E(X) - E(X \wedge 10,000)]}{1 - F(10,000)}$$

$$= \frac{1.5(20,000 - 6,000)}{1 - 0.60} = 52,500.$$

8.12 The ratio desired is

$$\frac{E(X \wedge 10,000)}{E(X \wedge 1,000)} = \frac{e^{6.9078 + 1.5174^2/2}\Phi\left(\frac{\ln 10,000 - 6.9078 - 1.5174^2}{1.5174}\right) + 10,000\left[1 - \Phi\left(\frac{\ln 10,000 - 6.9078}{1.5174}\right)\right]}{e^{6.9078 + 1.5174^2/2}\Phi\left(\frac{\ln 1,000 - 6.9078 - 1.5174^2}{1.5174}\right) + 1,000\left[1 - \Phi\left(\frac{\ln 1,000 - 6.9078}{1.5174}\right)\right]}$$

$$= \frac{e^{8.059}\Phi(0) + 10,000[1 - \Phi(1.5174)]}{e^{8.059}\Phi(-1.5174) + 1,000[1 - \Phi(0)]}$$

$$= \frac{3,162(0.5) + 10,000(0.0647)}{3,162(0.0647) + 1,000(0.5)} = 3.162.$$

This year, the probability of exceeding 1,000 is $\Pr(X > 1,000) = 1 - \Phi\left(\frac{\ln 1,000 - 6.9078}{1.5174}\right) = 0.5$. With 10% inflation, the distribution is lognormal with parameters $\mu = 6.9078 + \ln 1.1 = 7.0031$ and $\mu = 1.5174$. The probability is $1 - \Phi\left(\frac{\ln 1,000 - 7.0031}{1.5174}\right) = 1 - \Phi(-0.0628) = 0.525$, an increase of

5%. Alternatively, the original lognormal distribution could be used and then $\Pr(X > 1{,}000/1.1)$ computed.

8.13 The desired quantity is the expected value of a right truncated variable. It is

$$\frac{\int_0^{1.000} x f(x)}{F(1{,}000)} = \frac{E(X \wedge 1{,}000) - 1{,}000[1 - F(1{,}000)]}{F(1{,}000)} = \frac{E(X \wedge 1{,}000) - 400}{0.6}.$$

From the loss elimination ratio,

$$0.3 = \frac{E(X \wedge 1{,}000)}{E(X)} = \frac{E(X \wedge 1{,}000)}{2{,}000}$$

and so $E(X \wedge 1{,}000) = 600$, making the answer $200/0.6 = 333$.

8.3 SECTION 8.4

8.14 From Exercise 3.9 we have

$$E(X \wedge 150{,}000) = 30{,}000[1 - e^{-0.00001(150{,}000)}] = 23{,}306.10.$$

After 10% inflation the expected cost is

$$1.1E(X \wedge 150{,}000/1.1) = 33{,}000[1 - e^{-0.00001(150{,}000/1.1)}] = 24{,}560.94,$$

for an increase of 5.38%.

8.15 From Exercise 3.10 we have

$$e_X(d) = \frac{\theta + d}{\alpha - 1} = \frac{100 + d}{2 - 1} = 100 + d.$$

Therefore, the range is 100 to infinity. With 10% inflation, θ becomes 110 and the mean residual life is $e_Y(d) = 110 + d$. The ratio is $\frac{110+d}{100+d}$. As d increases, the ratio decreases from 1.1 to 1. The mean residual life is

$$\begin{aligned}
e_Z(d) &= \frac{\int_d^{500}(x - d)f(x)dx + \int_{500}^{\infty}(500 - d)f(x)dx}{1 - F_X(d)} \\
&= 100 + d - \frac{(100 + d)^2}{600}.
\end{aligned}$$

This function is a quadratic function of d. It starts at 83.33, increases to a maximum of 150 at $d = 200$, and decreases to 0 when $d = 500$. The range is 0 to 150.

8.4   SECTION 8.5

8.16 $25 = E(X) = \int_0^w (1 - x/w)dx = w/2$ for $w = 50$. $S(10) = 1 - 10/50 = 0.8$.
Then

$$
\begin{aligned}
\mathrm{E}(Y) &= \int_{10}^{50} (x - 10)(1/50)dx/0.8 = 20, \\
\mathrm{E}(Y^2) &= \int_{10}^{50} (x - 10)^2(1/50)dx/0.8 = 533.33, \\
\mathrm{Var}(Y) &= 533.33 - 20^2 = 133.33.
\end{aligned}
$$

8.17 The bonus is $B = 500{,}000(0.7 - L/500{,}000)/3 = (350{,}000 - L)/3$ if positive. The bonus is positive provided $L < 350{,}000$. The expected bonus is

$$
\begin{aligned}
\mathrm{E}(B) &= \frac{1}{3} \int_0^{350{,}000} (350{,}000 - l) f_L(l)dl \\
&= \frac{1}{3} \{350{,}000 F_L(350{,}000) - \mathrm{E}(L \wedge 350{,}000) \\
&\quad + 350{,}000[1 - F_L(350{,}000)]\} \\
&= \frac{1}{3} \left\{ 350{,}000 - \frac{600{,}000}{2} \left[1 - \left(\frac{600{,}000}{950{,}000} \right)^2 \right] \right\} \\
&= 56{,}556.
\end{aligned}
$$

8.18 The quantity we seek is

$$
\frac{1.1[\mathrm{E}(X \wedge 22/1.1) - \mathrm{E}(X \wedge 11/1.1)]}{\mathrm{E}(X \wedge 22) - \mathrm{E}(X \wedge 11)} = \frac{1.1(17.25 - 10)}{18.1 - 10.95} = 1.115.
$$

8.19 This exercise asks for quantities on a per-loss basis. The expected value is

$$
\mathrm{E}(X) - \mathrm{E}(X \wedge 100) = 1{,}000 - 1{,}000(1 - e^{-100/1{,}000}) = 904.84.
$$

To obtain the second moment, we need

$$
\begin{aligned}
\mathrm{E}[(X \wedge 100)^2] &= \int_0^{100} x^2 0.001 e^{-0.001x}dx + (100)^2 e^{-100/1{,}000} \\
&= -e^{-0.001x}(x^2 + 2{,}000x + 2{,}000{,}000)\big|_0^{100} + 9{,}048.37 \\
&= 9{,}357.68.
\end{aligned}
$$

The second moment is

$$E(X^2) - E[(X \wedge 100)^2] - 200E(X) + 200E(X \wedge 100)$$
$$= 2(1{,}000)^2 - 9{,}357.68 - 200(1{,}000) + 200(95.16)$$
$$= 1{,}809{,}674.32,$$

for a variance of $1{,}809{,}674.32 - 904.84^2 = 990{,}938.89$.

8.20 Under the old plan the expected cost is $500/1 = 500$. Under the new plan, the expected claim cost is K. The bonus is

$$B = \begin{cases} 0.5(500 - X), & X < 500 \\ 0.5(500 - 500), & X \geq 500, \end{cases}$$

which is 250 less a benefit with a limit of 500 and a coinsurance of 0.5. Therefore,

$$\begin{aligned} E(B) &= 250 - 0.5E(X \wedge 500) \\ &= 250 - 0.5\frac{K}{1}\left[1 - \left(\frac{K}{K + 500}\right)\right] \\ &= 250 - \frac{K}{2} + \frac{K^2}{2K + 1{,}000}. \end{aligned}$$

The equation to solve is

$$500 = K + 250 - \frac{K}{2} + \frac{K^2}{2K + 1{,}000}$$

and the solution is $K = 354$.

8.21 For year a, expected losses per claim are 2,000, and thus 5,000 claims are expected. Per loss, the reinsurer's expected cost is

$$\begin{aligned} E(X) - E(X \wedge 3{,}000) &= 2{,}000 - 2{,}000\left[1 - \left(\frac{2{,}000}{2{,}000 + 3{,}000}\right)\right] \\ &= 800, \end{aligned}$$

and, therefore, the total reinsurance premium is $1.1(5{,}000)(800) = 4{,}400{,}000$. For year b, there are still 5,000 claims expected. Per loss, the reinsurer's expected cost is

$$1.05[E(X) - E(X \wedge 3{,}000/1.05)]$$
$$= 1.05\left\{2{,}000 - 2{,}000\left[1 - \left(\frac{2{,}000}{2{,}000 + 3{,}000/1.05}\right)\right]\right\}$$
$$= 864.706,$$

and the total reinsurance premium is $1.1(5,000)(864.706) = 4,755,882$. The ratio is 1.0809.

8.22 For this uniform distribution,

$$
\begin{aligned}
\mathrm{E}(X \wedge u) &= \int_0^u x(0.00002)dx + \int_u^{50,000} u(0.00002)dx \\
&= 0.00001u^2 + 0.00002u(50,000 - u) \\
&= u - 0.00001u^2.
\end{aligned}
$$

From Theorem 8.7, the expected payment per payment is

$$
\frac{\mathrm{E}(X \wedge 25,000) - \mathrm{E}(X \wedge 5,000)}{1 - F(5000)} = \frac{18,750 - 4,750}{1 - \frac{5,000}{50,000}} = 15,556.
$$

8.23 This is a combination of franchise deductible and policy limit, so none of the results apply. From the definition of this policy, the expected cost per loss is

$$
\int_{50,000}^{100,000} xf(x)dx + 100,000[1 - F(100,000)]
$$
$$
= \int_0^{100,000} xf(x)dx + 100,000[1 - F(100,000)] - \int_0^{50,000} xf(x)dx
$$
$$
= \mathrm{E}(X \wedge 100,000) - \mathrm{E}(X \wedge 50,000) + 50,000[1 - F(50,000)].
$$

Alternatively, it could be argued that this policy has two components. The first is an ordinary deductible of 50,000 and the second is a bonus payment of 50,000 whenever there is a payment. The first two terms in the preceding formula reflect the cost of the ordinary deductible and the third term is the extra cost of the bonus. Using the lognormal distribution, the answer is

$$
e^{10.5}\Phi\left(\frac{\ln 100,000 - 10 - 1}{1}\right) + 100,000\left[1 - \Phi\left(\frac{\ln 100,000 - 10}{1}\right)\right]
$$
$$
-e^{10.5}\Phi\left(\frac{\ln 50,000 - 10 - 1}{1}\right)
$$
$$
= e^{10.5}\Phi(0.513) + 100,000[1 - \Phi(1.513)] - e^{10.5}\Phi(-0.180)
$$
$$
= e^{10.5}(0.6959) + 100,000(0.0652) - e^{10.5}(0.4285) = 16,231.
$$

8.24 $\mathrm{E}(Y^L) = \mathrm{E}(X) - \mathrm{E}(X \wedge 30,000) = 10,000 - 10,000(1 - e^{-3}) = 497.87$. $\mathrm{E}(Y^P) = 497.87/e^{-3} = 10,000$.

$$
\begin{aligned}
\mathrm{E}[(Y^L)^2] &= \mathrm{E}(X^2) - \mathrm{E}[(X \wedge 30,000)^2] - 60,000\mathrm{E}(X) \\
&\quad +60,000\mathrm{E}(X \wedge 30,000) \\
&= 2(10,000)^2 - 10,000^2(2)\Gamma(3;3) - 30,000^2 e^{-3} - 60,000(10,000) \\
&\quad +60,000(9,502.13) \\
&= 9,957,413.67.
\end{aligned}
$$

$\mathrm{E}[(Y^P)^2] = 9,957,413.67/e^{-3} = 200,000,000.$ Then $\mathrm{Var}(Y^L) = 9,957,413.67 - 497.87^2 = 9,709,539.14$, and the cv is $9,709,539.14^{1/2}/497.87 = 6.259$. For Y^P, the variance is $100,000,000$ and the cv is 1.

8.25 The density function over the respective intervals is $0.3/50 = 0.006$, $0.36/50 = 0.0072$, $0.18/100 = 0.0018$, and $0.16/200 = 0.0008$. The answer is

$$
\begin{aligned}
&\int_0^{50} x^2(0.006)dx + \int_{50}^{100} x^2(0.0072)dx + \int_{100}^{200} x^2(0.0018)dx \\
&+ \int_{200}^{350} x^2(0.0008)dx + \int_{350}^{400} 350^2(0.0008)dx = 20{,}750.
\end{aligned}
$$

8.26 The 10,000 payment by the insured is reached when losses hit 14,000. The breakpoints are at 1,000, 6,000, and 14,000. So the answer must be of the form

$$
a\mathrm{E}(X \wedge 1{,}000) + b\mathrm{E}(X \wedge 6{,}000) + c\mathrm{E}(X \wedge 14{,}000) + d\mathrm{E}(X).
$$

For the insurance to pay 90% above 14,000, it must be that $d = 0.9$. To pay nothing from 6,000 to 14,000, $c + d = 0$, so $c = -0.9$. To pay 80% from 1,000 to 6,000, $b + c + d = 0.8$, so $b = 0.8$. Finally, to pay nothing below 1,000, $a + b + c + d = 0$, so $a = -0.8$. The answer is

$$
-0.8(833.33) + 0.8(2{,}727.27) - 0.9(3{,}684.21) + 0.9(5{,}000) = 2{,}699.36.
$$

8.27 The expected payment is $\lambda = 3$. With the coinsurance, the expected payment is $\alpha 3$. For the deductible,

$$
\mathrm{E}(X \wedge 2) = (0)e^{-3} + (1)(3e^{-3}) + 2(1 - e^{-3} - 3e^{-3}) = 1.751065.
$$

The expected cost is $3 - 1.751065 = 1.248935$. Then, $\alpha = 1.248935/3 = 0.4163$.

8.28 The maximum loss is 95. The expected payment per payment is

$$0.8 \frac{E(X \wedge 95) - E(X \wedge 20)}{1 - F(20)} = 0.8 \frac{\int_0^{95} 1 - \frac{x^2}{10,000} dx - \int_0^{20} 1 - \frac{x^2}{10,000} dx}{1 - \frac{20^2}{10,000}}$$

$$= 0.8 \frac{75 - \frac{95^3 - 20^3}{3(10,000)}}{0.96} = 38.91.$$

8.5 SECTION 8.6

8.29 (a) For frequency, the probability of a claim is 0.03, and for severity, the probability of a 10,000 claim is $1/3$ and of a 20,000 claim is $2/3$.

(b) $\Pr(X = 0) = 1/3$ and $\Pr(X = 10,000) = 2/3$.

(c) For frequency, the probability of a claim is 0.02, and the severity distribution places probability 1 at 10,000.

8.30 $\nu = [1 - F(1,000)]/[1 - F(500)] = 9/16$. The original frequency distribution is P–ETNB with $\lambda = 3$, $r = -0.5$, and $\beta = 2$. The new frequency is P–ZMNB with $\lambda = 3$, $r = -0.5$, $\beta = 2(9/16) = 9/8$, and $p_0^T = \frac{0 - 3^{.5} + (17/8)^{.5} - 0(17/8)^{.5}}{1 - 3^{.5}} = 0.37472$. This is equivalent to a P–ETNB with $\lambda = 3(1 - 0.37472) = 1.87584$, $\beta = 9/8$, and $r = -0.5$, which is P–IG with $\lambda = 1.87584$ and $\beta = 9/8$.

The new severity distribution has cdf $F(x) = \frac{F(x+500) - F(500)}{1 - F(500)} = 1 - \left(\frac{1,500}{1,500+x}\right)^2$, which is Pareto with $\alpha = 2$ and $\theta = 1,500$.

8.31 The value of p_0^M will be negative and so there is no appropriate frequency distribution to describe effect of lowering the deductible.

8.32 We have

$$\begin{aligned} P_{N^P}(z) &= P_N(1 - v + vz) \\ &= 1 - [1 - (1 - v + vz)]^{-r} \\ &= 1 - (v - vz)^{-r} \\ &= 1 - v^{-r}(1 - z)^{-r} \\ &= 1 - v^{-r}[1 - P_{N^L}(z)] \\ &= 1 - v^{-r} + v^{-r} P_{N^L}(z). \end{aligned}$$

Therefore,

$$\Pr(N^P = 0) = 1 - v^{-r},$$

and

$$\Pr\left(N^P = n\right) = \left[1 - \Pr\left(N^P = 0\right)\right]\Pr\left(N^L = n\right); \quad n = 1, 2, 3, \dots .$$

8.33 Before the deductible, the expected number of losses is $r\beta = 15$. From the Weibull distribution, $S(200) = \exp[-(200/1{,}000)^{0.3}] = 0.5395$. The expected number of payments is $15(0.5395) = 8.0925$.

8.34 $S(20) = 1 - (20/100)^2 = 0.96$. The expected number of claims without the deductible is $4/0.96 = 4.1667$.

CHAPTER 9

CHAPTER 9 SOLUTIONS

9.1 SECTION 9.1

9.1 The number of claims, N, has a binomial distribution with $m = $ number of policies and $q = 0.1$. The claim amount variables, $X_1, X_2, \ldots$, all are discrete with $\Pr(X_j = 5{,}000) = 1$ for all j.

9.2 (a) An individual model is best because each insured has a unique distribution. (b) A collective model is best because each malpractice claim has the same distribution and there are a random number of such claims. (c) Each family can be modeled with a collective model using a compound frequency distribution. There is a distribution for the number of family members and then each family member has a random number of claims.

Student Solutions Manual to Accompany Loss Models: From Data to Decisions, Fourth **67** *Edition.* By Stuart A. Klugman, Harry H. Panjer, Gordon E. Willmot Copyright © 2012 John Wiley & Sons, Inc.

9.2   SECTION 9.2

9.3
$$
\begin{aligned}
\mathrm{E}(N) &= P^{(1)}(1), \\
P^{(1)}(z) &= \alpha Q(z)^{\alpha-1} Q^{(1)}(z), \\
P^{(1)}(1) &= \alpha Q(1)^{\alpha-1} Q^{(1)}(1) \propto \alpha.
\end{aligned}
$$

9.4 The Poisson and all compound distributions with a Poisson primary distribution have a pgf of the form $P(z) = \exp\{\lambda[P_2(z) - 1]\} = [Q(z)]^\lambda$, where $Q(z) = \exp[P_2(z) - 1]$.

The negative binomial and geometric distributions and all compound distributions with a negative binomial or geometric primary distribution have $P(z) = \{1 - \beta[P_2(z) - 1]\}^{-r} = [Q(z)]^r$, where $Q(z) = \{1 - \beta[P_2(z) - 1]\}^{-1}$.

The same is true for the binomial distribution and binomial-X compound distributions with $\alpha = m$ and $Q(z) = 1 + q[P_2(z) - 1]$.

The zero-truncated and zero-modified distributions cannot be written in this form.

9.3   SECTION 9.3

9.5 To simplify writing the expressions, let
$$
\begin{aligned}
Njp &= \mu'_{Nj} = \mathrm{E}(N^j), \\
Nj &= \mu_{Nj} = \mathrm{E}[(N - N1p)^j], \\
Xjp &= \mu'_{Xj} = \mathrm{E}(X^j), \\
Xj &= \mu_{Xj} = \mathrm{E}[(XN - X1p)^j],
\end{aligned}
$$

and similarly for S. For the first moment, $P_S^{(1)}(z) = P_N^{(1)}[P_X(z)]P_X^{(1)}(z)$, and so
$$
\begin{aligned}
\mathrm{E}(S) &= P_S^{(1)}(1) = P_N^{(1)}[P_X(1)]P_X^{(1)}(1) \\
&= P_N^{(1)}(1)P_X^{(1)}(1) = (N1p)(X1p) = \mathrm{E}(N)\mathrm{E}(X).
\end{aligned}
$$

For the second moment use
$$
\begin{aligned}
P_S^{(2)}(1) &= S2p - S1p = P_N^{(2)}[P_X(z)][P_X^{(1)}(z)]^2 + P_N^{(1)}[P_X(z)]P_X^{(2)}(z) \\
&= (N2p - N1p)(Xp1)^2 + N1p(X2p - X1p).
\end{aligned}
$$

$$
\begin{aligned}
\mathrm{Var}(S) &= S2 = S2p - (S1p)^2 = S2p - S1p + S1p - (S1p)^2 \\
&= (N2p - N1p)(X1p)^2 + N1p(X2p - X1p) + (N1p)(X1p) \\
&\quad -(N1p)^2(X1p)^2 \\
&= N1p[X2p - (X1p)^2] + [N2p - (N1p)^2](X1p)^2 \\
&= (N1p)(X2) + (N2)(X1p)^2.
\end{aligned}
$$

For the third moment use

$$
\begin{aligned}
P_S^{(3)} &= S3p - 3S2p + 2S1p = P_N^{(3)}[P_X(z)][P_X^{(1)}(z)]^3 \\
&\quad + 3P_N^{(2)}[P_X(z)]P_X^{(1)}(z)P_X^{(2)}(z) + P_N^{(1)}[P_X(z)]P_X^{(3)}(z) \\
&= (N3p - 3N2p + 2N1p)(X1p)^3 \\
&\quad + 3(N2p - N1p)(X1p)(X2p - X1p) \\
&\quad + N1p(X3p - 3X2p + 2X1p).
\end{aligned}
$$

$$
\begin{aligned}
S3 &= S3p - 3(S2p)(S1p) + 2(S1p)^3 \\
&= S3p - 3S2p + 2S1p + 3[S2 + (S1p)^2](1 - 3S1p) + 2(S1p)^3 \\
&= (N3p - 3N2p + 2N1p)(X1p)^3 \\
&\quad + 3(N2p - N1p)(X1p)(X2p - X1p) \\
&\quad + N1p(X3p - 3X2p + 2X1p) \\
&\quad + 3\{N1p[X2p - (X1p)^2] \\
&\qquad + [N2p - (N1p)^2](X1p)^2 \\
&\qquad + (N1p)^2(X1p)^2\}[1 - 3(N1p)(X1p)] \\
&\quad + 2(N1p)^3(X1p)^3 \\
&= N1p(X3) + 3(N2)(X1p)(X2) + N3(X1p)^3.
\end{aligned}
$$

9.6
$$
\begin{aligned}
E(X) &= 1{,}000 + 0.8(500) = 1{,}400. \\
Var(X) &= Var(X_1) + Var(X_2) + 2Cov(X_1, X_2) \\
&= 500^2 + 0.64(300)^2 + 2(0.8)(100{,}000) \\
&= 467{,}600. \\
E(S) &= E(N)E(X) = 4(1{,}400) = 5{,}600. \\
Var(S) &= E(N)\,Var(X) + Var(N)E(X)^2 \\
&= 4(467{,}600) + 4(1{,}400)^2 = 9{,}710{,}400.
\end{aligned}
$$

9.7 $E(S) = 15(5)(5) = 375.$
$Var(S) = 15(5)(100/12) + 15(5)(6)(5)^2 = 11{,}875.$ $StDev(S) = 108.97.$
The 95th percentile is $375 + 1.645(108.97) = 554.26.$

9.8
$$
\begin{aligned}
Var(N) &= E[Var(N|\lambda)] + Var[E(N|\lambda)] = E(\lambda) + Var(\lambda), \\
E(\lambda) &= 0.25(5) + 0.25(3) + 0.5(2) = 3, \\
Var(\lambda) &= 0.25(25) + 0.25(9) + 0.5(4) - 9 = 1.5, \\
Var(N) &= 4.5.
\end{aligned}
$$

9.9 The calculations appear in Table 9.1.

Table 9.1 Results for Exercise 9.9.

x	$f_1(x)$	$f_2(x)$	$f_{1+2}(x)$	$f_3(x)$	$f_S(x)$
0	0.9	0.5	0.45	0.25	0.1125
1	0.1	0.3	0.32	0.25	0.1925
2		0.2	0.21	0.25	0.2450
3			0.02	0.25	0.2500
4					0.1375
5					0.0575
6					0.0050

9.10 The calculations appear in Table 9.2.

Table 9.2 Results for Exercise 9.10.

x	$f_2(x)$	$f_3(x)$	$f_{2+3}(x)$	$f_1(x)$	$f_S(x)$
0	0.6	0.25	0.150	p	$0.15p$
1	0.2	0.25	0.200	$1-p$	$0.15 + 0.05p$
2	0.1	0.25	0.225		$0.2 + 0.025p$
3	0.1	0.25	0.250		$0.225 + 0.025p$
4			0.100		$0.25 - 0.15p$
5			0.050		$0.1 - 0.05p$
6			0.025		$0.05 - .025p$
7					$0.025 - 0.025p$

$$0.06 = f_S(5) = 0.1 - 0.05p, \ p = 0.8.$$

9.11 If all 10 do not have AIDS,

$$
\begin{aligned}
\mathrm{E}(S) &= 10(1,000) = 10,000, \\
\mathrm{Var}(S) &= 10(250,000) = 2,500,000,
\end{aligned}
$$

and so the premium is $10,000 + 0.1(2,500,000)^{1/2} = 10,158$.

If the number with AIDS has the binomial distribution with $m = 10$ and $q = 0.01$, then, letting N be the number with AIDS,

$$
\begin{aligned}
\mathrm{E}(S) &= \mathrm{E}[\mathrm{E}(S|N)] = \mathrm{E}[70{,}000N + 1{,}000(10 - N)] \\
&= 10{,}000 + 69{,}000[10(0.01)] \\
&= 16{,}900, \\
\mathrm{Var}(S) &= \mathrm{Var}[\mathrm{E}(S|N)] + \mathrm{E}[\mathrm{Var}(S|N)] \\
&= \mathrm{Var}[70{,}000N + 1{,}000(10 - N)] \\
&\quad + \mathrm{E}[1{,}600{,}000N + 250{,}000(10 - N)] \\
&= 69{,}000^2[10(0.01)(0.99)] + 2{,}500{,}000 + 1{,}350{,}000[10(0.01)] \\
&= 473{,}974{,}000,
\end{aligned}
$$

and so the premium is $16{,}900 + 0.1(473{,}974{,}000)^{1/2} = 19{,}077$. The ratio is $10{,}158/19{,}077 = 0.532$.

9.12 Let M be the random number of males and C be the number of cigarettes smoked. Then $\mathrm{E}(C) = \mathrm{E}[\mathrm{E}(C|M)] = \mathrm{E}[6M + 3(8 - M)] = 3\mathrm{E}(M) + 24$. But M has the binomial distribution with mean $8(0.4) = 3.2$, and so $\mathrm{E}(C) = 3(3.2) + 24 = 33.6$.

$$
\begin{aligned}
\mathrm{Var}(C) &= \mathrm{E}[\mathrm{Var}(C|M)] + \mathrm{Var}[\mathrm{E}(C|M)] \\
&= \mathrm{E}[64M + 31(8 - M)] + \mathrm{Var}(3M + 24) \\
&= 33\mathrm{E}(M) + 248 + 9\,\mathrm{Var}(M) \\
&= 33(3.2) + 9(8)(0.4)(0.6) = 370.88.
\end{aligned}
$$

The answer is $33.6 + \sqrt{370.88} = 52.86$.

9.13 For insurer A, the group pays the net premium, so the expected total cost is just the expected total claims, that is, $\mathrm{E}(S) = 5$.

For insurer B, the cost to the group is $7 - D$, where D is the dividend. We have

$$
D = \begin{cases} 7k - S, & S < 7k, \\ 0, & S \geq 7k. \end{cases}
$$

Then $\mathrm{E}(D) = \int_0^{7k}(7k - s)(0.1)ds = 2.45k^2$. We want $5 = \mathrm{E}(7 - D) = 7 - 2.45k^2$, and so $k = 0.9035$.

9.14 Let θ be the underwriter's estimated mean. The underwriter computes the premium as

$$
\begin{aligned}
2\mathrm{E}[(S - 1.25\theta)_+] &= 2\int_{1.25\theta}^{\infty} (s - 1.25\theta)\theta^{-1}e^{-s/\theta}ds \\
&= -2(s - 1.25\theta)e^{-s/\theta} - 2\theta e^{-s/\theta}\Big|_{1.25\theta}^{\infty} \\
&= 2\theta e^{-1.25}.
\end{aligned}
$$

Let μ be the true mean. Then $\theta = 0.9\mu$. The true expected loss is

$$
\mathrm{E}[(S - 1.25(0.9)\mu)_+] = 2\int_{1.125\mu}^{\infty} (s - 1.125\mu)\mu^{-1}e^{-s/\mu}ds = \mu e^{-1.125}.
$$

The loading is

$$
\frac{2(0.9)\mu e^{-1.25}}{\mu e^{-1.125}} - 1 = 0.5885.
$$

9.15 A convenient relationship is, for discrete distributions on whole numbers, $\mathrm{E}[(X - d - 1)_+] = \mathrm{E}[(X - d)_+] - 1 + F(d)$. For this problem, $\mathrm{E}[(X - 0)_+] = \mathrm{E}(X) = 4$. $\mathrm{E}[(X - 1)_+] = 4 - 1 + 0.05 = 3.05$, $\mathrm{E}[(X - 2)_+] = 3.05 - 1 + 0.11 = 2.16$, $\mathrm{E}[(X - 3)_+] = 2.16 - 1 + 0.36 = 1.52$. Then, by linear interpolation, $d = 2 + (2 - 2.16)/(1.52 - 2.16) = 2.25$.

9.16 $15 = \int_{100}^{\infty}[1 - F(s)]ds$, $10 = \int_{120}^{\infty}[1 - F(s)]ds$, $F(120) - F(80) = 0$. Subtracting the second equality from the first yields $5 = \int_{100}^{120}[1 - F(s)]ds$, but over this range $F(s) = F(80)$, and so

$$
5 = \int_{100}^{120}[1 - F(s)]ds = \int_{100}^{120}[1 - F(80)]ds = 20[1 - F(80)]
$$

and, therefore, $F(80) = 0.75$.

9.17

$$
\begin{aligned}
\mathrm{E}(A) &= \int_{50k}^{100} \left(\frac{x}{k} - 50\right)(0.01)dx = \left(\frac{x^2}{2k} - 50x\right)(0.01)\Big|_{50k}^{100} \\
&= 50k^{-1} - 50 + 12.5k. \\
\mathrm{E}(B) &= \int_{0}^{100} kx(0.01)dx = \frac{kx^2}{2}(0.01)\Big|_{0}^{100} = 50k.
\end{aligned}
$$

The solution to $50k^{-1} - 50 + 12.5k = 50k$ is $k = 2/3$.

9.18 $E(X) = 440$, $F(30) = 0.3$, $f(x) = 0.01$ for $0 < x \leq 30$.

$$\begin{aligned}
E(\text{benefits}) &= \int_0^{30} 20x(0.01)dx + \int_{30}^{\infty} [600 + 100(x - 30)]f(x)dx \\
&= 90 + \int_{30}^{\infty} (-2,400)f(x)dx + 100 \int_{30}^{\infty} xf(x)dx \\
&= 90 - 2,400[1 - F(30)] + 100 \int_0^{\infty} xf(x)dx \\
&\quad -100 \int_0^{30} xf(x)dx \\
&= 90 - 2,400(0.7) + 100(440) - 100 \int_0^{30} x(0.01)dx \\
&= 90 - 1,680 + 44,000 - 450 = 41,960.
\end{aligned}$$

9.19
$$\begin{aligned}
E(S) &= E(N)E(X) = [0(0.5) + 1(0.4) + 3(0.1)][1(0.9) + 10(0.1)] \\
&= 0.7(1.9) = 1.33.
\end{aligned}$$

We require $\Pr(S > 3.99)$. Using the calculation in Table 9.3, $\Pr(S > 3.99) = 1 - 0.5 - 0.36 - 0.0729 = 0.0671$.

Table 9.3   Calculations for Exercise 9.19.

x	$f_X^{*0}(x)$	$f_X^{*1}(x)$	$f_X^{*2}(x)$	$f_X^{*3}(x)$	$f_S(x)$
0	1	0	0	0	0.5000
1	0	0.9	0	0	0.3600
2	0	0	0.81	0	0
3	0	0	0	0.729	0.0729
p_n	0.5	0.4	0	0.1	

9.20 For 100 independent lives, $E(S) = 100mq$ and $\text{Var}(S) = 100m^2q(1-q) = 250,000$. The premium is $100mq + 500$. For this particular group,

$$\begin{aligned}
E(S) &= 97(mq) + (3m)q = 100mq, \\
\text{Var}(S) &= 97m^2q(1 - q) + (3m)^2q(1 - q) \\
&= 106m^2q(1 - q) = 265,000,
\end{aligned}$$

and the premium is $100mq + 514.18$. The difference is 14.78.

9.21
$$\begin{aligned}
E(S) &= 1(8,000)(0.025) + 2(8,000)(0.025) = 600, \\
\text{Var}(S) &= 1(8,000)(0.025)(0.975) \\
&\quad +2^2(8,000)(0.025)(0.975) = 975.
\end{aligned}$$

The cost of reinsurance is $0.03(2)(4,500) = 270$.

$$\begin{aligned} \Pr(S + 270 > 1,000) &= \Pr(S > 730) \\ &= \Pr\left(\frac{S - 600}{\sqrt{975}} > \frac{730 - 600}{\sqrt{975}} = 4.163\right), \end{aligned}$$

so $K = 4.163$.

9.22
$$\begin{aligned} E(Z) &= \int_{10}^{100} 0.8(y - 10)(0.02)(1 - 0.01y)dy \\ &= 0.016 \int_{10}^{100} -0.01y^2 + 1.1y - 10dy = 19.44. \end{aligned}$$

9.23
$$\begin{aligned} \Pr(S > 100) &= \sum_{n=0}^{3} \Pr(N = n)\Pr(X^{*n} > 100) \\ &= 0.5(0) + 0.2\Pr(X > 100) \\ &\quad + 0.2\Pr(X^{*2} > 100) + 0.1\Pr(X^{*3} > 100). \end{aligned}$$

Because $X \sim N(100, 9)$, $X^{*2} \sim N(200, 18)$, and $X^{*3} \sim N(300, 27)$, and so

$$\begin{aligned} \Pr(S > 100) &= 0.2\Pr\left(Z > \frac{100 - 100}{3}\right) + 0.2\Pr\left(Z > \frac{100 - 200}{\sqrt{18}}\right) \\ &\quad + 0.2\Pr\left(Z > \frac{100 - 300}{\sqrt{27}}\right) \\ &= 0.2(0.5) + 0.2(1) + 0.1(1) = 0.4. \end{aligned}$$

9.24 The calculations are in Table 9.4. The expected retained payment is $2,000(0.1) + 3,000(0.15) + 4,000(0.06) + 5,000(0.6275) = 4,027.5$, and the total cost is $4,027.5 + 1,472 = 5,499.5$.

Table 9.4   Calculations for Exercise 9.24.

x	$f_X^{*0}(x)$	$f_X^{*1}(x)$	$f_X^{*2}(x)$	$f_S(x)$
0	1	0	0	0.0625
1	0	0	0	0.0000
2	0	0.4	0	0.1000
3	0	0.6	0	0.1500
4	0	0	0.16	0.0600
p_k	1/16	1/4	3/8	

9.25 In general, paying for days a through b, the expected number of days is

$$\sum_{k=a}^{b}(k - a + 1)p_k + (b - a + 1)[1 - F(b)]$$

$$= \sum_{k=a}^{b}\sum_{j=a}^{k}p_k + (b - a + 1)[1 - F(b)]$$

$$= \sum_{j=a}^{b}\sum_{k=j}^{b}p_k + (b - a + 1)[1 - F(b)]$$

$$= \sum_{j=a}^{b}[F(b) - F(j - 1)] + (b - a + 1)[1 - F(b)]$$

$$= \sum_{j=a}^{b}[1 - F(j - 1)] = \sum_{j=a}^{b}(0.8)^{j-1}$$

$$= \frac{(0.8)^{a-1} - (0.8)^b}{.2}.$$

For the 4 through 10 policy, the expected number of days is $(0.8^3 - 0.8^{10})/0.2 = 2.02313$. For the 4 through 17 policy, the expected number of days is $(0.8^3 - 0.8^{17})/0.2 = 2.44741$. This is a 21% increase.

9.26

$$\begin{aligned}
E(S) &= \int_{1}^{\infty} x3x^{-4}dx = 3/2, \\
E(X^2) &= \int_{1}^{\infty} x^23x^{-4}dx = 3, \\
Var(S) &= 3 - (3/2)^2 = 3/4.
\end{aligned}$$

$$\begin{aligned}
0.9 &= \Pr[S \le (1 + \theta)(3/2)] = \int_{1}^{(1+\theta)(3/2)} 3x^{-4}dx \\
&= 1 - [(1 + \theta)(3/2)]^{-3},
\end{aligned}$$

and so $\theta = 0.43629$.

$$\begin{aligned}
0.9 &= \Pr[S \le 1.5 + \lambda\sqrt{3/4}] = \int_{1}^{1.5+\lambda\sqrt{3/4}} 3x^{-4}dx \\
&= 1 - [1.5 + \lambda\sqrt{3/4}]^{-3},
\end{aligned}$$

and so $\lambda = 0.75568$.

9.27 The answer is the sum of the following:
$0.80R_{100}$ pays 80% of all in excess of 100,
$0.10R_{1100}$ pays an additional 10% in excess of 1,100, and
$0.10R_{2100}$ pays an additional 10% in excess of 2,100.

9.28 $\Pr(S = 0) = \sum_{n=0}^{\infty} p_n \Pr(B_n = 0)$ where $B_n \sim \text{bin}(n, 0.25)$. Thus

$$\Pr(S = 0) = \sum_{n=0}^{\infty} \frac{e^{-2}2^n}{n!}(0.75)^n = e^{-2}e^{1.5} = e^{-1/2}.$$

9.29 Let μ be the mean of the exponential distribution. Then,

$$
\begin{aligned}
\mathrm{E}(S) &= \mathrm{E}[\mathrm{E}(S|\mu)] \\
&= \mathrm{E}(\mu) \\
&= 3{,}000{,}000.
\end{aligned}
$$

9.30 $\mathrm{E}(N) = 0.1$.

$$
\begin{aligned}
\mathrm{E}(X) &= \int_0^{30} 100t f(t)dt + 3{,}000\Pr(T > 30) \\
&= \int_0^{10} 100t(0.04)dt + \int_{10}^{20} 100t(0.035)dt \\
&\quad + \int_{20}^{30} 100t(0.02)dt + 3{,}000(0.05) \\
&= 200 + 525 + 500 + 150 = 1{,}350. \\
\mathrm{E}(S) &= 0.1(1{,}350) = 135.
\end{aligned}
$$

9.31 Total claims are compound Poisson with $\lambda = 5$ and severity distribution

$$
\begin{aligned}
f_X(x) &= 0.4f_1(x) + 0.6f_2(x) \\
&= \begin{cases} 0.4(0.001) + 0.6(0.005) = 0.0034, & 0 < x \le 200, \\ 0.4(0.001) + 0.6(0) = 0.0004, & 200 < x \le 1{,}000. \end{cases}
\end{aligned}
$$

Then,

$$\begin{aligned}
\mathrm{E}[(X-100)_+] &= \int_{100}^{\infty} (x-100) f_X(x) dx \\
&= \int_{100}^{200} (x-100)(0.0034) dx \\
&\quad + \int_{200}^{\infty} (x-100)(0.0004) dx \\
&= 177.
\end{aligned}$$

9.32 The calculations appear in Table 9.5.

Table 9.5 Calculations for Exercise 9.32.

s	$\Pr(S=s)$	d	$d\Pr(S=s)$
0	0.031676	4	0.12671
1	0.126705	3	0.38012
2	0.232293	2	0.46459
3	0.258104	1	0.25810
4+	0.351222	0	0
Total			1.22952

9.33 The negative binomial probabilities are $p_0 = 0.026$, $p_1 = 0.061$, and $p_2 = 0.092$, and the remaining probability is 0.821. The mean is 6, and so the total expected payments are 600. The expected policyholder payment is

$$0(0.026) + 100(0.061) + 200(0.092) + 300(0.821) = 270.80.$$

The insurance company expected payment is $600 - 270.80 = 329.20$.

9.34 Because the only two ways to get 600 in aggregate claims are one 100+500 and six 100s, their probabilities are

$$\frac{e^{-5}5^2}{2!}2(0.80)(0.16) = 0.02156 \text{ and } \frac{e^{-5}5^6}{6!}(0.80)^6 = 0.03833$$

for a total of 0.05989. The recursive formula can also be used.

9.35 The moments are $\mathrm{E}(N) = 16(6) = 96$, $\mathrm{Var}(N) = 16(6)(7) = 672$, $\mathrm{E}(X) = 8/2 = 4$. $\mathrm{Var}(X) = 8^2/12 = 5.33$, $\mathrm{E}(S) = 96(4) = 384$, $\mathrm{Var}(S) = 96(5.33) + 672(4)^2 = 11{,}264$. The 95th percentile is, from the normal distribution, $384 + 1.645(11{,}264)^{1/2} = 558.59$.

9.36 The moments are (noting that X has a Pareto distribution) $E(N) = 3$, $Var(N) = 3$, $E(X) = 2/(3-1) = 1$. $Var(X) = 2^2 2/[(3-1)(3-2)] - 1^2 = 3$, $Var(S) = 3(3) + 3(1)^2 = 12$.

9.4   SECTION 9.4

9.37 Because this is a compound distribution defined on the nonnegative integers, we can use Theorem 7.4. With an appropriate adaptation of notation,

$$P_N[P_X(z; \beta)] = P_N\{P_X(z); \beta[1 - f_X(0)]\}.$$

So just replace β by $\beta^* = \beta[1 - f_X(0)]$.

9.38 (a)
$$f_S(x) = \sum_{n=1}^{\infty} \frac{\beta^n}{n(1+\beta)^n \ln(1+\beta)} \frac{x^{n-1}e^{-x/\theta}}{\theta^n(n-1)!}$$

$$= \frac{1}{\ln(1+\beta)} \sum_{n=1}^{\infty} \left[\frac{\beta}{\theta(1+\beta)}\right]^n \frac{1}{n!} x^{n-1} e^{-x/\theta}.$$

(b)
$$f_S(x) = \frac{e^{-x/\theta}}{x \ln(1+\beta)} \sum_{n=1}^{\infty} \left[\frac{x\beta}{\theta(1+\beta)}\right]^n \frac{1}{n!}$$

$$= \frac{e^{-x/\theta}}{x \ln(1+\beta)} \left\{\exp\left[\frac{x\beta}{\theta(1+\beta)}\right] - 1\right\}$$

$$= \frac{\exp\left[-\frac{x}{\theta(1+\beta)}\right] - \exp\left(-\frac{x}{\theta}\right)}{x \ln(1+\beta)}.$$

9.39 To use (9.15) we need the binomial probabilities $p_0 = 0.6^3 = 0.216$, $p_1 = 3(0.6)^2 0.4 = 0.432$, $p_2 = 3(0.6)0.4^2 = 0.288$, and $p_3 = 0.4^3 = 0.064$. Then, $\bar{P}_0 = 0.432 + 0.288 + 0.064 = 0.784$, $\bar{P}_1 = 0.288 + 0.064 = 0.352$, and $\bar{P}_2 = 0.064$. Then

$$F_S(300) = 1 - e^{-300/100} \left[0.784\frac{(300/100)^0}{0!} + 0.352\frac{(300/100)^1}{1!} \right.$$
$$\left. + 0.064\frac{(300/100)^2}{2!}\right]$$

$$= 0.89405.$$

9.40 For the three policies the means are $10,000(0.01) = 100$, $20,000(0.02) = 400$, and $40,000(0.03) = 1,200$. Because the Poisson variance is equal to the mean, the variances are $10,000^2(0.01) = 1,000,000$, $20,000^2(0.02) = 8,000,000$, and $40,000(0.03) = 48,000,000$. The overall mean is $5,000(100) + 3,000(400) + 1,000(1,200) = 2,900,000$ and the variance is $5,000(1,000,000) + 3,000(8,000,000) + 1,000(48,000,000) = 7,7 \times 10^{10}$. Total claims are the sum of 9,000 compound Poisson distributions which itself is a compound Poisson distribution with $\lambda = 5,000(0.01) + 3,000(0.02) + 1,000(0.03) = 140$ and the severity distribution places probability $50/140$ on 10,000, $60/140$ on 20,000, and $30/140$ on 40,000. Using the recursive formula with units of 10,000,

$$\Pr(S = 0) = e^{-140},$$

$$\Pr(S = 1) = \frac{140}{1}\frac{5}{14}e^{-140} = 50e^{-140},$$

$$\Pr(S = 2) = \frac{140}{2}\left[\frac{5}{14}50e^{-140} + 2\frac{6}{14}e^{-140}\right] = 1{,}310e^{-140},$$

$$\Pr(S = 3) = \frac{140}{3}\left[\frac{5}{14}1{,}310e^{-140} + 2\frac{6}{14}50e^{-140} + 3\frac{3}{14}e^{-140}\right] = 24{,}196.67e^{-140},$$

$$\Pr(S > 3) = 1 - 25{,}557.67e^{-140}.$$

9.5 SECTION 9.6

9.41

$$
\begin{aligned}
m_0^k &= \int_{kh}^{(k+1)h} \frac{x - kh - h}{-h} f(x)dx \\
&= -\int_0^{(k+1)h} \frac{x}{h}dx + \int_0^{kh} \frac{x}{h}dx + (k+1)\{F[(k+1)h] - F(kh)\} \\
&= -\frac{1}{h}E[X \wedge (k+1)h] + (k+1)\{1 - F[(k+1)h]\} \\
&\quad +\frac{1}{h}E(X \wedge kh) - k[1 - F(kh)] \\
&\quad +(k+1)\{F[(k+1)h] - F(kh)\} \\
&= \frac{1}{h}E(X \wedge kh) - \frac{1}{h}E[X \wedge (k+1)h] + 1 - F(kh),
\end{aligned}
$$

$$
\begin{aligned}
m_1^k &= \int_{kh}^{(k+1)h} \frac{x - kh}{h} f(x)dx \\
&= \frac{1}{h}E[X \wedge (k+1)h] - \frac{1}{h}E(X \wedge kh) - 1 + F[(k+1)h].
\end{aligned}
$$

For $k = 1, 2, \ldots$,

$$
\begin{aligned}
f_k &= m_1^{k-1} + m_0^k \\
&= \frac{1}{h} E(X \wedge kh) - \frac{1}{h} E[X \wedge (k-1)h] - 1 + F(kh) \\
&\quad + \frac{1}{h} E(X \wedge kh) - \frac{1}{h} E[X \wedge (k+1)h] + 1 - F(kh) \\
&= \frac{1}{h} \{2E(X \wedge kh) - E[X \wedge (k-1)h] - E[X \wedge (k+1)h]\}.
\end{aligned}
$$

Also, $f_0 = m_0^0 = 1 - E(X \wedge h)/h$. All of the m_j^k have nonnegative integrands and, therefore, all of the f_k are nonnegative. To be a valid probability function, they must add to one,

$$
\begin{aligned}
f_0 + \sum_{k=1}^{\infty} f_k &= 1 - \frac{1}{h} E(X \wedge h) + \frac{1}{h} \sum_{k=1}^{\infty} \{E(X \wedge kh) - E[X \wedge (k-1)h]\} \\
&\quad + \frac{1}{h} \sum_{k=1}^{\infty} \{E(X \wedge kh) - E[X \wedge (k+1)h]\} \\
&= 1 - \frac{1}{h} E(X \wedge h) + \frac{1}{h} E(X \wedge h) = 1,
\end{aligned}
$$

because both sums are telescoping.

The mean of the discretized distribution is

$$
\begin{aligned}
\sum_{k=1}^{\infty} hk f_k &= \sum_{k=1}^{\infty} k\{E(X \wedge kh) - E[X \wedge (k-1)h]\} \\
&\quad + \sum_{k=1}^{\infty} k\{E(X \wedge kh) - E[X \wedge (k+1)h]\} \\
&= E(X \wedge h) + \sum_{k=1}^{\infty} (k+1)\{E[X \wedge (k+1)h] - E(X \wedge (kh))\} \\
&\quad + \sum_{k=1}^{\infty} k\{E(X \wedge kh) - E[X \wedge (k+1)h]\} \\
&= E(X \wedge h) + \sum_{k=1}^{\infty} \{E[X \wedge (k+1)h] - E(X \wedge (kh))\} \\
&= E(X)
\end{aligned}
$$

because $E(X \wedge \infty) = E(X)$.

9.42 Assume $x = 1$. Then $g_0 = \exp[-200(1 - 0.76)] = \exp(-48)$. The recursive formula gives

$$
g_k = \frac{200}{k}(0.14 g_{k-1} + 0.10 g_{k-2} + 0.06 g_{k-3} + 0.12 g_{k-4})
$$

with $g_k = 0$ for $k < 0$. Now use a spreadsheet to recursively compute probabilities until the probabilities sum to 0.05, which happens at $k = 62$. Then $62x = 4{,}000{,}000$ for $x = 64{,}516$. The expected compensation is

$$200(0.14 + 0.10 + 0.06 + 0.12)(64{,}516) = 5{,}419{,}344.$$

9.43 (a) $P_N(z) = wP_1(z) + (1 - w)P_2(z)$.

(b)
$$\begin{aligned} P_S(z) &= P_N(P_X(z)) \\ &= wP_1(P_X(z)) + (1 - w)P_2(P_X(z)) \\ &= wP_{S_1}(z) + (1 - w)P_{S_2}(z), \end{aligned}$$

$$f_S(x) = wf_{S_1} + (1 - w)f_{S_2}(x), \quad x = 0, 1, 2, \dots .$$

Hence, first use (9.22) to compute $f_{S_1}(x)$. Then take a weighted average of the results.

(c) Yes. Any distributions $P_1(z)$ and $P_2(z)$ using (9.22) can be used.

9.44 From (9.22), the recursion for the compound Poisson distribution,

$$f_S(0) = e^{-5},$$

$$f_S(x) = \frac{5}{x} \sum_{y=1}^{5} yf_X(y)f_S(x - y).$$

Then

$$f_S(1) = 5f_X(1)e^{-5},$$

and so $f_X(1) = \frac{1}{5}$ since $f_S(1) = e^{-5}$. Then,

$$\begin{aligned} f_S(2) &= \tfrac{5}{2}[f_X(1)f_S(1) + 2f_X(2)f_S(0)] \\ &= \tfrac{5}{2}\left[\tfrac{1}{5}e^{-5} + 2f_X(2)e^{-5}\right] \end{aligned}$$

and, since $f_S(2) = \tfrac{5}{2}e^{-5}$, we obtain $f_X(2) = \tfrac{2}{5}$.

9.45 $f_S(7) = \tfrac{6}{7}[1f_X(1)f_S(6) + 2f_X(2)f_S(5) + 4f_X(4)f_S(4)f_S(3)]$. Therefore, $0.041 = \tfrac{6}{7}[\tfrac{1}{3}f_S(6) + \tfrac{2}{3}0.0271 + \tfrac{4}{3}0.0132]$ for $f_S(6) = 0.0365$.

9.46 From (9.21) with $f_X(0) = 0$ and x replaced by z:

$$f_S(z) = \sum_{y=1}^{M} \left(a + b\frac{y}{z} \right) f_X(y) f_S(z - y)$$

$$= \sum_{y=1}^{M-1} \left(a + b\frac{y}{z} \right) f_X(y) f_S(z - y)$$

$$+ \left(a + b\frac{M}{z} \right) f_X(M) f_S(z - M).$$

Let $z = x + M$,

$$f_S(x + M) = \sum_{y=1}^{M-1} \left(a + b\frac{y}{x + M} \right) f_X(y) f_S(x + M - y)$$

$$+ \left(a + b\frac{M}{x + M} \right) f_X(M) f_S(x).$$

Rearrangement gives the result.

(b) The maxmimum number of claims is m and the maximum claim amount is M. Thus, the maximum value of S is mM with probability $[qf_X(M)]^m$. This becomes the starting point for a backward recursion.

9.47 We are looking for $6 - E(S) - E(D)$.

$$E(X) = \tfrac{1}{4}(1) + \tfrac{3}{4}(2) = \frac{7}{4} \text{ and } E(S) = \tfrac{7}{4}(2) = \tfrac{7}{2}.$$

$$D = \begin{cases} 4.5 - S, & S < 4.5 \\ 0, & S \geq 4.5. \end{cases}$$

$$
\begin{aligned}
f_S(0) &= e^{-2}, \\
f_S(1) &= \tfrac{2}{1}1\tfrac{1}{4}e^{-2} = \tfrac{1}{2}e^{-2}, \\
f_S(2) &= \tfrac{2}{2}\left(1\tfrac{1}{4}\tfrac{1}{2}e^{-2} + 2\tfrac{3}{4}e^{-2}\right) = \tfrac{13}{8}e^{-2}, \\
f_S(3) &= \tfrac{2}{3}\left(1\tfrac{1}{4}\tfrac{13}{8}e^{-2} + 2\tfrac{3}{4}\tfrac{1}{2}e^{-2}\right) = \tfrac{37}{48}e^{-2}, \\
f_S(4) &= \tfrac{2}{4}\left(1\tfrac{1}{4}\tfrac{37}{48}e^{-2} + 2\tfrac{3}{4}\tfrac{13}{8}e^{-2}\right) = \tfrac{505}{384}e^{-2}.
\end{aligned}
$$

Then $E(D) = (4.5 + 3.5\tfrac{1}{2} + 2.5\tfrac{13}{8} + 1.5\tfrac{37}{48} + 0.5\tfrac{505}{384})e^{-2} = 1.6411$. The answer is $6 - 3.5 - 1.6411 = 0.8589$.

9.48 For adults, the distribution is compound Poisson with $\lambda = 3$ and severity distribution with probabilities 0.4 and 0.6 on 1 and 2 (in units of 200). For children it is $\lambda = 2$ and severity probabilities of 0.9 and 0.1. The sum of the two distributions is also compound Poisson, with $\lambda = 5$. The probability at 1 is $[3(0.4) + 2(0.9)]/5 = 0.6$ and the remaining probability is at 2. The initial aggregate probabilities are

$$
\begin{aligned}
f_S(0) &= e^{-5}, \\
f_S(1) &= \tfrac{5}{1} 1\tfrac{3}{5} e^{-5} = 3e^{-5}, \\
f_S(2) &= \tfrac{5}{2} \left(1\tfrac{3}{5} 3e^{-5} + 2\tfrac{2}{5} e^{-5}\right) = \tfrac{13}{2} e^{-5}, \\
f_S(3) &= \tfrac{5}{3} \left(1\tfrac{3}{5} \tfrac{13}{2} e^{-5} + 2\tfrac{2}{5} 3e^{-5}\right) = \tfrac{21}{2} e^{-5}, \\
f_S(4) &= \tfrac{5}{4} \left(1\tfrac{3}{5} \tfrac{21}{2} e^{-5} + 2\tfrac{2}{5} \tfrac{13}{2} e^{-5}\right) = \tfrac{115}{8} e^{-5}.
\end{aligned}
$$

The probability of claims being 800 or less is the sum

$$
\left(1 + 3 + \frac{13}{2} + \frac{21}{2} + \frac{115}{8}\right) e^{-5} = 35.375 e^{-5} = 0.2384.
$$

9.49 The aggregate distribution is 2 times a Poisson variable. The probabilities are $\Pr(S = 0) = e^{-1}$, $\Pr(S = 2) = \Pr(N = 1) = e^{-1}$, $\Pr(S = 4) = \Pr(N = 2) = \tfrac{1}{2} e^{-1}$. $E(D) = (6 - 0)e^{-1} + (6 - 2)e^{-1} + (6 - 4)\tfrac{1}{2} e^{-1} = 11e^{-1} = 4.0467$.

9.50 $\lambda = 1 + 1 = 2$, $f_X(1) = [1(1) + 1(0.5)]/2 = 0.75$, $f_X(2) = 0.25$. The calculations appear in Table 9.6. The answer is $F_X^{*4}(6) = (81 + 108 + 54)/256 = 243/256 = 0.94922$.

Table 9.6   Calculations for Exercise 9.50

x	$f_X^{*0}(x)$	$f_X^{*1}(x)$	$f_X^{*2}(x)$	$f_X^{*3}(x)$	$f_X^{*4}(x)$
0	1	0	0	0	0
1	0	3/4	0	0	0
2	0	1/4	9/16	0	0
3	0	0	6/16	27/64	0
4	0	0	1/16	27/64	81/256
5	0	0	0	9/64	108/256
6	0	0	0	1/64	54/256

9.51 $56 = 29E(X)$, so $E(X) = 56/29$. $126 = 29E(X^2)$, so $E(X^2) = 126/29$. Let $f_i = \Pr(X = i)$. Then there are three equations:

$$
\begin{aligned}
f_1 + f_2 + f_3 &= 1, \\
f_1 + 2f_2 + 3f_3 &= 56/29, \\
f_1 + 4f_2 + 9f_3 &= 126/29.
\end{aligned}
$$

The solution is $f_2 = 11/29$. (Also, $f_1 = 10/29$ and $f_3 = 8/29$) and the expected count is $29(11/29) = 11$.

9.52 Let $f_j = \Pr(X = j)$. $0.16 = \lambda f_1$, $k = 2\lambda f_2$, $0.72 = 3\lambda f_3$. Then $f_1 = 0.16/\lambda$ and $f_3 = 0.24/\lambda$, and so $f_2 = 1 - 0.16/\lambda - 0.24/\lambda$. $1.68 = \lambda[1(0.16/\lambda) + 2(1 - 0.4/\lambda) + 3(0.24/\lambda)] = 0.08 + 2\lambda$, and so $\lambda = 0.8$.

9.53 $1 - F(6) = 0.04 - 0.02$, $F(6) = 0.98$. $1 - F(4) = 0.20 - 0.10$, $F(4) = 0.90$. $\Pr(S = 5 \text{ or } 6) = F(6) - F(4) = 0.08$.

9.54 For 1,500 lives, $\lambda = 0.01(1,500) = 15$. In units of 20, the severity distribution is $\Pr(X = 0) = 0.5$ and $\Pr(X = x) = 0.1$ for $x = 1, 2, 3, 4, 5$. Then $E(X^2) = 0.5(0) + 0.1(1 + 4 + 9 + 16 + 25) = 5.5$ and $\text{Var}(S) = 15(5.5) = 82.5$. In payment units it is $20^2(82.5) = 33,000$.

9.55 $\Pr(N = 2) = \frac{1}{4}\Pr(N = 2|\text{class I}) + \frac{3}{4}\Pr(N = 2|\text{class II})$. $\Pr(N = 2|\text{class I}) = \int_0^1 \frac{\beta^2}{(1+\beta)^3} 1 d\beta = 0.068147$. [Hint: Use the substitution $y = \beta/(1 + \beta)$]. $\Pr(N = 2|\text{class II}) = (0.25)^2/(1.25)^3 = 0.032$. $\Pr(N = 2) = 0.25(0.068147) + 0.75(0.32) = 0.04104$.

9.56 With $E(N) = 5$ and $E(X) = 5(0.6) + k(0.4) = 3 + 0.4k$, $E(S) = 15 + 2k$. With $\Pr(S = 0) = e^{-5} = 0.006738$, the expected cost not covered by the insurance is $0(0.006738) + 5(0.993262) = 4.96631$. Therefore, $28.03 = 15 + 2k - 4.96631$ for $k = 8.9982$.

9.57 Using the recursive formula, $\Pr(S = 0) = e^{-3}$, $\Pr(S = 1) = \frac{3}{1}(0.4)e^{-3} = 1.2e^{-3}$, $\Pr(S = 1) = \frac{3}{2}[0.4(1.2)e^{-3} + 2(0.3)e^{-3}] = 1.62e^{-3}$, $\Pr(S = 3) = \frac{3}{3}[0.4(1.62)e^{-3} + 2(0.3)(1.2)e^{-3} + 3(0.2)e^{-3}] = 1.968e^{-3}$. $\Pr(S \le 3) = 5.788e^{-3} = 0.28817$.

9.58 Using the recursive formula, $\Pr(S = 0) = (1 + 0.5)^{-6} = 0.08779$. $a = 0.5/(1 + 0.5) = 1/3$, $b = (6 - 1)(1/3) = 5/3$.

$$\Pr(S=1) = \left(\frac{1}{3} + \frac{5/3}{1}\right)(0.4)(0.08779) = 0.07023,$$

$$\Pr(S=2) = \left(\frac{1}{3} + \frac{5/3}{2}\right)(0.4)(0.07023) + \left(\frac{1}{3} + \frac{(5/3)2}{2}\right)(0.3)(0.08779)$$

$$= 0.08545,$$

$$\Pr(S=3) = \left(\frac{1}{3} + \frac{5/3}{3}\right)(0.4)(0.08545) + \left(\frac{1}{3} + \frac{(5/3)2}{3}\right)(0.3)(0.07023)$$

$$+ \left(\frac{1}{3} + \frac{(5/3)3}{3}\right)(0.2)(0.08779) = 0.09593.$$

Then, $\Pr(S \leq 3) = 0.33940$.

9.59 The result is 0.016.

9.60 The result is 0.055. Using a normal approximation with a mean of 250 and a variance 8,000, the probability is 0.047.

9.61 If $F_X(x) = 1 - e^{-\mu x}, x > 0$, then

$$f_0 = F_X\left(\frac{h}{2}\right) = 1 - e^{-\frac{\mu h}{2}},$$

and for $j = 1, 2, 3, \dots$,

$$\begin{aligned}
f_j &= F_X\left[\left(j+\frac{1}{2}\right)h\right] - F_X\left[\left(j-\frac{1}{2}\right)h\right] \\
&= 1 - e^{-\mu h\left(j+\frac{1}{2}\right)} - 1 + e^{-\mu h\left(j-\frac{1}{2}\right)} \\
&= e^{-\mu h\left(j-\frac{1}{2}\right)}\left(1 - e^{-\mu h}\right) \\
&= e^{-\frac{\mu h}{2}}\left(1 - e^{-\mu h}\right)e^{-\mu h(j-1)} \\
&= (1 - f_0)(1 - \phi)\phi^{j-1},
\end{aligned}$$

where $\phi = e^{-\mu h}$.

9.6   SECTION 9.7

9.62 In this case, $v = 1 - F_X(d) = e^{-\mu d}$, and from (9.30),

$$P_{NP}(z) = B\left[\theta(1 - v + vz - 1)\right] = B\left[\theta v(z-1)\right] = B\left[\theta e^{-\mu d}(z-1)\right].$$

Also, $Y^P = \alpha Z$, where

$$\Pr(Z > z) = \Pr(X > z + d)/\Pr(X > d) = e^{-\mu(z+d)}/e^{-\mu d} = e^{-\mu z}.$$

That is, $F_{Y^P}(y) = 1 - \Pr(Y^P > y) = 1 - \Pr(Z > y/\alpha) = 1 - e^{-\frac{\mu}{\alpha}y}$.

9.63 (a) The cumulative distribution function of the individual losses is, from Appendix A, given by $F_X(x) = 1 - \left(1 + \frac{x}{100}\right)e^{-\frac{x}{100}}$, $x \geq 0$. Also, $\mathrm{E}(X \wedge x) = 200\Gamma\left(3; \frac{x}{100}\right) + x\left[1 - \Gamma\left(2; \frac{x}{100}\right)\right]$. Then

$$
\begin{aligned}
\mathrm{E}(X \wedge 175) &= 200(0.25603) + 175(1 - 0.52212) = 134.835, \\
\mathrm{E}(X \wedge 50) &= 200(0.01439) + 50(1 - 0.09020) = 48.368,
\end{aligned}
$$

and the individual mean payment amount on a per-loss basis is

$$\mathrm{E}(Y^L) = \mathrm{E}(X \wedge 175) - \mathrm{E}(X \wedge 50) = 134.835 - 48.368 = 86.467.$$

Similarly, for the second moment,

$$\mathrm{E}\left[(X \wedge x)^2\right] = 60{,}000\Gamma\left(4; \frac{x}{100}\right) + x^2\left[1 - \Gamma\left(2; \frac{x}{100}\right)\right],$$

and, in particular,

$$
\begin{aligned}
\mathrm{E}\left[(X \wedge 175)^2\right] &= 60{,}000(0.10081) + 30{,}625(1 - 0.52212) = 20{,}683.645, \\
\mathrm{E}\left[(X \wedge 50)^2\right] &= 60{,}000(0.00175) + 2{,}500(1 - 0.09020) = 2{,}379.587.
\end{aligned}
$$

Therefore,

$$
\begin{aligned}
\mathrm{E}\left[(Y^L)^2\right] &= \mathrm{E}\left[(X \wedge 175)^2\right] - \mathrm{E}\left[(X \wedge 50)^2\right] \\
&\quad -100\mathrm{E}(X \wedge 175) + 100\mathrm{E}(X \wedge 50) \\
&= 20{,}683.645 - 2{,}379.587 - 100(134.835) + 100(48.368) \\
&= 9{,}657.358.
\end{aligned}
$$

Consequently,

$$\mathrm{Var}(Y^L) = 9{,}657.358 - (86.467)^2 = 2{,}180.816 = (46.70)^2.$$

For the negative binomially distributed number of losses,

$$\mathrm{E}(N^L) = (2)(1.5) = 3 \text{ and } \mathrm{Var}(N^L) = (2)(1.5)(1 + 1.5) = 7.5.$$

The mean of the aggregate payments is, therefore,

$$\mathrm{E}(S) = \mathrm{E}(N^L)\mathrm{E}(Y^L) = (3)(86.467) = 259.401,$$

and using Equation (9.9), the variance is

$$
\begin{aligned}
\mathrm{Var}(S) &= \mathrm{E}(N^L)\mathrm{Var}(Y^L) + \mathrm{Var}(N^L)\left[\mathrm{E}(Y^L)\right]^2 \\
&= (3)(2{,}180.816) + (7.5)(86.467)^2 \\
&= 62{,}616.514 = (250.233)^2.
\end{aligned}
$$

(b) The number of payments N^P has a negative binomial distribution with $r^* = r = 2$ and $\beta^* = \beta\left[1 - F_X(50)\right] = (1.5)(1 - 0.09020) = 1.36469$.

(c) The maximum payment amount is $175 - 50 = 125$. Thus $F_{Y^P}(y) = 1$ for $y \geq 125$. For $y < 125$,

$$
\begin{aligned}
F_{Y^P}(y) &= 1 - \Pr\left(X > y + 50\right)/\Pr(X > 50) \\
&= 1 - \frac{\left(1 + \frac{y+50}{100}\right)e^{-\frac{y+50}{100}}}{\left(1 + \frac{50}{100}\right)e^{-\frac{50}{100}}} \\
&= 1 - \left(1 + \frac{y}{150}\right)e^{-\frac{y}{100}}.
\end{aligned}
$$

(d)
$$
\begin{aligned}
f_0 &= F_{Y^P}(20) = 0.072105, \\
f_1 &= F_{Y^P}(60) - F_{Y^P}(20) = 0.231664 - 0.072105 = 0.159559, \\
f_2 &= F_{Y^P}(100) - F_{Y^P}(60) = 0.386868 - 0.231664 = 0.155204, \\
f_3 &= F_{Y^P}(140) - F_{Y^P}(100) = 1 - 0.386868 = 0.613132.
\end{aligned}
$$

(e)
$$
\begin{aligned}
g_0 &= \left[1 + \beta^*(1 - 0.072105)\right]^{-2} = \left[1 + (1.36469)(1 - 0.072105)\right]^{-2} \\
&= 0.194702 \\
a &= 1.36469/2.36469 = 0.577112, \quad b = (2 - 1)\,a = 0.577112. \\
g_x &= \frac{\sum_{y=1}^{x}\left(a + b\frac{y}{x}\right)f_y g_{x-y}}{1 - af_0} = 0.602169\sum_{y=1}^{x}\left(1 + \frac{y}{x}\right)f_y g_{x-y}, \\
g_1 &= (0.602169)(2)(0.159559)(0.194702) = 0.037415, \\
g_2 &= (0.602169)\left[(1.5)(0.159559)(0.037415) + (2)(0.155204)(0.194702)\right] \\
&= 0.041786, \\
g_3 &= 0.602169\left[(4/3)(0.159559)(0.041786) + (5/3)(0.155204)(0.037415)\right. \\
&\quad \left. + (2)(0.613132)(0.194702)\right] = 0.154953.
\end{aligned}
$$

9.7   SECTION 9.8

9.64
$$
\mathrm{E}(S) = \sum_{j=1}^{n}\mathrm{E}(I_j B_j) = \sum_{j=1}^{n}\mathrm{E}[\mathrm{E}(I_j B_j | I_j)],
$$

and then $\mathrm{E}(I_j B_j | I_j) = 0$ with probability $1 - q_j$ and $= \mu_j$ with probability q_j. Then

$$
\mathrm{E}[\mathrm{E}(I_j B_j | I_j)] = 0(1 - q_j) + \mu_j q_j = \mu_j q_j,
$$

thus establishing (9.35). For the variance,

$$
\mathrm{Var}(S) = \sum_{j=1}^{n}\mathrm{Var}(I_j B_j) = \sum_{j=1}^{n}\mathrm{Var}[\mathrm{E}(I_j B_j | I_j)] + \mathrm{E}[\mathrm{Var}(I_j B_j | I_j)].
$$

For the first term,

$$
\begin{aligned}
\mathrm{Var}[\mathrm{E}(I_j B_j | I_j)] &= 0^2(1 - q_j) + \mu_j^2 q_j - (\mu_j q_j)^2 \\
&= \mu_j^2 q_j (1 - q_j).
\end{aligned}
$$

For the second term, $\mathrm{Var}(I_j B_j | I_j) = 0$ with probability $1 - q_j$ and $= \sigma_j^2$ with probability q_j. Then,

$$
\mathrm{E}[\mathrm{Var}(I_j B_j | I_j)] = 0(1 - q_j) + \sigma_j^2 q_j.
$$

Inserting the two terms into the sum establishes (9.36).

9.65 Let S be the true random variable and let S_1, S_2, and S_3 be the three approximations. For the true variable,

$$
\mathrm{E}(S) = \sum_{j=1}^{n} q_j b_j, \quad \mathrm{Var}(S) = \sum_{j=1}^{n} q_j(1 - q_j) b_j^2.
$$

For all three approximations,

$$
\mathrm{E}(S) = \sum_{j=1}^{n} \lambda_j b_j, \quad \mathrm{Var}(S) = \sum_{j=1}^{n} \lambda_j b_j^2.
$$

For the first approximation, with $\lambda_j = q_j$ it is clear that $\mathrm{E}(S_1) = \mathrm{E}(S_2)$, and because $q_j > q_j(1 - q_j)$, $\mathrm{Var}(S_1) > \mathrm{Var}(S)$.

For the second approximation with $\lambda_j = -\ln(1 - q_j)$, note that

$$
-\ln(1 - q_j) = q_j + \frac{q_j^2}{2} + \frac{q_j^3}{3} + \cdots > q_j,
$$

and then it is clear that $\mathrm{E}(S_2) > \mathrm{E}(S_1)$. Because the variance also involves λ_j, the same is true for the variance.

For the third approximation, again using a Taylor series expansion,

$$
\frac{q_j}{1 - q_j} = q_j + q_j^2 + q_j^3 + \cdots > q_j + \frac{q_j^2}{2} + \frac{q_j^3}{3} + \cdots,
$$

and, therefore, the quantities for this approximation are the highest of all.

9.66
$$
\begin{aligned}
B &= \mathrm{E}(S) + 2\mathrm{SD}(S) \\
&= 40(2) + 60(4) + 2\sqrt{40(4) + 60(10)} \\
&= 375.136.
\end{aligned}
$$

For A,
$$
\begin{aligned}
\mathrm{E}(S) &= \mathrm{E}[\mathrm{E}(S|N)] = \mathrm{E}[2N + 4(100 - N)] \\
&= 400 - 2\mathrm{E}(N) = 400 - 2(40) = 320.
\end{aligned}
$$

$$
\begin{aligned}
\mathrm{Var}(S) &= \mathrm{Var}[\mathrm{E}(S|N)] + \mathrm{E}[\mathrm{Var}(S|N)] \\
&= \mathrm{Var}(400 - 2N) + \mathrm{E}[4N + 10(100 - N)] \\
&= 4\,\mathrm{Var}(N) - 6\mathrm{E}(N) + 1000 \\
&= 4(100)(0.4)(0.6) - 6(100)(0.4) + 1{,}000 = 856.
\end{aligned}
$$

Therefore, $A = 320 + 2\sqrt{856} = 378.515$ and $A/B = 1.009$.

9.67 Premium per person is $1.1(1{,}000)[0.2(0.02) + 0.8(0.01)] = 13.20$. With 30% smokers,

$$
\begin{aligned}
\mathrm{E}(S) &= 1{,}000[0.3(0.02) + 0.7(0.01)] = 13, \\
\mathrm{Var}(S) &= 1{,}000^2[0.3(0.02)(0.98) + 0.7(0.01)0(0.99)] = 12{,}810.
\end{aligned}
$$

With n policies, the probability of claims exceeding premium is

$$
\begin{aligned}
\Pr(S > 13.2n) &= \Pr\left(Z > \frac{13.2n - 13n}{\sqrt{12{,}810n}} \right) \\
&= \Pr(Z > 0.0017671\sqrt{n}) = 0.20.
\end{aligned}
$$

Therefore, $0.0017671\sqrt{n} = 0.84162$ for $n = 226{,}836$.

9.68 Let the policy being changed be the nth policy and let $F_n(x)$ represent the distribution function using n policies. Then, originally, $F_n(x) = 0.8F_{n-1}(x) + 0.2F_{n-1}(x - 1)$. Starting with $x = 0$:

$$
\begin{array}{ll}
0.40 = 0.80F_{n-1}(0) + 0.2(0), & F_{n-1}(0) = 0.50, \\
0.58 = 0.80F_{n-1}(1) + 0.2(0.50), & F_{n-1}(1) = 0.60, \\
0.64 = 0.80F_{n-1}(2) + 0.2(0.60), & F_{n-1}(2) = 0.65, \\
0.69 = 0.80F_{n-1}(3) + 0.2(0.65), & F_{n-1}(3) = 0.70, \\
0.70 = 0.80F_{n-1}(4) + 0.2(0.70), & F_{n-1}(4) = 0.70, \\
0.78 = 0.80F_{n-1}(5) + 0.2(0.70), & F_{n-1}(5) = 0.80.
\end{array}
$$

With the amount changed, $F_n(5) = 0.8F_{n-1}(5) + 0.2F_{n-1}(3) = 0.8(0.8) + 0.2(0.7) = 0.78$.

9.69 $\mathrm{E}(S) = 400(0.03)(5) + 300(0.07)(3) + 200(0.10)(2) = 163$.
For a single insured with claim probability q and exponential mean θ,

$$
\begin{aligned}
\mathrm{Var}(S) &= \mathrm{E}(N)\,\mathrm{Var}(X) + \mathrm{Var}(N)\mathrm{E}(X)^2 \\
&= q\theta^2 + q(1 - q)\theta^2 \\
&= q(2 - q)\theta^2.
\end{aligned}
$$

$$\begin{aligned}\text{Var}(S) &= 400(0.03)(1.97)(25) + 300(0.07)(1.93)(9) \\ &\quad + 200(0.10)(1.90)(4) \\ &= 1,107.77.\end{aligned}$$

$$P = \text{E}(S) + 1.645\text{SD}(S) = 163 + 1.645\sqrt{1,107.77} = 217.75.$$

9.70 For one member, the mean is

$$0.7(160) + 0.2(600) + 0.5(240) = 352$$

and the variance is

$$0.7(4,900) + 0.21(160)^2 + 0.2(20,000) + 0.16(600)^2$$
$$+0.5(8,100) + 0.25(240)^2 = 88,856 \ .$$

For n members, the goal is

$$\begin{aligned}0.1 &> \Pr\left[S > 1.15(352)n\right] \\ &= \Pr\left(Z > \frac{1.15(352)n - 352n}{\sqrt{88,856n}}\right),\end{aligned}$$

and thus,

$$\frac{1.15(352)n - 352n}{\sqrt{88,856n}} > 1.28155,$$

which yields $n > 52.35$. So 53 members are needed.

9.71 The mean is

$$100,000 = 0.2k(3,500) + 0.6\alpha k(2,000) = (700 + 1,200\alpha)k,$$

and the variance is

$$\begin{aligned}\text{Var}(S) &= 0.2(0.8)k^2(3,500) + 0.6(0.4)(\alpha k)^2(2,000) \\ &= (560 + 480\alpha^2)k^2.\end{aligned}$$

Solving the first equation for k and substituting give

$$\text{Var}(S) = \frac{560 + 480\alpha^2}{(700 + 1200\alpha)^2}100,000^2.$$

Because the goal is to minimize the variance, constants can be removed, such as all the zeros, thus leaving

$$\frac{56 + 48\alpha^2}{(7 + 12\alpha)^2}.$$

Taking the derivatives leads to a numerator of (the denominator is not important because the next step is to set the derivative equal to zero)

$$(7 + 12\alpha)^2 96\alpha - (56 + 48\alpha^2)2(7 + 12\alpha)12.$$

Setting this expression equal to zero, dividing by 96, and rearranging lead to the quadratic equation

$$84\alpha^2 - 119\alpha - 98 = 0,$$

and the only positive root is the solution $\alpha = 2$.

9.72 $\lambda = 500(0.01) + 500(0.02) = 15$. $f_X(x) = 500(0.01)/15 = 1/3$, $f_X(2x) = 2/3$. $E(X^2) = (1/3)x^2 + (2/3)(2x)^2 = 3x^2$. $\text{Var}(S) = 15(3x^2) = 45x^2 = 4{,}500$. $x = 10$.

9.73 All work is done in units of 100,000. The first group of 500 policies is not relevant. The others have amounts 1, 2, 1, and 1.

$$\begin{aligned}
E(S) &= 500(0.02)(1) + 500(0.02)(2) + 300(0.1)(1) + 500(0.1)(1) \\
&= 110, \\
\text{Var}(S) &= 500(0.02)(0.98)(1) + 500(0.02)(0.98)(4) \\
&\quad +300(0.1)(0.9)(1) + 500(0.1)(0.9)(1) \\
&= 121.
\end{aligned}$$

(a) $P = 110 + 1.645\sqrt{121} = 128.095$.

(b) $\mu + \sigma^2/2 = \ln 110 = 4.70048$. $2\mu + 2\sigma^2 = \ln(121 + 110^2) = 9.41091$. $\mu = 4.695505$ and $\sigma = 0.0997497$. $\ln P = 4.695505 + 1.645(0.0997497) = 4.859593$, $P = 128.97$.

(c) $\alpha\theta = 110$, $\alpha\theta^2 = 121$, $\theta = 121/110 = 1.1$, $\alpha = 100$. This is a chi-square distribution with 200 degrees of freedom. The 95th percentile is (using the Excel®[1] GAMMAINV function) 128.70.

(d) $\lambda = 500(0.02) + 500(0.02) + 300(0.10) + 500(0.10) = 100$. $f_X(1) = (10 + 30 + 50)/100 = 0.9$ and $f_X(2) = 0.1$. Using the recursive formula for the compound Poisson distribution, we find $F_S(128) = 0.94454$ and $F_S(129) = 0.95320$, and so, to be safe at the 5% level, a premium of 129 is required.

---

[1] Excel® is either a registered trademark or trademark of Microsoft Corporation in the United States and/or other countries.

(e) One way to use the software is to note that $S = X_1 + 2X_2 + X_3$ where each X is binomial with $m = 500$, 500, and 800 and $q = 0.02$, 0.02, and 0.10. The results are $F_S(128) = 0.94647$ and $F_S(129) = 0.95635$, and so, to be safe at the 5% level, a premium of 129 is required.

9.74 From (9.35), $E(S) = 500(0.02)(500) + 250(0.03)(750) + 250(0.04)(1,000) = 20,625$. From (9.36),

$$
\begin{aligned}
\mathrm{Var}(S) &= 500[0.02(500)^2 + 0.02(0.98)(500)^2] \\
&= 250[0.03(750)^2 + 0.03(0.97)(750)^2] \\
&= 250[0.04(1,000)^2 + 0.04(0.96)(1,000)^2] = 32,860,937.5
\end{aligned}
$$

The compound Poisson model has $\lambda = 500(0.02) + 250(0.03) + 250(0.04) = 27.5$ and the claim amount distribution has density function, from (9.38),

$$
f_X(x) = \frac{10}{27.5} \frac{1}{500} e^{-x/500} + \frac{7.5}{27.5} \frac{1}{750} e^{-x/750} + \frac{10}{27.5} \frac{1}{1,000} e^{-x/1,000}.
$$

This mixture of exponentials distribution has mean

$$
[10(500) + 7.5(750) + 10(1,000)]/27.5 = 750
$$

and variance

$$
[10(2)(500)^2 + 7.5(2)(750)^2 + 10(2)(1,000)^2]/27.5 - 750^2 = 653,409.09.
$$

Then

$$
\begin{aligned}
E(S) &= 27.5(750) = 20{,}625, \\
\mathrm{Var}(S) &= 27.5(653{,}409.09) + 27.5(750)^2 = 33{,}437{,}500.
\end{aligned}
$$

CHAPTER 10

CHAPTER 10 SOLUTIONS

10.1 SECTION 10.2

10.1 When three observations are taken without replacement, there are only four possible results. They are 1,3,5; 1,3,9; 1,5,9; and 3,5,9. The four sample means are 9/3, 13/3, 15/3, and 17/3. The expected value (each has probability 1/4) is 54/12 or 4.5, which equals the population mean. The four sample medians are 3, 3, 5, and 5. The expected value is 4, and so the median is biased.

10.2
$$
\begin{aligned}
\mathrm{E}(\bar{X}) &= \mathrm{E}\left[\frac{1}{n}(X_1 + \cdots + X_n)\right] = \frac{1}{n}\left[\mathrm{E}(X_1) + \cdots + \mathrm{E}(X_n)\right] \\
&= \frac{1}{n}(\mu + \cdots + \mu) = \mu.
\end{aligned}
$$

10.3 For a sample of size 3 from a continuous distribution, the density function of the median is $6f(x)F(x)[1 - F(x)]$. For this exercise, $F(x) = (x - \theta + 2)/4$,

Student Solutions Manual to Accompany Loss Models: From Data to Decisions, Fourth Edition. By Stuart A. Klugman, Harry H. Panjer, Gordon E. Willmot
Copyright © 2012 John Wiley & Sons, Inc.

$\theta - 2 < x < \theta + 2$. The density function for the median is

$$f_{\mathrm{med}}(x) = 6(0.25)\frac{x - \theta + 2}{4}\frac{2 - x + \theta}{4}$$

and the expected value is

$$6 \int_{\theta-2}^{\theta+2} \frac{x(x - \theta + 2)(2 - x + \theta)}{64}\,dx = \frac{6}{64}\int_0^4 (y + \theta - 2)y(4 - y)dy$$

$$= \frac{6}{64}\int_0^4 -y^3 + (6 - \theta)y^2 + 4(\theta - 2)y\,dy$$

$$= \frac{6}{64}\left[-\frac{y^4}{4} + \frac{(6 - \theta)y^3}{3} + \frac{4(\theta - 2)y^2}{2} \right]\Big|_0^4$$

$$= \frac{6}{64}\left[-64 + \frac{(6 - \theta)64}{3} + 32(\theta - 2) \right]$$

$$= \theta,$$

where the first line used the substitution $y = x - \theta + 2$.

10.4 Because the mean of a Pareto distribution does not always exist, it is not reasonable to discuss unbiasedness or consistency. Had the problem been restricted to Pareto distributions with $\alpha > 1$, then consistency can be established. It turns out that for the sample mean to be consistent, only the first moment needs to exist (the variance having a limit of zero is a sufficient, but not a necessary, condition for consistency).

10.5 The mean is unbiased, so its MSE is its variance. It is

$$MSE_{\mathrm{mean}}(\theta) = \frac{\mathrm{Var}(X)}{3} = \frac{4^2}{12(3)} = \frac{4}{9}.$$

The median is also unbiased. The variance is

$$6 \int_{\theta-2}^{\theta+2} \frac{(x - \theta)^2(x - \theta + 2)(2 - x + \theta)}{64}\,dx = \frac{6}{64}\int_0^4 (y - 2)^2 y(4 - y)dy$$

$$= \frac{6}{64}\int_0^4 -y^4 + 8y^3 - 20y^2 + 16y\,dy$$

$$= \frac{6}{64}\left[-\frac{4^5}{5} + \frac{8(4)^4}{4} - \frac{20(4)^3}{3} + \frac{16(4)^2}{2} \right]$$

$$= 4/5,$$

and so the sample mean has the smaller MSE.

10.6 We have

$$\begin{aligned}
\text{Var}(\hat{\theta}_C) &= \text{Var}[w\hat{\theta}_A + (1-w)\hat{\theta}_B] \\
&= w^2(160{,}000) + (1-w)^2(40{,}000) \\
&= 200{,}000w^2 - 80{,}000w + 40{,}000.
\end{aligned}$$

The derivative is $400{,}000w - 80{,}000$, and setting it equal to zero provides the solution, $w = 0.2$.

10.7 $\text{MSE} = \text{Var} + \text{bias}^2$. $1 = \text{Var} + (0.2)^2$, $\text{Var} = 0.96$.

10.8 To be unbiased,

$$m = \text{E}(Z) = \alpha(0.8m) + \beta m = (0.8\alpha + \beta)m,$$

and so $1 = 0.8\alpha + \beta$ or $\beta = 1 - 0.8\alpha$. Then

$$\text{Var}(Z) = \alpha^2 m^2 + \beta^2 1.5m^2 = [\alpha^2 + (1-0.8\alpha)^2 1.5]m^2,$$

which is minimized when $\alpha^2 + 1.5 - 2.4\alpha + 0.96\alpha^2$ is minimized. This result occurs when $3.92\alpha - 2.4 = 0$ or $\alpha = 0.6122$. Then $\beta = 1 - 0.8(0.6122) = 0.5102$.

10.9 One way to solve this problem is to list the 20 possible samples of size 3 and assign probability $1/20$ to each. The population mean is $(1 + 1 + 2 + 3 + 5 + 10)/6 = 11/3$.

(a) The 20 sample means have an average of $11/3$, and so the bias is zero. The variance of the sample means (dividing by 20 because this is the population of sample means) is 1.9778, which is also the MSE.

(b) The 20 sample medians have an average of 2.7, and so the bias is $2.7 - 11/3 = -0.9667$. The variance is 1.81 and the MSE is 2.7444.
(c) The 20 sample midranges have an average of 4.15, and so the bias is $4.15 - 11/3 = 0.4833$. The variance is 2.65 and the MSE is 2.8861.

(d) $\text{E}(aX_{(1)} + bX_{(2)} + cX_{(3)}) = 1.25a + 2.7b + 7.05c$, where the expected values of the order statistics can be found by averaging the 20 values from the enumerated population. To be unbiased, the expected value must be $11/3$, and so the restriction is $1.25a + 2.7b + 7.05c = 11/3$. With this restriction, the MSE is minimized at $a = 1.445337$, $b = 0.043733$, and $c = 0.247080$ with an MSE of 1.620325. With no restrictions, the minimum is at $a = 1.289870$, $b = 0.039029$, and $c = 0.220507$ with an MSE of 1.446047 (and a bias of -0.3944).

10.10 bias$(\hat{\theta}_1) = 165/75 - 2 = 0.2$, Var$(\hat{\theta}_1) = 375/75 - (165/75)^2 = 0.16$, MSE$(\hat{\theta}_1) = 0.16 + (0.2)^2 = 0.2$. bias$(\hat{\theta}_2) = 147/75 - 2 = -0.04$, Var$(\hat{\theta}_2) = 312/75 - (147/75)^2 = 0.3184$, MSE$(\hat{\theta}_2) = 0.3184 + (-0.04)^2 = 0.32$. The relative efficiency is $0.2/0.32 = 0.625$, or $0.32/0.20 = 1.6$.

10.2 SECTION 10.3

10.11 (a) From the information given in the problem, we can begin with

$$0.95 = \Pr(a \leq \bar{X}/\theta \leq b),$$

where $\bar{X}/\theta$ is known to have the gamma distribution with $\alpha = 50$ and $\theta = 0.02$. This does not uniquely specify the endpoints. However, if 2.5% probability is allocated to each side, then $a = 0.7422$ and $b = 1.2956$. Inserting these values in the inequality, taking reciprocals, and multiplying through by $\bar{X}$ give

$$0.95 = \Pr(0.7718\bar{X} \leq \theta \leq 1.3473\bar{X}).$$

Inserting the sample mean gives an interval of 212.25 to 370.51.

(b) The sample mean has $\mathrm{E}(\bar{X}) = \theta$ and $\mathrm{Var}(\bar{X}) = \theta^2/50$. Then, using $275^2/50$ as the approximate variance,

$$\begin{aligned} 0.95 &\doteq \Pr\left(-1.96 \leq \frac{\bar{X} - \theta}{275/\sqrt{50}} \leq 1.96\right) \\ &= \Pr(-76.23 \leq \bar{X} - \theta \leq 76.23). \end{aligned}$$

Inserting the sample mean of 275 gives the interval 275 ± 76.23, or 198.77 to 351.23.

(c) Leaving the θ in the variance alone,

$$\begin{aligned} 0.95 &\doteq \Pr\left(-1.96 \leq \frac{\bar{X} - \theta}{\theta/\sqrt{50}} \leq 1.96\right) \\ &= \Pr(-0.2772\theta \leq \bar{X} - \theta \leq 0.2772\theta) \\ &= \Pr(\bar{X}/1.2772 \leq \theta \leq \bar{X}/0.7228) \end{aligned}$$

for an interval of 215.31 to 380.46.

10.12 The estimated probability of one or more claims is $400/2{,}000 = 0.2$. For this binomial distribution, the variance is estimated as $0.2(0.8)/2{,}000 = 0.00008$. The upper bound is $0.2 + 1.96\sqrt{0.00008} = 0.21753$.

10.3 SECTION 10.4

10.13 For the exact test, null should be rejected if $\bar{X} \leq c$. The value of c comes from

$$
\begin{aligned}
0.05 &= \Pr(\bar{X} \leq c | \theta = 325) \\
&= \Pr(\bar{X}/325 \leq c/325),
\end{aligned}
$$

where $\bar{X}/325$ has the gamma distribution with parameters 50 and 0.02. From that distribution, $c/325 = 0.7793$ for $c = 253.27$. Because the sample mean of 275 is not below this value, the null hypothesis is not rejected. The p-value is obtained from

$$
\Pr(\bar{X} \leq 275 | \theta = 325) = \Pr(\bar{X}/325 \leq 275/325).
$$

From the gamma distribution with parameters 50 and 0.02, this probability is 0.1353.

For the normal approximation,

$$
\begin{aligned}
0.05 &= \Pr(\bar{X} \leq c | \theta = 325) \\
&= \Pr\left(Z \leq \frac{c - 325}{325/\sqrt{50}} \right).
\end{aligned}
$$

Solving $(c - 325)/(325/\sqrt{50}) = -1.645$ produces $c = 249.39$. Again, the null hypothesis is not rejected. For the p-value,

$$
\Pr\left(Z \leq \frac{275 - 325}{325/\sqrt{50}} = -1.0879 \right) = 0.1383.
$$

CHAPTER 11

CHAPTER 11 SOLUTIONS

11.1 SECTION 11.2

11.1 When all information is available, the calculations are in Table 11.1. As in Example 11.4, values apply from the current y-value to the next one.

11.2 (a) $\hat{\mu} = \sum x_i/35 = 204{,}900$. $\hat{\mu}'_2 = \sum x_i^2/35 = 1.4134 \times 10^{11}$.
$\hat{\sigma} = 325{,}807$. $\hat{\mu}'_3 = 1.70087 \times 10^{17}$, $\hat{\mu}_3 = 9.62339 \times 10^{16}$,
$\hat{c} = 325{,}807/204{,}900 = 1.590078$, $\hat{\gamma}_1 = 2.78257$.

(b) $E_n(500{,}000) = [\sum_{j=1}^{30} y_j + 5(500{,}000)]/35 = 153{,}139$.
$E_n^{(2)}(500{,}000) = [\sum_{j=1}^{30} y_j^2 + 5(500{,}000)^2]/35 = 53{,}732{,}687{,}032$.

11.3 $\hat{\mu}'_1 = [2(2{,}000) + 6(4{,}000) + 12(6{,}000) + 10(8{,}000)]/30 = 6{,}000$,
$\hat{\mu}_2 = [2(-4{,}000)^2 + 6(-2{,}000)^2 + 12(0)^2 + 10(2{,}000)^2]/30 = 3{,}200{,}000$,
$\hat{\mu}_3 = [2(-4{,}000)^3 + 6(-2{,}000)^3 + 12(0)^3 + 10(2{,}000)^3]/30 = -3{,}200{,}000{,}000$.
$\hat{\gamma}_1 = -3{,}200{,}000{,}000/(3{,}200{,}000)^{1.5} = -0.55902$.

Table 11.1 Calculations for Exercise 11.1.

j	y_j	s_j	r_j	$F_{30}(x)$	$\hat{H}(x)$	$\hat{F}(x)^*$
1	0.1	1	30	$1 - 29/30 = 0.0333$	$1/30 = 0.0333$	0.0328
2	0.5	1	29	$1 - 28/30 = 0.0667$	$0.0333 + 1/29 = 0.0678$	0.0656
3	0.8	1	28	$1 - 27/30 = 0.1000$	$0.0678 + 1/28 = 0.1035$	0.0983
4	1.8	2	27	$1 - 25/30 = 0.1667$	$0.1035 + 2/27 = 0.1776$	0.1627
5	2.1	1	25	$1 - 24/30 = 0.2000$	$0.1776 + 1/25 = 0.2176$	0.1956
6	2.5	1	24	$1 - 23/30 = 0.2333$	$0.2176 + 1/24 = 0.2593$	0.2284
7	2.8	1	23	$1 - 22/30 = 0.2667$	$0.2593 + 1/23 = 0.3027$	0.2612
8	3.9	2	22	$1 - 20/30 = 0.3333$	$0.3027 + 2/22 = 0.3937$	0.3254
9	4.0	1	20	$1 - 19/30 = 0.3667$	$0.3937 + 1/20 = 0.4437$	0.3583
10	4.1	1	19	$1 - 18/30 = 0.4000$	$0.4437 + 1/19 = 0.4963$	0.3912
11	4.6	2	18	$1 - 16/30 = 0.4667$	$0.4963 + 2/18 = 0.6074$	0.4552
12	4.8	2	16	$1 - 14/30 = 0.5333$	$0.6074 + 2/16 = 0.7324$	0.5192
13	5.0	14	14	$1 - 0/30 = 1.0000$	$0.7324 + 14/14 = 1.7324$	0.8231

$^*\hat{F}(x) = 1 - e^{-\hat{H}(x)}$.

Table 11.2 Calculations for Exercise 11.4.

Payment range	Number of payments	Ogive value	Histogram value
0–25	6	$\frac{6}{392} = 0.0153$	$\frac{6}{392(25)} = 0.000612$
25–50	24	$\frac{30}{392} = 0.0765$	$\frac{24}{392(25)} = 0.002449$
50–75	30	$\frac{60}{392} = 0.1531$	$\frac{30}{392(25)} = 0.003061$
75–100	31	$\frac{91}{392} = 0.2321$	$\frac{31}{392(25)} = 0.003163$
100–150	57	$\frac{148}{392} = 0.3776$	$\frac{57}{392(50)} = 0.002908$
150–250	80	$\frac{228}{392} = 0.5816$	$\frac{80}{392(100)} = 0.002041$
250–500	85	$\frac{313}{392} = 0.7985$	$\frac{85}{392(250)} = 0.000867$
500–1,000	54	$\frac{367}{392} = 0.9362$	$\frac{54}{392(500)} = 0.000276$
1,000–2,000	15	$\frac{382}{392} = 0.9745$	$\frac{15}{392(1000)} = 0.000038$
2,000–4,000	10	$\frac{392}{392} = 1.0000$	$\frac{10}{392(2000)} = 0.000013$

11.2 SECTION 11.3

11.4 There are 392 observations and the calculations are in Table 11.2. For each interval, the ogive value is for the right-hand endpoint of the interval, while the histogram value is for the entire interval. Graphs of the ogive and histogram appear in Figures 11.1 and 11.2.

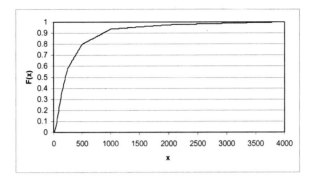

Figure 11.1   Ogive for Exercise 11.4.

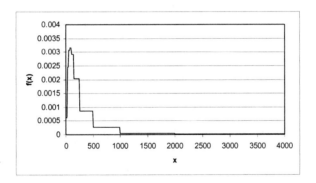

Figure 11.2   Histogram for Exercise 11.4.

11.5 (a) The ogive connects the points $(0.5, 0)$, $(2.5, 0.35)$, $(8.5, 0.65)$, $(15.5, 0.85)$, and $(29.5, 1)$.

(b) The histogram has height $0.35/2 = 0.175$ on the interval $(0.5, 2.5)$, height $0.3/6 = 0.05$ on the interval $(2.5, 8.5)$, height $0.2/7 = 0.028571$ on the interval $(8.5, 15.1)$, and height $0.15/14 = 0.010714$ on the interval $(15.5, 29.5)$.

11.6 The plot appears in Figure 11.3. The points are the complements of the survival probabilities at the indicated times.

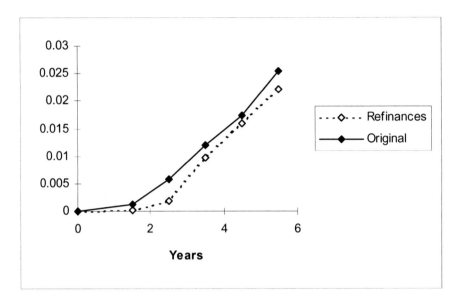

Figure 11.3   Ogive for mortgage lifetime for Exercise 11.6.

Because one curve lies completely above the other, it appears possible that original issues have a shorter lifetime.

11.7 The heights of the histogram bars are, respectively, $0.5/2 = 0.25$, $0.2/8 = 0.025$, $0.2/90 = 0.00222$, $0.1/900 = 0.000111$. The histogram appears in Figure 11.4.

11.8 The empirical model places probability $1/n$ at each data point. Then

$$
\begin{aligned}
E(X \wedge 2) &= \sum_{x_j < 2} x_j(1/40) + \sum_{x_j \geq 2} 2(1/40) \\
&= (20 + 15)(1/40) + (14)(2)(1/40) \\
&= 1.575.
\end{aligned}
$$

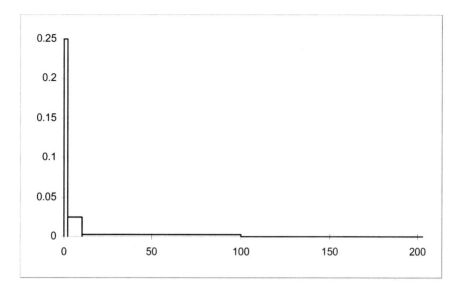

Figure 11.4   Histogram for Exercise 11.7.

11.9 We have

$$
\begin{aligned}
\mathrm{E}(X \wedge 7{,}000) &= \frac{1}{2{,}000}\left(\sum_{x_j \le 7{,}000} x_j + \sum_{x_j > 7{,}000} 7{,}000\right) \\
&= \frac{1}{2{,}000}\left(\sum_{x_j \le 6{,}000} x_j + \sum_{x_j > 6{,}000} 6{,}000 \right. \\
&\quad + \left. \sum_{6{,}000 < x_j \le 7{,}000}(x_j - 6{,}000) + \sum_{x_j > 7{,}000} 1{,}000\right) \\
&= \mathrm{E}(X \wedge 6{,}000) + [200{,}000 - 30(6{,}000) + 270(1{,}000)]/2{,}000 \\
&= 1{,}955.
\end{aligned}
$$

11.10 Let n be the sample size. The equations are

$$0.21 = \frac{36}{n} + \frac{0.4x}{n} \text{ and } 0.51 = \frac{36}{n} + \frac{x}{n} + \frac{0.6y}{n}.$$

Also, $n = 200 + x + y$. The equations can be rewritten as

$$0.21(200 + x + y) = 36 + 0.4x \text{ and } 0.51(200 + x + y) = 36 + x + 0.6y.$$

The linear equations can be solved for $x = 120$.

CHAPTER 12

CHAPTER 12 SOLUTIONS

12.1 SECTION 12.1

12.1 The calculations are in Tables 12.1 and 12.2.

Student Solutions Manual to Accompany Loss Models: From Data to Decisions, Fourth **105**
Edition. By Stuart A. Klugman, Harry H. Panjer, Gordon E. Willmot
Copyright © 2012 John Wiley & Sons, Inc.

Table 12.1 Calculations for Exercise 12.1.

i	d_i	u_i	x_i	i	d_i	u_i	x_i
1	0	–	0.1	16	0	4.8	–
2	0	–	0.5	17	0	–	4.8
3	0	–	0.8	18	0	–	4.8
4	0	0.8	–	19–30	0	–	5.0
5	0	–	1.8	31	0.3	–	5.0
6	0	–	1.8	32	0.7	–	5.0
7	0	–	2.1	33	1.0	4.1	–
8	0	–	2.5	34	1.8	3.1	–
9	0	–	2.8	35	2.1	–	3.9
10	0	2.9	–	36	2.9	–	5.0
11	0	2.9	–	37	2.9	–	4.8
12	0	–	3.9	38	3.2	4.0	–
13	0	4.0	–	39	3.4	–	5.0
14	0	–	4.0	40	3.9	–	5.0
15	0	–	4.1				

Table 12.2 Further calculations for Exercise 12.1.

j	y_j	s_j	r_j
1	0.1	1	$30 - 0 - 0 = 30$ or $0 + 30 - 0 - 0 = 30$
2	0.5	1	$31 - 1 - 0 = 30$ or $30 + 1 - 1 - 0 = 30$
3	0.8	1	$32 - 2 - 0 = 30$ or $30 + 1 - 1 - 0 = 30$
4	1.8	2	$33 - 3 - 1 = 29$ or $30 + 1 - 1 - 1 = 29$
5	2.1	1	$34 - 5 - 1 = 28$ or $29 + 1 - 2 - 0 = 28$
6	2.5	1	$35 - 6 - 1 = 28$ or $28 + 1 - 1 - 0 = 28$
7	2.8	1	$35 - 7 - 1 = 27$ or $28 + 0 - 1 - 0 = 27$
8	3.9	2	$39 - 8 - 4 = 27$ or $27 + 4 - 1 - 3 = 27$
9	4.0	1	$40 - 10 - 4 = 26$ or $27 + 1 - 2 - 0 = 26$
10	4.1	1	$40 - 11 - 6 = 23$ or $26 + 0 - 1 - 2 = 23$
11	4.8	3	$40 - 12 - 7 = 21$ or $23 + 0 - 1 - 1 = 21$
12	5.0	17	$40 - 15 - 8 = 17$ or $21 + 0 - 3 - 1 = 17$

12.2

$$S_{40}(t) = \begin{cases} 1, & 0 \le t < 0.1, \\ \frac{30-1}{30} = 0.9667, & 0.1 \le t < 0.5, \\ 0.9667\frac{30-1}{30} = 0.9344, & 0.5 \le t < 0.8, \\ 0.9344\frac{30-1}{30} = 0.9033, & 0.8 \le t < 1.8, \\ 0.9033\frac{29-2}{29} = 0.8410, & 1.8 \le t < 2.1, \\ 0.8410\frac{28-1}{28} = 0.8110, & 2.1 \le t < 2.5, \\ 0.8110\frac{28-1}{28} = 0.7820, & 2.5 \le t < 2.8, \\ 0.7820\frac{27-1}{27} = 0.7530, & 2.8 \le t < 3.9, \\ 0.7530\frac{27-2}{27} = 0.6973, & 3.9 \le t < 4.0, \\ 0.6973\frac{26-1}{26} = 0.6704, & 4.0 \le t < 4.1, \\ 0.6704\frac{23-1}{23} = 0.6413, & 4.1 \le t < 4.8, \\ 0.6413\frac{21-3}{21} = 0.5497, & 4.8 \le t < 5.0, \\ 0.5497\frac{17-17}{17} = 0, & t \ge 5.0. \end{cases}$$

12.3

$$
\hat{H}(t) =
\begin{cases}
0, & 0 \le t < 0.1, \\[4pt]
\frac{1}{30} = 0.0333, & 0.1 \le t < 0.5, \\[4pt]
0.0333 + \frac{1}{30} = 0.0667, & 0.5 \le t < 0.8, \\[4pt]
0.0667 + \frac{1}{30} = 0.1000, & 0.8 \le t < 1.8, \\[4pt]
0.1000 + \frac{2}{29} = 0.1690, & 1.8 \le t < 2.1, \\[4pt]
0.1690 + \frac{1}{28} = 0.2047, & 2.1 \le t < 2.5, \\[4pt]
0.2047 + \frac{1}{28} = 0.2404, & 2.5 \le t < 2.8, \\[4pt]
0.2404 + \frac{1}{27} = 0.2774, & 2.8 \le t < 3.9, \\[4pt]
0.2774 + \frac{2}{27} = 0.3515, & 3.9 \le t < 4.0, \\[4pt]
0.3515 + \frac{1}{26} = 0.3900, & 4.0 \le t < 4.1, \\[4pt]
0.3900 + \frac{1}{23} = 0.4334, & 4.1 \le t < 4.8, \\[4pt]
0.4334 + \frac{3}{21} = 0.5763, & 4.8 \le t < 5.0, \\[4pt]
0.5763 + \frac{17}{17} = 1.5763, & t \ge 5.0.
\end{cases}
$$

$$
\hat{S}(t) =
\begin{cases}
e^{-0} = 1, & 0 \le t < 0.1, \\
e^{-0.0333} = 0.9672, & 0.1 \le t < 0.5, \\
e^{-0.0667} = 0.9355, & 0.5 \le t < 0.8, \\
e^{-0.1000} = 0.9048, & 0.8 \le t < 1.8, \\
e^{-0.1690} = 0.8445, & 1.8 \le t < 2.1, \\
e^{-0.2047} = 0.8149, & 2.1 \le t < 2.5, \\
e^{-0.2404} = 0.7863, & 2.5 \le t < 2.8, \\
e^{-0.2774} = 0.7578, & 2.8 \le t < 3.9, \\
e^{-0.3515} = 0.7036, & 3.9 \le t < 4.0, \\
e^{-0.3900} = 0.6771, & 4.0 \le t < 4.1, \\
e^{-0.4334} = 0.6483, & 4.1 \le t < 4.8, \\
e^{-0.5763} = 0.5620, & 4.8 \le t < 5.0, \\
e^{-1.5763} = 0.2076, & t \ge 5.0.
\end{cases}
$$

12.4 Using the raw data, the results are in Table 12.3. When the deductible and limit are imposed, the results are as in Table 12.4. Because 1,000 is a censoring point and not an observed loss value, there is no change in the survival function at 1,000.

Table 12.3   Calculations for Exercise 12.4.

Value(x)	r	s	$S_{KM}(x)$	$H_{NA}(x)$	$S_{NA}(x)$
27	20	1	0.95	0.0500	0.9512
82	19	1	0.90	0.1026	0.9025
115	18	1	0.85	0.1582	0.8537
126	17	1	0.80	0.2170	0.8049
155	16	1	0.75	0.2795	0.7562
161	15	1	0.70	0.3462	0.7074
243	14	1	0.65	0.4176	0.6586
294	13	1	0.60	0.4945	0.6099
340	12	1	0.55	0.5779	0.5611
384	11	1	0.50	0.6688	0.5123
457	10	1	0.45	0.7688	0.4636
680	9	1	0.40	0.8799	0.4148
855	8	1	0.35	1.0049	0.3661
877	7	1	0.30	1.1477	0.3174
974	6	1	0.25	1.3144	0.2686
1,193	5	1	0.20	1.5144	0.2199
1,340	4	1	0.15	1.7644	0.1713
1,884	3	1	0.10	2.0977	0.1227
2,558	2	1	0.05	2.5977	0.0744
15,743	1	1	0.00	3.5977	0.0274

Table 12.4   Further calculations for Exercise 12.4.

Value(x)	r	s	$S_{KM}(x)$	$H_{NA}(x)$	$S_{NA}(x)$
115	18	1	0.9444	0.0556	0.9459
126	17	1	0.8889	0.1144	0.8919
155	16	1	0.8333	0.1769	0.8379
161	15	1	0.7778	0.2435	0.7839
243	14	1	0.7222	0.3150	0.7298
294	13	1	0.6667	0.3919	0.6758
340	12	1	0.6111	0.4752	0.6218
384	11	1	0.5556	0.5661	0.5677
457	10	1	0.5000	0.6661	0.5137
680	9	1	0.4444	0.7773	0.4596
855	8	1	0.3889	0.9023	0.4056
877	7	1	0.3333	1.0451	0.3517
974	6	1	0.2778	1.2118	0.2977

12.5 Suppose the lapse was at time 1. The estimate of $S(4)$ is $(3/4)(2/3)(1/2) = 0.25$. If it is at time 2, the estimate is $(4/5)(2/3)(1/2)=0.27$. If it is at time 3, the estimate is $(4/5)(3/4)(1/2) = 0.3$. If it is at time 4, the estimate is $(4/5)(3/4)(2/3) = 0.4$. If it is at time 5, the estimate is $(4/5)(3/4)(2/3)(1/2) = 0.20$. Therefore, the answer is time 5.

Table 12.5   Calculations for Exercise 12.7.

Age(t)	#ds	#xs	#us	r	$\hat{S}(t)$
0	300				
1		6		300	$\frac{294}{300} = 0.98$
2	20				
3		10		314	$0.98\frac{304}{314} = 0.94879$
4	30	10		304	$0.94879\frac{294}{304} = 0.91758$
5		a		324	$0.91758\frac{324-a}{324} = 0.892$
7			45		$\implies a = 9$
9		b		$279-a = 270$	$0.892\frac{270-b}{270}$
10			35		
12		6		$244-a-b = 235 - b$	$0.892\frac{270-b}{270}\frac{229-b}{235-b} = 0.856$
13			15		$\implies b = 4$

12.6 $\hat{H}(12) = \frac{2}{15} + \frac{1}{12} + \frac{1}{10} + \frac{2}{6} = 0.65$. The estimate of the survival function is $\hat{S}(12) = e^{-0.65} = 0.522$.

12.7 The information may be organized as in Table 12.5

12.8 $\hat{H}(t_{10}) - \hat{H}(t_9) = \frac{1}{n-9} = 0.077$, $n = 22$. $\hat{H}(t_3) = \frac{1}{22} + \frac{1}{21} + \frac{1}{20} = 0.14307$, $\hat{S}(t_3) = e^{-0.14307} = 0.8667$.

12.9 $0.60 = 0.72\frac{r_4-2}{r_4}$, $r_4 = 12$. $0.50 = 0.60\frac{r_5-1}{r_5}$, $r_5 = 6$. With two deaths at the fourth death time and the risk set decreasing by 6, there must have been four censored observations.

12.10 $0.575 = \hat{S}(10) = e^{-\hat{H}(10)}$. $\hat{H}(10) = -\ln(0.575) = 0.5534 = \frac{1}{50} + \frac{3}{49} + \frac{5}{k} + \frac{7}{12}$. The solution is $k = 36$.

12.11 With no censoring, the r-values are 12, 9, 8, 7, 6, 4, and 3, and the s values are 3, 1, 1, 1, 2, 1, and 1. Then

$$\hat{H}(7,000) = \frac{3}{12} + \frac{1}{9} + \frac{1}{8} + \frac{1}{7} + \frac{2}{6} + \frac{1}{4} + \frac{1}{3} = 1.5456.$$

With censoring, there are only five uncensored values with r values 9, 8, 7, 4, and 3, and all five s values are 1. Then

$$\hat{H}(7,000) = \frac{1}{9} + \frac{1}{8} + \frac{1}{7} + \frac{1}{4} + \frac{1}{3} = 0.9623.$$

12.12 $\frac{0.5}{0.65} = \frac{r_4-s_4}{r_4} = \frac{r_4-3}{r_4} \implies r_4 = 13$. The risk set at the fifth death time is the 13 from the previous death time less the 3 who died and less the 6 who were censored. That leaves $r_5 = 13 - 3 - 6 = 4$. Then, $\frac{0.25}{0.5} = \frac{r_5 - s_5}{r_5} = \frac{4 - s_5}{4} \implies s_5 = 2$.

12.2 SECTION 12.2

12.13 To proceed, we need the estimated survival function at whole number durations. From Exercise 11.1, we have $S_{30}(1) = 27/30$, $S_{30}(2) = 25/30$, $S_{30}(3) = 22/30$, $S_{30}(4) = 19/30$, and $S_{30}(5) = 14/30$. Then the mortality estimates are $\hat{q}_0 = 3/30$, $\hat{q}_1 = 2/27$, $\hat{q}_2 = 3/25$, $\hat{q}_3 = 3/22$, $\hat{q}_4 = 5/19$, $_5\hat{p}_0 = 14/30$. The six variances are

$$
\begin{aligned}
\mathrm{Var}(\hat{q}_0) &= 3(27)/30^3 = 0.003, \\
\mathrm{Var}(\hat{q}_1) &= 2(25)/27^3 = 0.002540, \\
\mathrm{Var}(\hat{q}_2) &= 3(22)/25^3 = 0.004224, \\
\mathrm{Var}(\hat{q}_3) &= 3(19)/22^3 = 0.005353, \\
\mathrm{Var}(\hat{q}_4) &= 5(14)/19^3 = 0.010206, \\
\mathrm{Var}(_5\hat{p}_0) &= 14(16)/30^3 = 0.008296.
\end{aligned}
$$

The first and last variances are unconditional.

12.14 From the data set, there were 1,915 out of 94,935 that had two or more accidents. The estimated probability is $1{,}915/94{,}935 = 0.02017$, and the estimated variance is

$$0.02017(0.97983)/94{,}935 = 2.08176 \times 10^{-7}.$$

12.15 From Exercise 12.13, $S_{30}(3) = 22/30$, and the direct estimate of its variance is $22(8)/30^3 = 0.0065185$. Using Greenwood's formula, the estimated variance is

$$
\left(\frac{22}{30}\right)^2 \left(\frac{1}{30(29)} + \frac{1}{29(28)} + \frac{1}{28(27)} + \frac{2}{27(25)}\right.
$$
$$
\left. + \frac{1}{25(24)} + \frac{1}{24(23)} + \frac{1}{23(22)}\right) = \frac{22(8)}{30^3}.
$$

For $_2\hat{q}_3$, the point estimate is $8/22$, and the direct estimate of the variance is $8(14)/22^3 = 0.010518$. Greenwood's estimate is

$$
\left(\frac{14}{22}\right)^2 \left(\frac{2}{22(20)} + \frac{1}{20(19)} + \frac{1}{19(18)} + \frac{2}{18(16)} + \frac{2}{16(14)}\right) = \frac{8(14)}{22^3}.
$$

12.16 From Exercise 12.2, $S_{40}(3) = 0.7530$, and Greenwood's formula provides a variance of

$$0.7530^2 \left(\frac{1}{30(29)} + \frac{1}{30(29)} + \frac{1}{30(29)} + \frac{2}{29(27)} \right.$$
$$\left. + \frac{1}{28(27)} + \frac{1}{28(27)} + \frac{1}{27(26)} \right) = 0.00571.$$

Also, $_2\hat{q}_3 = (0.7530 - 0.5497)/0.7530 = 0.26999$, and the variance is estimated as

$$0.73001^2 \left(\frac{2}{27(25)} + \frac{1}{26(25)} + \frac{1}{23(22)} + \frac{3}{21(18)} \right) = 0.00768.$$

12.17 Using the log-transformed method,

$$U = \exp \left(\frac{1.96\sqrt{0.00571}}{0.753 \ln 0.753} \right) = 0.49991.$$

The lower limit is $0.753^{1/0.49991} = 0.56695$, and the upper limit is $0.753^{0.49991} = 0.86778$.

12.18 From Exercise 12.3, $\hat{H}(3) = 0.2774$. The variance is estimated as

$$\widehat{\text{Var}}[\hat{H}(3)] = \frac{1}{30^2} + \frac{1}{30^2} + \frac{1}{30^2} + \frac{2}{29^2} + \frac{1}{28^2} + \frac{1}{28^2} + \frac{1}{27^2} = 0.0096342.$$

The linear confidence interval is

$$0.2774 \pm 1.96\sqrt{0.0096342} \text{ or } 0.0850 \text{ to } 0.4698.$$

The log-transformed interval requires

$$U = \exp \left[\pm \frac{1.96\sqrt{0.0096342}}{0.2774} \right] = 2.00074, \text{ or } 0.49981.$$

The lower limit is $0.2774(0.49981) = 0.13865$ and the upper limit is $0.2774(2.00074) = 0.55501$.

12.19 Without any distributional assumptions, the variance is estimated as $(1/5)(4/5)/5 = 0.032$. From the distributional assumption, the true value of $_3q_7$ is $[(8/15) - (5/15)]/(8/15) = 3/8$, and the variance is $(3/8)(5/8)/5 = 0.046875$. The difference is -0.014875.

12.20 First, obtain the estimated survival probability as

$$\hat{S}(4) = \frac{12}{15} \frac{56}{80} \frac{20}{25} \frac{54}{60} = 0.4032.$$

Greenwood's formula gives

$$(0.4032)^2 \left(\frac{3}{15(12)} + \frac{24}{80(56)} + \frac{5}{25(20)} + \frac{6}{60(54)} \right) = 0.00551.$$

12.21 The Nelson–Åalen estimates are the centers of the confidence intervals, which are 0.15 and 0.27121. Therefore, $s_{i+1}/r_{i+1} = 0.12121$. From the first confidence interval, the estimated variance is $(0.07875/1.96)^2 = 0.0016143$, while for the second interval it is $(0.11514/1.96)^2 = 0.0034510$ and, therefore, $s_{i+1}/r_{i+1}^2 = 0.0018367$. Dividing the first result by the second gives $r_{i+1} = 66$. The first equation then yields $s_{i+1} = 8$.

12.22 Greenwood's estimate is

$$V = S^2 \left(\frac{2}{50(48)} + \frac{4}{45(41)} + \frac{8}{(41-c)(33-c)} \right).$$

Then,

$$0.011467 = \frac{V}{S^2} = 0.003001 + \frac{8}{(41-c)(33-c)},$$

$$(41-c)(33-c) = \frac{8}{0.008466} = 945.$$

Solving the quadratic equation yields $c = 6$.

12.23 For the Nelson–Åalen estimate,

$$1.5641 = \hat{H}(35) = \frac{2}{15} + \frac{3}{13} + \frac{2}{10} + \frac{d}{8} + \frac{2}{8-d},$$

$$(1.5641 - 0.5641)8(8-d) = d(8-d) + 16,$$

$$0 = d^2 - 16d + 48,$$

$$d = 4.$$

The variance is

$$\frac{2}{15^2} + \frac{3}{13^2} + \frac{2}{10^2} + \frac{4}{8^2} + \frac{2}{4^2} = 0.23414.$$

12.24 The standard deviation is

$$\left(\frac{15}{100^2} + \frac{20}{65^2} + \frac{13}{40^2} \right)^{1/2} = 0.11983.$$

Table 12.6   Data for Exercise 12.28.

y_j	$p(y_j)$
0.1	0.0333
0.5	0.0323
0.8	0.0311
1.8	0.0623
2.1	0.0300
2.5	0.0290
2.8	0.0290
3.9	0.0557
4.0	0.0269
4.1	0.0291
4.8	0.0916

12.25 The uncensored observations are 4 and 8, the two r-values are 10 and 5, and the two s-values are 2 and 1. Then $\hat{S}(11) = \frac{8}{10}\frac{4}{5} = 0.64$. Greenwood's estimate is

$$(0.64)^2 \left[\frac{2}{10(8)} + \frac{1}{5(4)} \right] = 0.03072.$$

12.26 At day 8 (the first uncensored time), $r = 7$ $(8-1)$ and $s = 1$. At day 12, $r = 5$ and $s = 2$. Then $\hat{H}(12) = \frac{1}{7} + \frac{2}{5} = 0.5429$. Also, $\text{Vâr}[\hat{H}(12)] = \frac{1}{7^2} + \frac{2}{5^2} = 0.1004$. The interval is $0.5429 \pm 1.645\sqrt{0.1004}$, which is $(0.0217, 1.0641)$.

12.3   SECTION 12.3

12.27 In order for the mean to be equal to y, we must have $\theta/(\alpha - 1) = y$. Letting α be arbitrary (and greater than 1), use a Pareto distribution with $\theta = y(\alpha - 1)$. This makes the kernel function

$$k_y(x) = \frac{\alpha[(\alpha - 1)y]^\alpha}{[(\alpha - 1)y + x]^{\alpha+1}}.$$

12.28 The data points and probabilities can be taken from Exercise 12.2. They are given in Table 12.6

The probability at 5.0 is discrete and so should not be spread out by the kernel density estimator. Because of the value at 0.1, the largest available bandwidth is 0.1. Using this bandwidth and the triangular kernel produces the graph in Figure 12.1.

This graph is clearly not satisfactory. The gamma kernel is not available because there would be positive probability at values greater than 5. Your

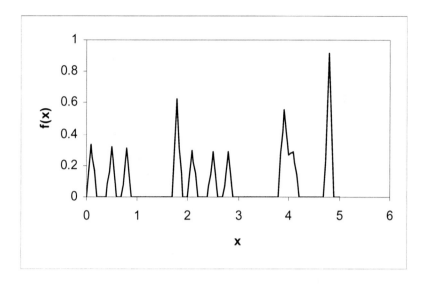

Figure 12.1   Triangular kernel for Exercise 12.28.

author tried to solve this by using the beta distribution. With θ known to be 5, the mean (to be set equal to y) is $5a/(a+b)$. To have some smoothing control and to determine parameter values, the sum $a+b$ was fixed. Using a value of 50 for the sum, the kernel is

$$k_y(x) = \frac{\Gamma(50)}{\Gamma(10y)\Gamma(50-10y)} \left(\frac{x}{5}\right)^{10y} \left(1-\frac{x}{5}\right)^{50-10y-1} \frac{1}{x}, \ 0 < x < 5$$

and the resulting smoothed estimate appears in Figure 12.2.

12.29 With a bandwidth of 60, the height of the kernel is $1/120$. At a value of 100, the following data points contribute probability $1/20$: 47, 75, and 156. Therefore, the height is $3(1/20)(1/120) = 1/800$.

12.30 The uniform kernel spreads the probability of 0.1 to 10 units on either side of an observation. The observation at 25 contributes a density of 0.005 from 15 to 35, thus contributing nothing to survival past age 40. The same applies to the point at 30. The points at 35 each contribute probability from 25 to 45 and 0.25 of that probability is above 40. Together they contribute $2(0.25)(0.1) = 0.05$. The point at 37 contributes $(7/20)(0.1) = 0.035$. The next four points contribute a total of $(9/20+15/20+17/20+19/20)(0.1) = 0.3$. The final point (at 55) contributes all its probability at points above 40 and so contributes 0.1 to the total, which is $0.05 + 0.035 + 0.3 + 0.1 = 0.485$.

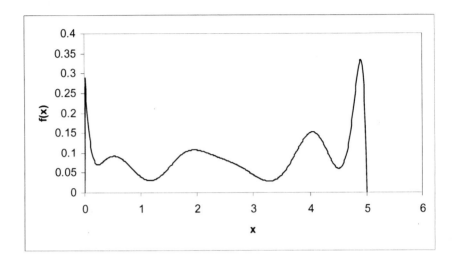

Figure 12.2   Beta kernel for Exercise 12.28.

12.31 (a) With two of the five points below 150, the empirical estimate is $2/5 = 0.4$.

(b) The point at 82 has probability 0.2 spread from 32 to 132; all is below 150, so the contribution is 0.2. The point at 126 has probability from 76 to 176; the contribution below 150 is $(74/100)(0.2) = 0.148$. The point at 161 contributes $(39/100)(0.2) = 0.078$. The last two points contribute nothing, so the estimate is $0.2 + 0.148 + 0.078 = 0.426$.

(c) As in part (b), the first point contributes 0.2 and the last two points contribute nothing. The triangle has base 100 and area 0.2, so the height must be 0.004. For the point at 126, the probability excluded is the triangle from 150 to 176, which has base 26 and height at 150 of $0.004(26/50) = 0.00208$. The area is $0.5(26)(0.00208) = 0.02704$ and the contribution is 0.17296. For the point at 161, the area included is the triangle from 111 to 150, which has base 39 and height at 150 of $0.004(39/50) = 0.00312$. The area is $0.5(39)(0.00312) = 0.06084$. The estimate is $0.2 + 0.17296 + 0.06084 = 0.4338$.

12.4   SECTION 12.4

12.32 The only change is the entries in the d_j and w_j^m columns are swapped. The exposures then change. For example, at $j = 2$, the exposure is $28 + 0 + 3(1/2) - 2(1/2) = 28.5$.

Table 12.7   Kaplan–Meier calculations for Exercise 12.33.

x	r	s	$\hat{S}(x)$
45.3	8	1	$7/8 = 0.875$
45.4	7	1	$0.875(6/7) = 0.750$
46.2	8	1	$0.750(7/8) = 0.656$
46.4	6	1	$0.656(5/6) = 0.549$
46.7	5	1	$0.549(4/5) = 0.438$

Table 12.8   Calculations for Exercise 12.34.

c_j	P_j	n_j^b	w_j^e	d_j	$q_j'^{(d)}$	$\hat{S}(c_j)$
250	0	7	0	1	1/7	1.000
500	6	8	0	2	2/14	$1.000(6/7) = 0.857$
1,000	12	7	1	4	4/19	$0.857(12/14) = 0.735$
2,750	14	0	1	1	1/14	$0.735(15/19) = 0.580$
3,000	12	0	0	0	0/12	$0.580(13/14) = 0.539$
3,500	12	0	1	6	6/12	$0.539(12/12) = 0.539$
5,250	5	0	1	0	0/5	$0.539(6/12) = 0.269$
5,500	4	0	1	1	1/4	$0.269(5/5) = 0.269$
6,000	2	0	0	1	1/2	$0.269(3/4) = 0.202$
10,250	1	0	1	0	0/1	$0.202(1/2) = 0.101$
10,500	0	0	0	0	–	$0.101(1/1) = 0.101$

12.33 The Kaplan–Meier calculations appear in Table 12.7. Then $\hat{q}_{45} = 1 - 0.750 = 0.250$ and $\hat{q}_{46} = 1 - 0.438/0.750 = 0.416$.

For exact exposure at age 45, the first eight individuals contribute $1 + 1 + 0.3 + 1 + 0.4 + 1 + 0.4 + 0.8 = 5.9$ of exposure for $\hat{q}_{45} = 1 - e^{-2/5.9} = 0.28751$. For age 46, eight individuals contribute for an exposure of $0.7 + 1 + 1 + 1 + 0.3 + 0.2 + 0.4 + 0.9 = 5.5$ for $\hat{q}_{46} = 1 - e^{-3/5.5} = 0.42042$.

For actuarial exposure at age 45 the two deaths add 1.3 to the exposure for $\hat{q}_{45} = 2/7.2 = 0.27778$. For age 46, the three deaths add 1.7 for $\hat{q}_{46} = 3/7.2 = 0.41667$.

12.34 The calculations are in Table 12.8. The intervals were selected so that all deductibles and limits are at the boundaries and so no assumption is needed about the intermediate values. This setup means that no assumptions need to be made about the timing of entrants and withdrawals. When working with the observations, the deductible must be added to the payment in order to produce the loss amount. The requested probability is $\hat{S}(5{,}500)/\hat{S}(500) = 0.269/0.857 = 0.314$.

12.35 For the intervals, the n-values are 6, 6, 7, 0, 0, 0, and 0, the w-values are 0, 1, 1, 1, 0, 0, and 0, and the d-values are 1, 2, 4, 7, 1, 1, and 0. the

P-values are then 6, $6-0-1+6=11$, $11-1-2+7=15$, $15-1-4+0=10$, $10-1-7+0=2$, $2-0-1+0=1$, and $1-0-1+0=0$. The estimates are $\hat{S}(500)=5/6$ and $\hat{S}(6{,}000)=(5/6)(9/11)(11/15)(3/10)(1/2)=3/40$, where both estimates are conditioned on survival to 250. The answer is the ratio $(3/40)/(5/6)=9/100=0.09$.

CHAPTER 13

CHAPTER 13 SOLUTIONS

13.1 SECTION 13.1

13.1 The mean of the data is $\hat{\mu}_1' = [27 + 82 + 115 + 126 + 155 + 161 + 243 + 13(250)]/20 = 207.95$. The expected value of a single observation censored at 250 is $E(X \wedge 250) = \theta(1 - e^{-250/\theta})$. Setting the two equal and solving produce $\hat{\theta} = 657.26$.

13.2 The equations to solve are

$$
\begin{aligned}
\exp(\mu + \sigma^2/2) &= 1{,}424.4, \\
\exp(2\mu + 2\sigma^2) &= 13{,}238{,}441.9.
\end{aligned}
$$

Taking logarithms yields

$$
\begin{aligned}
\mu + \sigma^2/2 &= 7.261506, \\
2\mu + 2\sigma^2 &= 16.398635.
\end{aligned}
$$

The solution of these two equations is $\hat{\mu} = 6.323695$ and $\hat{\sigma}^2 = 1.875623$, and then $\hat{\sigma} = 1.369534$.

Student Solutions Manual to Accompany Loss Models: From Data to Decisions, Fourth Edition. By Stuart A. Klugman, Harry H. Panjer, Gordon E. Willmot
Copyright © 2012 John Wiley & Sons, Inc.

13.3 The two equations to solve are

$$0.2 = 1 - e^{-(5/\theta)^\tau},$$
$$0.8 = 1 - e^{-(12/\theta)^\tau}.$$

Moving the 1 to the left-hand side and taking logarithms produces

$$0.22314 = (5/\theta)^\tau,$$
$$1.60944 = (12/\theta)^\tau.$$

Dividing the second equation by the first equation produces

$$7.21269 = 2.4^\tau.$$

Taking logarithms again produces

$$1.97584 = 0.87547\tau,$$

and so $\hat{\tau} = 2.25689$. Using the first equation,

$$\hat{\theta} = 5/(0.22314^{1/2.25689}) = 9.71868.$$

Then $\hat{S}(8) = e^{-(8/9.71868)^{2.25689}} = 0.52490.$

13.4 The equations to solve are

$$0.5 = 1 - \exp[-(10{,}000/\theta)^\tau],$$
$$0.9 = 1 - \exp[-(100{,}000/\theta)^\tau].$$

Then

$$\ln 0.5 = -0.69315 = -(10{,}000/\theta)^\tau,$$
$$\ln 0.1 = -2.30259 = -(100{,}000/\theta)^\tau.$$

Dividing the second equation by the first gives

$$3.32192 = 10^\tau,$$
$$\ln 3.32192 = 1.20054 = \tau \ln 10 = 2.30259\tau,$$
$$\hat{\tau} = 1.20054/2.30259 = 0.52139.$$

Then

$$0.69315 = (10{,}000/\theta)^{0.52139},$$
$$0.69315^{1/0.52139} = 0.49512 = 10{,}000/\theta,$$
$$\hat{\theta} = 20{,}197.$$

13.5 The two moment equations are

$$\frac{4 + 5 + 21 + 99 + 421}{5} = 110 = \frac{\theta}{\alpha - 1},$$

$$\frac{4^2 + 5^2 + 21^2 + 99^2 + 421^2}{5} = 37,504.8 = \frac{2\theta^2}{(\alpha - 1)(\alpha - 2)}.$$

Dividing the second equation by the square of the first equation gives

$$\frac{37,504.8}{110^2} = 3.0996 = \frac{2(\alpha - 1)}{\alpha - 2}.$$

The solution is $\hat{\alpha} = 3.8188$. From the first equation, $\hat{\theta} = 110(2.8188) = 310.068$. For the 95th percentile,

$$0.95 = 1 - \left(\frac{310.068}{310.068 + \pi_{0.95}}\right)^{3.8188}$$

for $\hat{\pi}_{0.95} = 369.37$.

13.6 After inflation, the 100 claims from year 1 total $100(10,000)(1.1)^2 = 1,210,000$, and the 200 claims from year 2 total $200(12,500)(1.1) = 2,750,000$. The average of the 300 inflated claims is $3,960,000/300 = 13,200$. The moment equation is $13,200 = \theta/(3 - 1)$, which yields $\hat{\theta} = 26,400$.

13.7 The equations to solve are

$$0.2 = F(18.25) = \Phi\left(\frac{\ln 18.25 - \mu}{\sigma}\right),$$

$$0.8 = F(35.8) = \Phi\left(\frac{\ln 35.8 - \mu}{\sigma}\right).$$

The 20th and 80th percentiles of the normal distribution are -0.842 and 0.842, respectively. The equations become

$$-0.842 = \frac{2.904 - \mu}{\sigma},$$

$$0.842 = \frac{3.578 - \mu}{\sigma}.$$

Dividing the first equation by the second yields

$$-1 = \frac{2.904 - \mu}{3.578 - \mu}.$$

The solution is $\hat{\mu} = 3.241$ and substituting in either equation yields $\hat{\sigma} = 0.4$. The probability of exceeding 30 is

$$\Pr(X > 30) = 1 - F(30) = 1 - \Phi\left(\frac{\ln 30 - 3.241}{0.4}\right) = 1 - \Phi(0.4)$$

$$= 1 - \Phi(0.4) = 1 - 0.6554 = 0.3446.$$

13.8 For a mixture, the mean and second moment are a combination of the individual moments. The first two moments are

$$
\begin{aligned}
\mathrm{E}(X) &= p(1) + (1-p)(10) = 10 - 9p, \\
\mathrm{E}(X^2) &= p(2) + (1-p)(200) = 200 - 198p, \\
\mathrm{Var}(X) &= 200 - 198p - (10 - 9p)^2 = 100 - 18p - 81p^2 = 4.
\end{aligned}
$$

The only positive root of the quadratic equation is $\hat{p} = 0.983$.

13.9 We need the $0.6(21) = 12.6$th smallest observation. It is $0.4(38) + 0.6(39) = 38.6$.

13.10 We need the $0.75(21) = 15.75$th smallest observation. It is $0.25(13) + 0.75(14) = 13.75$.

13.11 $\hat{\mu} = 975$, $\hat{\mu}'_2 = 977{,}916\frac{2}{3}$, $\hat{\sigma}^2 = 977{,}916\frac{2}{3} - 975^2 = 27{,}291\frac{2}{3}$. The moment equations are $975 = \alpha\theta$ and $27{,}291\frac{2}{3} = \alpha\theta^2$. The solutions are $\hat{\alpha} = 34.8321$ and $\hat{\theta} = 27.9915$.

13.12 $F(x) = (x/\theta)^{\gamma}/[1 + (x/\theta)^{\gamma}]$. The equations are $0.2 = (100/\theta)^{\gamma}/[1 + (100/\theta)^{\gamma}]$ and $0.8 = (400/\theta)^{\gamma}/[1 + (400/\theta)^{\gamma}]$. From the first equation $0.2 = 0.8(100/\theta)^{\gamma}$ or $\theta^{\gamma} = 4(100)^{\gamma}$. Insert this result in the second equation to get $0.8 = 4^{\gamma-1}/(1 + 4^{\gamma-1})$, and so $\hat{\gamma} = 2$ and then $\hat{\theta} = 200$.

13.13 $\mathrm{E}(X) = \int_0^1 p x^p dx = p/(1+p) = \bar{x}$. $\hat{p} = \bar{x}/(1 - \bar{x})$.

13.14 $\hat{\mu} = 3{,}800 = \alpha\theta$. $\mu'_2 = 16{,}332{,}000$, $\hat{\sigma}^2 = 1{,}892{,}000 = \alpha\theta^2$. $\hat{\alpha} = 7.6321$, $\hat{\theta} = 497.89$.

13.15 $\hat{\mu} = 2{,}000 = \exp(\mu + \sigma^2/2)$, $\hat{\mu}'_2 = 6{,}000{,}000 = \exp(2\mu + 2\sigma^2)$. $7.690090 = \mu + \sigma^2/2$ and $15.60727 = 2\mu + 2\sigma^2$. The solutions are $\hat{\mu} = 7.39817$ and $\hat{\sigma} = 0.636761$.

$$
\begin{aligned}
\Pr(X > 4{,}500) &= 1 - \Phi[(\ln 4{,}500 - 7.39817)/0.636761] \\
&= 1 - \Phi(1.5919) = 0.056.
\end{aligned}
$$

13.16 $\hat{\mu} = 4.2 = (\beta/2)\sqrt{2\pi}$. $\hat{\beta} = 3.35112$.

13.17 X is Pareto, and so $\mathrm{E}(X) = 1{,}000/(\alpha - 1) = \bar{x} = 318.4$. $\hat{\alpha} = 4.141$.

13.18 $r\beta = 0.1001$, $r\beta(1 + \beta) = 0.1103 - 0.1001^2 = 0.10027999$. $1 + \beta = 1.0017981$, $\hat{\beta} = 0.0017981$, $\hat{r} = 55.670$.

13.19 $r\beta = 0.166$, $r\beta(1 + \beta) = 0.252 - 0.166^2 = 0.224444$. $1 + \beta = 1.352072$, $\hat{\beta} = 0.352072$, $\hat{r} = 0.47149$.

13.20 With $n+1 = 16$, we need the $0.3(16) = 4.8$ and $0.65(16) = 10.4$ smallest observations. They are $0.2(280) + 0.8(350) = 336$ and $0.6(450) + 0.4(490) = 466$. The equations are

$$0.3 = 1 - \left(\frac{\theta^\gamma}{\theta^\gamma + 336^\gamma}\right)^2 \text{ and } 0.65 = 1 - \left(\frac{\theta^\gamma}{\theta^\gamma + 466^\gamma}\right)^2,$$

$$(0.7)^{-1/2} = 1 + (336/\theta)^\gamma \text{ and } (0.35)^{-1/2} = 1 + (466/\theta)^\gamma,$$

$$\frac{(0.7)^{-1/2} - 1}{(0.35)^{-1/2} - 1} = 0.282814 = \left(\frac{336}{466}\right)^\gamma,$$

$$\ln(0.282814) = \ln(336/466), \gamma = 3.8614,$$

$$(0.7)^{-1/2} - 1 = (336/\theta)^{3.8614},$$

$$(0.19523)^{1/3.8614} = 336/\theta, \theta = 558.74.$$

13.21 With $n+1 = 17$, we need the $0.2(17) = 3.4$ and $0.7(17) = 11.9$ smallest observations. They are $0.6(75) + 0.4(81) = 77.4$ and $0.1(122) + 0.9(125) = 124.7$. The equations are

$$0.2 = 1 - e^{-(77.4/\theta)^\tau} \text{ and } 0.7 = 1 - e^{-(124/7/\theta)^\tau},$$

$$-\ln 0.8 = 0.22314 = (77.4/\theta)^\tau \text{ and } -\ln 0.3 = 1.20397 = (124.7/\theta)^\tau,$$

$$1.20397/0.22314 = 5.39558 = (124.7/77.4)^\tau,$$

$$\tau = \ln(5.39558)/\ln(124.7/77.4) = 3.53427,$$

$$\theta = 77.4/0.22314^{1/3.53427} = 118.32.$$

13.22 Shifting adds δ to the mean and median. The median of the unshifted distribution is the solution to $0.5 = S(m) = e^{-m/\theta}$ for $m = \theta \ln(2)$. The equations to solve are

$$300 = \theta + \delta \text{ and } 240 = \theta \ln(2) + \delta.$$

Subtracting the second equation from the first gives $60 = \theta[1 - \ln(2)]$ for $\theta = 195.53$. From the first equation, $\delta = 104.47$.

13.2 SECTION 13.2

13.23 For the inverse exponential distribution,

$$l(\theta) = \sum_{j=1}^{n}(\ln\theta - \theta x_j^{-1} - 2\ln x_j) = n\ln\theta - ny\theta - 2\sum_{j=1}^{n}\ln x_j,$$

$$l'(\theta) = n\theta^{-1} - ny, \ \hat{\theta} = y^{-1}, \text{ where } y = \frac{1}{n}\sum_{j=1}^{n}\frac{1}{x_j}.$$

For Data Set B, we have $\hat{\theta} = 197.72$ and the loglikelihood value is -159.78. Because the mean does not exist for the inverse exponential distribution, there is no traditional method-of-moments estimate available. However, it is possible to obtain a method-of-moments estimate using the negative first moment rather than the positive first moment. That is, equate the average reciprocal to the expected reciprocal:

$$\frac{1}{n}\sum_{j=1}^{n}\frac{1}{x_j} = \mathrm{E}(X^{-1}) = \theta^{-1}.$$

This special method-of-moments estimate is identical to the maximum likelihood estimate.

For the inverse gamma distribution with $\alpha = 2$,

$$f(x|\theta) = \frac{\theta^2 e^{-\theta/x}}{x^3\Gamma(2)}, \ \ln f(x|\theta) = 2\ln\theta - \theta x^{-1} - 3\ln x,$$

$$l(\theta) = \sum_{j=1}^{n}(2\ln\theta - \theta x_j^{-1} - 3\ln x_j) = 2n\ln\theta - ny\theta - 3\sum_{j=1}^{n}\ln x_j,$$

$$l'(\theta) = 2n\theta^{-1} - ny, \ \hat{\theta} = 2/y.$$

For Data Set B, $\hat{\theta} = 395.44$ and the value of the loglikelihood function is -169.07. The method-of-moments estimate solves the equation

$$1,424.4 = \frac{\theta}{\alpha - 1} = \frac{\theta}{2 - 1}, \ \hat{\theta} = 1,424.4,$$

which differs from the maximum likelihood estimate.

For the inverse gamma distribution with both parameters unknown,

$$f(x|\theta) = \frac{\theta^\alpha e^{-\theta/x}}{x^{\alpha+1}\Gamma(\alpha)}, \ \ln f(x|\theta) = \alpha\ln\theta - \theta x^{-1} - (\alpha + 1)\ln x - \ln\Gamma(\alpha).$$

The likelihood function must be maximized numerically. The answer is $\hat{\alpha} = 0.70888$ and $\hat{\theta} = 140.16$ and the loglikelihood value is -158.88. The method-

Table 13.1   Estimates for Exercise 13.25.

Model	Original	Censored
Exponential	$\hat{\theta} = 1,424.4$	$\hat{\theta} = 594.14$
Gamma	$\hat{\alpha} = 0.55616, \hat{\theta} = 2,561.1$	$\hat{\alpha} = 1.5183, \hat{\theta} = 295.69$
Inv. exponential	$\hat{\theta} = 197.72$	$\hat{\theta} = 189.78$
Inv. gamma	$\hat{\alpha} = 0.70888, \hat{\theta} = 140.16$	$\hat{\alpha} = 0.41612, \hat{\theta} = 86.290$

of-moments estimate is the solution to the two equations

$$1,424.4 = \frac{\theta}{\alpha - 1},$$

$$13,238,441.9 = \frac{\theta^2}{(\alpha - 1)(\alpha - 2)}.$$

Squaring the first equation and dividing it into the second equation give

$$6.52489 = \frac{\alpha - 1}{\alpha - 2},$$

which leads to $\hat{\alpha} = 2.181$ and then $\hat{\theta} = 1,682.2$. This result does not match the maximum likelihood estimate (which had to be the case because the mle produces a model that does not have a mean).

13.24 For the inverse exponential distribution, the cdf is $F(x) = e^{-\theta/x}$. Numerical maximization yields $\hat{\theta} = 6,662.39$ and the value of the loglikelihood function is -365.40. For the gamma distribution, the cdf requires numerical evaluation. In Excel® the function GAMMADIST(x, α, θ,true) can be used. The estimates are $\hat{\alpha} = 0.37139$ and $\hat{\theta} = 83,020$. The value of the loglikelihood function is -360.50. For the inverse gamma distribution, the cdf is available in Excel® as $1-$ GAMMADIST($1/x, \alpha, 1/\theta$,true). The estimates are $\hat{\alpha} = 0.83556$ and $\hat{\theta} = 5,113$. The value of the loglikelihood function is -363.92.

13.25 In each case the likelihood function is $f(27)f(82) \cdots f(243)[1-F(250)]^{13}$. Table 13.1 provides the estimates for both the original and censored data sets. The censoring tended to disguise the true nature of these numbers and, in general, had a large impact on the estimates.

13.26 The calculations are done as in Example 13.6, but with θ unknown. The likelihood must be numerically maximized. For the shifted data, the estimates are $\hat{\alpha} = 1.4521$ and $\hat{\theta} = 907.98$. The two expected costs are $907.98/0.4521 = 2,008$ and $1,107.98/0.4521 = 2,451$ for the 200 and 400 deductibles, respectively. For the unshifted data, the estimates are $\hat{\alpha} = 1.4521$

Table 13.2   Probabilities for Exercise 13.29

Event	Probability
Observed at age 35.4 and died	$\frac{F(1)-F(0.4)}{1-F(0.4)} = \frac{w-0.4w}{1-0.4w} = \frac{0.6w}{1-0.4w}$
Observed at age 35.4 and survived	$1 - \frac{0.6w}{1-0.4w} = \frac{1-w}{1-0.4w}$
Observed at age 35 and died	$F(1) = w$
Observed at age 35 and survived	$1 - w$

and $\hat{\theta} = 707.98$. The three expected costs are $707.98/0.4521 = 1{,}566$, $2{,}008$, and $2{,}451$ for the 0, 200, and 400 deductibles, respectively. While it is always the case that for the Pareto distribution the two approaches produce identical answers, that will not be true in general.

13.27 Table 13.1 can be used. The only difference is that observations that were surrenders are now treated as x-values and deaths are treated as y-values. Observations that ended at 5.0 continue to be treated as y-values. Once again there is no estimate for a Pareto model. The gamma parameter estimates are $\hat{\alpha} = 1.229$ and $\hat{\theta} = 6.452$.

13.28 The contribution to the likelihood for the first five values (number of drivers having zero through four accidents) is unchanged. However, for the last seven drivers, the contribution is

$$[\Pr(X \geq 5)]^7 = [1 - p(0) - p(1) - p(2) - p(3) - p(4)]^7,$$

and the maximum must be obtained numerically. The estimated values are $\hat{\lambda} = 0.16313$ and $\hat{q} = 0.02039$. These answers are similar to those for Example 13.8 because the probability of six or more accidents is so small.

13.29 There are four cases, with the likelihood function being the product of the probabilities for those cases raised to a power equal to the number of times each occurred. Table 13.2 provides the probabilities.

The likelihood function is

$$L = \left(\frac{0.6w}{1-0.4w}\right)^6 \left(\frac{1-w}{1-0.4w}\right)^4 w^8(1-w)^{12} \propto \frac{w^{14}(1-w)^{16}}{(1-0.4w)^{10}},$$

and its logarithm is

$$l = 14\ln w + 16\ln(1-w) - 10\ln(1-0.4w).$$

The derivative is

$$l' = \frac{14}{w} - \frac{16}{1-w} + \frac{4}{1-0.4w}.$$

Set the derivative equal to zero and clear the denominators to produce the equation

$$
\begin{aligned}
0 &= 14(1-w)(1-0.4w) - 16w(1-0.4w) + 4w(1-w) \\
&= 14 - 31.6w + 8w^2,
\end{aligned}
$$

and the solution is $w = q_{35} = 0.508$ (the other root is greater than one and so cannot be the solution).

13.30 The survival function is

$$
S(t) = \begin{cases} e^{-\lambda_1 t}, & 0 \le t < 2, \\ e^{-2\lambda_1 - (t-2)\lambda_2}, & t \ge 2 \end{cases}
$$

and the density function is

$$
f(t) = -S'(t) = \begin{cases} \lambda_1 e^{-\lambda_1 t}, & 0 \le t < 2 \\ \lambda_2 e^{-2\lambda_1 - (t-2)\lambda_2}, & t \ge 2. \end{cases}
$$

The likelihood function is

$$
\begin{aligned}
L &= f(1.7)S(1.5)S(2.6)f(3.3)S(3.5) \\
&= \lambda_1 e^{-1.7\lambda_1} e^{-1.5\lambda_1} e^{-2\lambda_1 - 0.6\lambda_2} \lambda_2 e^{-2\lambda_1 - 1.3\lambda_2} e^{-2\lambda_1 - 1.5\lambda_2} \\
&= \lambda_1 \lambda_2 e^{-9.2\lambda_1 - 3.4\lambda_2}.
\end{aligned}
$$

The logarithm and partial derivatives are

$$
\begin{aligned}
l &= \ln \lambda_1 + \ln \lambda_2 - 9.2\lambda_1 - 3.4\lambda_2, \\
\frac{\partial l}{\partial \lambda_1} &= \frac{1}{\lambda_1} - 9.2 = 0, \\
\frac{\partial l}{\partial \lambda_2} &= \frac{1}{\lambda_2} - 3.4 = 0,
\end{aligned}
$$

and the solutions are $\hat{\lambda}_1 = 0.10870$ and $\hat{\lambda}_2 = 0.29412$.

13.31 Let $f(t) = w$ be the density function. For the eight lives that lived the full year, the contribution to the likelihood is $\Pr(T > 1) = 1 - w$. For the one censored life, the contribution is $\Pr(T > 0.5) = 1 - 0.5w$. For the one death, the contribution is $\Pr(T \le 1) = w$. Then

$$
\begin{aligned}
L &= (1-w)^8 (1-0.5w)w, \\
\ln L &= 8\ln(1-w) + \ln(1-0.5w) + \ln w, \\
\frac{d\ln L}{dw} &= -\frac{8}{1-w} - \frac{0.5}{1-0.5w} + \frac{1}{w}.
\end{aligned}
$$

Setting the derivative equal to zero and clearing the denominators give

$$0 = -8w(1 - 0.5w) - 0.5w(1 - w) + (1 - w)(1 - 0.5w).$$

The only root of this quadratic that is less than one is $w = 0.10557 = \hat{q}_x$.

13.32 For the two lives that died, the contribution to the likelihood function is $f(10)$, while for the eight lives that were censored, the contribution is $S(10)$. We have

$$f(t) = -S'(t) = \frac{0.5}{k}\left(1 - \frac{t}{k}\right)^{-0.5},$$

$$L = f(10)^2 S(10)^8 = \left(\frac{0.5}{k}\right)^2 \left(1 - \frac{10}{k}\right)^{-1} \left(1 - \frac{10}{k}\right)^4 \propto \frac{(k-10)^3}{k^5},$$

$$\ln L = 3\ln(k - 10) - 5\ln k,$$

$$\frac{d\ln L}{dk} = \frac{3}{k - 10} - \frac{5}{k} = 0,$$

$$0 = 3k - 5(k - 10) = 50 - 2k.$$

Therefore, $\hat{k} = 25$.

13.33 We have

$$\begin{aligned}
L &= f(1{,}100)f(3{,}200)f(3{,}300)f(3{,}500)f(3{,}900)[S(4{,}000)]^{495} \\
&= \theta^{-1}e^{-1{,}100/\theta}\theta^{-1}e^{-3{,}200/\theta}\theta^{-1}e^{-3{,}300/\theta}\theta^{-1}e^{-3{,}500/\theta} \\
&\quad \times \theta^{-1}e^{-3{,}900/\theta}[e^{-4{,}000/\theta}]^{495} \\
&= \theta^{-5}e^{-1{,}995{,}000/\theta}, \\
\ln L &= -5\ln\theta - \frac{1{,}995{,}000}{\theta}, \\
\frac{d\ln L}{d\theta} &= -\frac{5}{\theta} + \frac{1{,}995{,}000}{\theta^2} = 0,
\end{aligned}$$

and the solution is $\hat{\theta} = 1{,}995{,}000/5 = 399{,}000$.

13.34 For maximum likelihood, the contributions to the likelihood function are (where q denotes the constant value of the time-to-death density function)

Event	Contribution
Survive to 36	$\Pr(T > 1) = 1 - q$
Censored at 35.6	$\Pr(T > 0.6) = 1 - 0.6q$
Die prior to 35.6	$\Pr(T \leq 0.6) = 0.6q$
Die after 35.6	$\Pr(0.6 < T \leq 1) = 0.4q$

Then,

$$L = (1-q)^{72}(1-0.6q)^{15}(0.6q)^{10}(0.4q)^3 \propto (1-q)^{72}(1-0.6q)^{15}q^{13},$$
$$\ln L = 72\ln(1-q) + 15\ln(1-0.6q) + 13\ln q,$$
$$\frac{d\ln L}{dq} = -\frac{72}{1-q} - \frac{9}{1-0.6q} + \frac{13}{q} = 0.$$

The solution to the quadratic equation is $\hat{q} = 0.13911 = \hat{q}_{35}$.

For the product-limit estimate, the risk set at time zero has 100 members. The first 10 observations are all deaths, and so the successive factors are $(99/100)$, $(98/99)$, ..., $(90/91)$ and, therefore, $\hat{S}(0.6) = 90/100 = 0.9$. The 15 censored observations reduce the risk set to 75. The next three deaths each reduce the risk set by one, and so $\hat{S}(1) = 0.9(74/75)(73/74)(72/73) = 0.864$. Then $\hat{q}_{35} = 1 - 0.864 = 0.136$.

13.35 The density function is $f(t) = -S'(t) = 1/w$. For actuary X, the likelihood function is

$$f(1)f(3)f(4)f(4)S(5) = \left(\frac{1}{w}\right)^4\left(1-\frac{5}{w}\right) = \frac{1}{w^4} - \frac{5}{w^5}.$$

Setting the derivative equal to zero gives

$$0 = -\frac{4}{w^5} + \frac{25}{w^6}, \quad 4w = 25, \quad \hat{w} = 6.25.$$

For actuary Y the likelihood function is

$$f(1)f(3)f(4)f(4)f(6) = w^{-5}.$$

This function appears to be strictly decreasing and, therefore, is maximized at $w = 0$, an unsatisfactory answer. Most of the time the support of the random variable can be ignored, but not this time. In this case, $f(t) = 1/w$ only for $0 \le t \le w$ and is zero otherwise. Therefore, the likelihood function is only w^{-5} when all the observed values are less than or equal to w, otherwise the function is zero. In other words,

$$L(w) = \begin{cases} 0, & w < 6, \\ w^{-5}, & w \ge 6. \end{cases}$$

This result makes sense because the likelihood that w is less than 6 should be zero. After all, such values of w are not possible, given the sampled values. This likelihood function is not continuous and, therefore, derivatives cannot be used to locate the maximum. Inspection quickly shows that the maximum occurs at $\hat{w} = 6$.

13.36 The likelihood function is

$$L(w) = \frac{f(4)f(5)f(7)S(3+r)}{S(3)^4} = \frac{w^{-1}w^{-1}w^{-1}(w-3-r)w^{-1}}{(w-3)^4w^{-4}} = \frac{w-3-r}{(w-3)^4},$$

$$l(w) = \ln(w-3-r) - 4\ln(w-3).$$

The derivative of the logarithm is

$$l'(w) = \frac{1}{w-3-r} - \frac{4}{w-3}.$$

Inserting the estimate of w and setting the derivative equal to zero yield

$$
\begin{aligned}
0 &= \frac{1}{10.67 - r} - \frac{4}{10.67} \\
&= 10.67 - 4(10.67 - r) = -32.01 + 4r, \\
r &= 8.
\end{aligned}
$$

13.37 The survival function is

$$
S(t) = \begin{cases}
e^{-t\lambda_1}, & 0 < t < 5, \\
e^{-5\lambda_1 - (t-5)\lambda_2}, & 5 \le t < 10, \\
e^{-5\lambda_1 - 5\lambda_2 - (t-10)\lambda_3}, & t \ge 10,
\end{cases}
$$

and the density function is

$$
f(t) = -S'(t) = \begin{cases}
\lambda_1 e^{-t\lambda_1}, & 0 < t < 5, \\
\lambda_2 e^{-5\lambda_1 - (t-5)\lambda_2}, & 5 \le t < 10, \\
\lambda_3 e^{-5\lambda_1 - 5\lambda_2 - (t-10)\lambda_3}, & t \ge 10.
\end{cases}
$$

The likelihood function and its logarithm are

$$
\begin{aligned}
L(\lambda_1, \lambda_2, \lambda_3) &= \lambda_1 e^{-3\lambda_1} \lambda_2^2 e^{-10\lambda_1 - 5\lambda_2} \lambda_3^4 e^{-20\lambda_1 - 20\lambda_2 - 11\lambda_3} \\
&\quad \times (e^{-5\lambda_1 - 5\lambda_2 - 5\lambda_3})^3 \\
&= \lambda_1 e^{-48\lambda_1} \lambda_2^2 e^{-40\lambda_2} \lambda_3^4 e^{-26\lambda_3}, \\
\ln L(\lambda_1, \lambda_2, \lambda_3) &= \ln \lambda_1 - 48\lambda_1 + 2\ln\lambda_2 - 40\lambda_2 + 4\ln\lambda_3 - 26\lambda_3.
\end{aligned}
$$

The partial derivative with respect to λ_1 is $\lambda_1^{-1} - 48 = 0$ for $\hat{\lambda}_1 = 1/48$. Similarly, $\hat{\lambda}_2 = 2/40$ and $\hat{\lambda}_3 = 4/26$.

13.38 The density function is the derivative $f(x) = \alpha 500^\alpha x^{-\alpha-1}$. The likelihood function is

$$L(\alpha) = \alpha^5 500^{5\alpha} (\Pi x_j)^{-\alpha-1},$$

and its logarithm is

$$
\begin{aligned}
l(\alpha) &= 5\ln\alpha + (5\alpha)\ln 500 - (\alpha+1)\Sigma \ln x_j \\
&= 5\ln\alpha + 31.073\alpha - 33.111(\alpha+1).
\end{aligned}
$$

Setting the derivative equal to zero gives

$$0 = 5\alpha^{-1} - 2.038.$$

The estimate is $\hat{\alpha} = 5/2.038 = 2.45$.

13.39 The coefficient $(2\pi x)^{-1/2}$ is not relevant because it does not involve μ. The logarithm of the likelihood function is

$$l(\mu) = -\frac{1}{22}(11-\mu)^2 - \frac{1}{30.4}(15.2-\mu)^2 - \frac{1}{36}(18-\mu)^2 - \frac{1}{42}(21-\mu)^2 - \frac{1}{51.6}(25.8-\mu)^2.$$

The derivative is

$$l'(\mu) = \frac{11-\mu}{11} + \frac{15.2-\mu}{15.2} + \frac{18-\mu}{18} + \frac{21-\mu}{21} + \frac{25.8-\mu}{25.8} = 5 - 0.29863\mu.$$

Setting the derivative equal to zero yields $\hat{\mu} = 16.74$.

13.40 The distribution and density function are

$$F(x) = 1 - e^{-(x/\theta)^2}, \quad f(x) = \frac{2x}{\theta^2}e^{-(x/\theta)^2}.$$

The likelihood function is

$$
\begin{aligned}
L(\theta) &= f(20)f(30)f(45)[1 - F(50)]^2 \\
&\propto \theta^{-2}e^{-(20/\theta)^2}\theta^{-2}e^{-(30/\theta)^2}\theta^{-2}e^{-(45/\theta)^2}\left[e^{-(50/\theta)^2}\right]^2 \\
&= \theta^{-6}e^{-8,325/\theta^2}.
\end{aligned}
$$

The logarithm and derivative are

$$
\begin{aligned}
l(\theta) &= -6\ln\theta - 8{,}325\theta^{-2}, \\
l'(\theta) &= -6\theta^{-1} + 16{,}650\theta^{-3}.
\end{aligned}
$$

Setting the derivative equal to zero yields $\hat{\theta} = (16{,}650/6)^{1/2} = 52.68$.

13.41 For the exponential distribution, the maximum likelihood estimate is the sample mean, and so $\bar{x}_P = 1000$ and $\bar{x}_S = 1500$. The likelihood with the restriction is (using i to index observations from Phil's bulbs and j to index observations from Sylvia's bulbs)

$$L(\theta^*) = \prod_{i=1}^{20}(\theta^*)^{-1}\exp(-x_i/\theta^*)\prod_{j=1}^{10}(2\theta^*)^{-1}\exp(-x_j/2\theta^*)$$

$$\propto (\theta^*)^{-30}\exp\left(-\sum_{i=1}^{20}\frac{x_i}{\theta^*} - \sum_{j=1}^{10}\frac{x_j}{2\theta^*}\right)$$

$$= (\theta^*)^{-30}\exp(-20\bar{x}_P/\theta^* - 10\bar{x}_S/2\theta^*)$$

$$= (\theta^*)^{-30}\exp(-20{,}000/\theta^* - 7{,}500/\theta^*).$$

Taking logarithms and differentiating yields

$$l(\theta^*) = -30\ln\theta^* - 27{,}500/\theta^*,$$

$$l'(\theta^*) = -30(\theta^*)^{-1} + 27{,}500(\theta^*)^{-2}.$$

Setting the derivative equal to zero gives $\hat{\theta}^* = 27{,}500/30 = 916.67$.

13.42 For the first part,

$$L(\theta) = F(1{,}000)^{62}[1 - F(1{,}000)]^{38}$$

$$= (1 - e^{-1{,}000/\theta})^{62}(e^{-1{,}000/\theta})^{38}.$$

Let $x = e^{-1{,}000/\theta}$. Then

$$L(x) = (1 - x)^{62}x^{38},$$

$$l(x) = 62\ln(1 - x) + 38\ln x,$$

$$l'(x) = -\frac{62}{1 - x} + \frac{38}{x}.$$

Setting the derivative equal to zero yields

$$0 = -62x + 38(1 - x)$$

$$= 38 - 100x,$$

$$x = 0.38,$$

and then $\hat{\theta} = -1{,}000/\ln 0.38 = 1{,}033.50$.

With additional information,

$$L(\theta) = \left[\prod_{j=1}^{62} f(x_j)\right][1 - F(1{,}000)]^{38} = \left(\prod_{j=1}^{62}\theta^{-1}e^{-x_j/\theta}\right)e^{-38{,}000/\theta}$$

$$= \theta^{-62}e^{-28{,}140/\theta}e^{-38{,}000/\theta} = \theta^{-62}e^{-66{,}140/\theta},$$

$$l(\theta) = -62\ln\theta - 66{,}140/\theta,$$

$$l'(\theta) = -62/\theta + 66{,}140/\theta^2 = 0,$$

$$0 = -62\theta + 66{,}140,$$

$$\hat{\theta} = 66{,}140/62 = 1{,}066.77.$$

Table 13.3   Likelihood contributions for Exercise 13.44.

Observation	Probability			Loglikelihood
1997-1	$\frac{\Pr(N=1)}{\Pr(N=1)+\Pr(N=2)}$	$= \frac{(1-p)p}{(1-p)p+(1-p)p^2}$	$= \frac{1}{1+p}$	$-3\ln(1+p)$
1997-2	$\frac{\Pr(N=2)}{\Pr(N=1)+\Pr(N=2)}$	$= \frac{(1-p)p^2}{(1-p)p+(1-p)p^2}$	$= \frac{p}{1+p}$	$\ln p - \ln(1+p)$
1998-0	$\frac{\Pr(N=0)}{\Pr(N=0)+\Pr(N=1)}$	$= \frac{(1-p)}{(1-p)+(1-p)p}$	$= \frac{1}{1+p}$	$-5\ln(1+p)$
1998-1	$\frac{\Pr(N=1)}{\Pr(N=0)+\Pr(N=1)}$	$= \frac{(1-p)p}{(1-p)+(1-p)p}$	$= \frac{p}{1+p}$	$2\ln p - 2\ln(1+p)$
1999-0	$\frac{\Pr(N=0)}{\Pr(N=0)}$	$= 1$		0

13.43 The density function is

$$f(x) = 0.5x^{-0.5}\theta^{-0.5}e^{-(x/\theta)^{0.5}}.$$

The likelihood function and subsequent calculations are

$$L(\theta) = \prod_{j=1}^{10} 0.5x_j^{-0.5}\theta^{-0.5}e^{-x_j^{0.5}\theta^{-0.5}} \propto \theta^{-5}\exp\left(-\theta^{-0.5}\sum_{j=1}^{10}x_j^{0.5}\right)$$

$$= \theta^{-5}\exp(-488.97\theta^{-0.5}),$$
$$l(\theta) = -5\ln\theta - 488.97\theta^{-0.5},$$
$$l'(\theta) = -5\theta^{-1} + 244.485\theta^{-1.5} = 0,$$
$$0 = -5\theta^{0.5} + 244.485,$$

and so $\hat{\theta} = (244.485/5)^2 = 2{,}391.$

13.44 Each observation has a uniquely determined conditional probability. The contribution to the loglikelihood is given in Table 13.3. The total is $l(p) = 3\ln p - 11\ln(1+p)$. Setting the derivative equal to zero gives $0 = l'(p) = 3p^{-1} - 11(1+p)^{-1}$, and the solution is $\hat{p} = 3/8$.

13.45 $L = 2^n\theta^n(\prod x_j)\exp(-\theta\sum x_j^2)$, $l = n\ln 2 + n\ln\theta + \sum\ln x_j - \theta\sum x_j^2$, $l' = n\theta^{-1} - \sum x_j^2 = 0$, $\hat{\theta} = n/\sum x_j^2$.

13.46 $f(x) = px^{p-1}$, $L = p^n(\prod x_j)^{p-1}$, $l = n\ln p + (p-1)\sum\ln x_j$, $l' = np^{-1} + \sum\ln x_j = 0$, $\hat{p} = -n/\sum\ln x_j$.

13.47 (a) $L = (\prod x_j)^{\alpha-1}\exp(-\sum x_j/\theta)[\Gamma(\alpha)]^{-n}\theta^{-n\alpha}$.

$$l = (\alpha-1)\sum\ln x_j - \theta^{-1}\sum x_j - n\ln\Gamma(\alpha) - n\alpha\ln\theta$$
$$= 81.61837(\alpha-1) - 38{,}000\theta^{-1} - 10\ln\Gamma(\alpha) - 10\alpha\ln\theta.$$
$$\partial l/\partial\theta = 38{,}000\theta^{-2} - 10\alpha\theta^{-1} = 0,$$

$\hat{\theta} = 38{,}000/(10 \cdot 12) = 316.67.$

(b) l is maximized at $\hat{\alpha} = 6.341$ and $\hat{\theta} = 599.3$ (with $l = -86.835$).

13.48 $\hat{\mu} = \frac{1}{5} \sum \ln x_i = 7.33429.$ $\hat{\sigma}^2 = \frac{1}{5} \sum (\ln x_i)^2 - 7.33429^2 = 0.567405,$ $\hat{\sigma} = 0.753263.$

$$
\begin{aligned}
\Pr(X > 4{,}500) &= 1 - \Phi[(\ln 4{,}500 - 7.33429)/0.753263] \\
&= 1 - \Phi(1.4305) = 0.076.
\end{aligned}
$$

13.49 $L = \theta^{-n} \exp(-\sum x_j/\theta).$ $l = -n \ln \theta - \theta^{-1} \sum x_j.$ $l' = -n\theta^{-1} + \theta^{-2} \sum x_j = 0.$ $\hat{\theta} = \sum x_j/n.$

13.50 $L = \beta^{-10}(\prod x_j) \exp[-\sum x_j^2/(2\beta^2)].$ $l = -10 \ln \beta + \sum \ln x_j - \sum x_j^2/(2\beta^2).$ $l' = -10\beta^{-1} + \beta^{-3} \sum x_j^2 = 0.$ $\hat{\beta} = \sqrt{\sum x_j^2/10} = 3.20031.$

13.51 $f(x) = \alpha x^{-\alpha-1}.$ $L = \alpha^n (\prod x_j)^{-\alpha-1}.$ $l = n \ln \alpha - (\alpha + 1) \sum \ln x_j.$ $l' = n\alpha^{-1} - \sum \ln x_j = 0.$ $\hat{\alpha} = n/\sum \ln x_j.$

13.52

$$
\begin{aligned}
L(\theta) &= \left(1 - \frac{\theta}{10}\right)^9 \left(\frac{\theta}{10} - \frac{\theta}{25}\right)^6 \left(\frac{\theta}{25}\right)^5 \propto (10 - \theta)^9 \theta^{11}, \\
l(\theta) &= 9 \ln(10 - \theta) + 11 \ln(\theta), \\
l'(\theta) &= -\frac{9}{10 - \theta} + \frac{11}{\theta} = 0, \\
9\theta &= 11(10 - \theta), \\
\theta &= 110/20 = 5.5.
\end{aligned}
$$

13.53

$$
\begin{aligned}
L(w) &= \frac{\frac{1}{w}\frac{1}{w}\frac{1}{w}\left(\frac{4-w-p}{w}\right)^2}{\left(\frac{w-4}{w}\right)^5} = \frac{(w - 4 - p)^2}{(w - 4)^5}, \\
l(w) &= 2 \ln(w - 4 - p) - 5 \ln(w - 4), \\
l'(w) &= \frac{2}{w - 4 - p} - \frac{5}{w - 4} = 0, \\
0 &= l'(29) = \frac{2}{25 - p} - \frac{5}{25}, \\
25 - p &= 10, \; p = 15.
\end{aligned}
$$

13.54 The density function is $f(x) = \theta x^{-2} e^{-\theta/x}$. The likelihood function is

$$
\begin{aligned}
L(\theta) &= \theta(66^{-2})e^{-\theta/66}\theta(91^{-2})e^{-\theta/91}\theta(186^{-2})e^{-\theta/186}(e^{-\theta/66})^7 \\
&\propto \theta^3 e^{-0.148184\theta}, \\
l(\theta) &= 3\ln\theta - 0.148184\theta, \\
l'(\theta) &= 3\theta^{-1} - 0.148184 = 0, \\
\theta &= 3/0.148184 = 20.25.
\end{aligned}
$$

The mode is $\theta/2 = 10.125$.

13.55

$$
\begin{aligned}
L(\alpha) &= \prod_{j=1}^{7} \frac{f(x_j|\alpha)}{1 - F(100|\alpha)} = \frac{\displaystyle\prod_{j=1}^{7}\frac{\alpha 400^\alpha}{(400+x_j)^{\alpha+1}}}{\left[\left(\dfrac{400}{400+100}\right)^\alpha\right]^7}, \\
l(\alpha) &= 7\ln\alpha + 7\alpha\ln 400 - (\alpha+1)\sum_{j=1}^{7}\ln(400+x_j) - 7\alpha\ln 0.8 \\
&= 7\ln\alpha - 3.79\alpha - 47.29, \\
l'(\alpha) &= 7\alpha^{-1} - 3.79 = 0, \\
\alpha &= 7/3.79 = 1.847.
\end{aligned}
$$

13.56

$$
\begin{aligned}
L &= \alpha^5\lambda^{5\alpha}[\textstyle\prod(\lambda+x_j)]^{-\alpha-1}, \\
l &= 5\ln\alpha + 5\alpha\ln 1{,}000 - (\alpha+1)\sum\ln(1{,}000+x_j), \\
l' &= 5\alpha^{-1} + 34.5388 - 35.8331 = 0, \\
\hat\alpha &= 3.8629.
\end{aligned}
$$

13.57 (a) Three observations exceed 200. The empirical estimate is $3/20 = 0.15$.

(b) $E(X) = 100\alpha/(\alpha - 1) = \bar{x} = 154.5$, $\hat\alpha = 154.5/54.5 = 2.835$, $\Pr(X > 200) = (100/200)^{2.835} = 0.140$.

(c) $f(x) = \alpha 100^\alpha x^{-\alpha-1}$. $L = \alpha^{20} 100^{20\alpha}(\prod x_j)^{-\alpha-1}$.

$$
\begin{aligned}
l &= 20\ln\alpha + 20\alpha\ln 100 - (\alpha+1)\sum\ln x_j, \\
l' &= 20\alpha^{-1} + 20\ln 100 - \sum\ln x_j = 0, \\
\hat\alpha &= 20/(\textstyle\sum\ln x_j - 20\ln 100) = 20/(99.125 - 92.103) = 2.848.
\end{aligned}
$$

$\Pr(X > 200) = (100/200)^{2.848} = 0.139$.

13.58 The maximum likelihood estimate is $\hat{\theta} = 93.188$.

13.59 (a)
$$
\begin{aligned}
\sum \frac{(x_j - \mu)^2}{x_j} &= \sum \left(x_j - 2\mu + \frac{\mu^2}{x_j} \right) \\
&= \sum \left(\frac{\mu^2}{x_j} - \frac{\mu^2}{\bar{x}} \right) + \sum \left(\frac{\mu^2}{\bar{x}} - 2\mu + x_j \right) \\
&= \mu^2 \sum \left(\frac{1}{x_j} - \frac{1}{\bar{x}} \right) + \frac{n\mu^2}{\bar{x}} - 2n\mu + n\bar{x} \\
&= \mu^2 \sum \left(\frac{1}{x_j} - \frac{1}{\bar{x}} \right) + \frac{n}{\bar{x}}(\bar{x} - \mu)^2.
\end{aligned}
$$

(b)
$$
\begin{aligned}
L &\propto \theta^{n/2} \exp\left[-\frac{\theta}{2\mu^2} \sum \frac{(x_j - \mu)^2}{x_j} \right], \\
l &= \ln L = \frac{n}{2} \ln \theta - \frac{\theta}{2\mu^2} \sum \frac{(x_j - \mu)^2}{x_j} \\
&= \frac{n}{2} \ln \theta - \frac{\theta}{2\mu^2} \left[\mu^2 \sum \left(\frac{1}{x_j} - \frac{1}{\bar{x}} \right) + \frac{n}{\bar{x}}(\bar{x} - \mu)^2 \right] \\
&= \frac{n}{2} \ln \theta - \frac{\theta}{2} \sum \left(\frac{1}{x_j} - \frac{1}{\bar{x}} \right) - \frac{n\theta}{2\mu^2 \bar{x}}(\bar{x} - \mu)^2, \\
\frac{\partial l}{\partial \mu} &= -\frac{n\theta}{2\bar{x}} \frac{-\mu^2 2(\bar{x} - \mu) - (\bar{x} - \mu)^2 2\mu}{\mu^4} = 0, \\
\hat{\mu} &= \bar{x}.
\end{aligned}
$$

$$
\begin{aligned}
\frac{\partial l}{\partial \theta} &= \frac{n}{2\theta} - \frac{1}{2} \sum \left(\frac{1}{x_j} - \frac{1}{\bar{x}} \right) + \frac{n}{2\mu^2 \bar{x}}(\bar{x} - \mu)^2 = 0, \\
\hat{\theta} &= \frac{n}{\sum \left(\frac{1}{x_j} - \frac{1}{\bar{x}} \right)}.
\end{aligned}
$$

13.60
$$
\begin{aligned}
L(\mu, \theta) &= \prod_{j=1}^{n} f\left[x_j; \mu, (\theta m_j)^{-1} \right] \\
&= \prod_{j=1}^{n} \left(\frac{2\pi}{\theta m_j} \right)^{-\frac{1}{2}} \exp\left[-\frac{(x_j - \mu)^2 m_j \theta}{2} \right] \\
&\propto \theta^{n/2} \exp\left[-\frac{\theta}{2} \sum m_j (x_j - \mu)^2 \right].
\end{aligned}
$$

$$\ell(\mu, \theta) = \frac{n}{2} \ln \theta - \frac{\theta}{2} \sum m_j (x_j - \mu)^2 + \text{constant},$$

$$\frac{\partial \ell}{\partial \mu} = \theta \sum m_j (x_j - \mu) = 0 \Rightarrow \hat{\mu} = \frac{\sum m_j x_j}{\sum m_j} = \frac{\sum m_j x_j}{m},$$

$$\frac{\partial^2 \ell}{\partial \mu} = -\theta \sum m_j < 0, \text{ hence, maximum.}$$

$$\frac{\partial \ell}{\partial \theta} = \frac{n}{2}\frac{1}{\theta} - \frac{1}{2} \sum m_j (x_j - \mu)^2 = 0 \Rightarrow \hat{\theta}^{-1} = \frac{1}{n} \sum m_j (x_j - \hat{\mu})^2,$$

$$\hat{\theta} = n \left[\sum m_j (x_j - \bar{x})^2 \right]^{-1},$$

$$\frac{\partial^2 \ell}{\partial \theta^2} = -\frac{n}{2}\frac{1}{\theta^2} < 0, \text{ hence, maximum.}$$

13.61

$$L(\theta) = \prod_{j=1}^{n} f(x_j; \theta) = \prod_{j=1}^{n} \frac{p(x_j) e^{r(\theta) x_j}}{q(\theta)},$$

$$\ell(\theta) = \sum_{j=1}^{n} \ln p(x_j) + r(\theta) \sum_{j=1}^{n} x_j - n \ln q(\theta),$$

$$\ell'(\theta) = r'(\theta) \sum_{j=1}^{n} x_j - n\frac{q'(\theta)}{q(\theta)}.$$

Therefore,

$$\frac{q'(\hat{\theta})}{r'(\hat{\theta}) q(\hat{\theta})} = \bar{x}.$$

But,

$$\frac{q'(\theta)}{r'(\theta) q(\theta)} = \text{E}(X) = \mu(\theta),$$

and so $\mu(\hat{\theta}) = \bar{x}$.

13.3   SECTION 13.3

13.62 In general, for the exponential distribution,

$$l'(\theta) = -n\theta^{-1} + n\bar{x}\theta^{-2},$$
$$l''(\theta) = n\theta^{-2} - 2n\bar{x}\theta^{-3},$$
$$\text{E}[l''(\theta)] = n\theta^{-2} - 2n\theta\theta^{-3} = -n\theta^{-2},$$
$$\text{Var}(\hat{\theta}) = \theta^2/n,$$

where the third line follows from $\text{E}(\bar{X}) = \text{E}(X) = \theta$. The estimated variance for Data Set B is $\widehat{\text{Var}}(\hat{\theta}) = 1{,}424.4^2/20 = 101{,}445.77$ and the 95% confidence interval is $1{,}424.4 \pm 1.96(101{,}445.77)^{1/2}$, or $1{,}424.4 \pm 624.27$. Note that in this particular case Theorem 13.5 gives the exact value of the variance, because

$$\operatorname{Var}(\hat{\theta}) = \operatorname{Var}(\bar{X}) = \operatorname{Var}(X)/n = \theta^2/n.$$

For the gamma distribution,

$$
\begin{aligned}
l(\alpha, \theta) &= (\alpha - 1)\sum_{j=1}^{n} \ln x_j - \sum_{j=1}^{n} x_j \theta^{-1} - n \ln \Gamma(\alpha) - n\alpha \ln \theta, \\
\frac{\partial l(\alpha, \theta)}{\partial \alpha} &= \sum_{j=1}^{n} \ln x_j - \frac{n\Gamma'(\alpha)}{\Gamma(\alpha)} - n \ln \theta, \\
\frac{\partial l(\alpha, \theta)}{\partial \theta} &= \sum_{j=1}^{n} x_j \theta^{-2} - n\alpha\theta^{-1}, \\
\frac{\partial^2 l(\alpha, \theta)}{\partial \alpha^2} &= -n\frac{\Gamma(\alpha)\Gamma''(\alpha) - \Gamma'(\alpha)^2}{\Gamma(\alpha)^2}, \\
\frac{\partial^2 l(\alpha, \theta)}{\partial \alpha \partial \theta} &= -n\theta^{-1}, \\
\frac{\partial^2 l(\alpha, \theta)}{\partial \theta^2} &= -2\sum_{j=1}^{n} x_j \theta^{-3} + n\alpha\theta^{-2} = -2n\bar{x}\theta^{-3} + n\alpha\theta^{-2}.
\end{aligned}
$$

The first two second partial derivatives do not contain x_j, and so the expected value is equal to the indicated quantity. For the final second partial derivative, $\operatorname{E}(\bar{X}) = \operatorname{E}(X) = \alpha\theta$. Therefore,

$$
I(\alpha, \theta) = \begin{bmatrix} n\frac{\Gamma(\alpha)\Gamma''(\alpha) - \Gamma'(\alpha)^2}{\Gamma(\alpha)^2} & n\theta^{-1} \\ n\theta^{-1} & n\alpha\theta^{-2} \end{bmatrix}.
$$

The derivatives of the gamma function are available in some better computer packages, but are not available in Excel®. Using numerical derivatives of the gamma function yields

$$
I(\hat{\alpha}, \hat{\theta}) = \begin{bmatrix} 82.467 & 0.0078091 \\ 0.0078091 & 0.0000016958 \end{bmatrix}
$$

and the covariance matrix is

$$
\begin{bmatrix} 0.021503 & -99.0188 \\ -99.0188 & 1{,}045{,}668 \end{bmatrix}.
$$

Numerical second derivatives of the likelihood function (using $h_1 = 0.00005$ and $h_2 = 0.25$) yield

$$
I(\hat{\alpha}, \hat{\theta}) = \begin{bmatrix} 82.467 & 0.0078091 \\ 0.0078091 & 0.0000016959 \end{bmatrix},
$$

and covariance matrix

$$\begin{bmatrix} 0.021502 & -99.0143 \\ -99.0143 & 1{,}045{,}620 \end{bmatrix}.$$

The confidence interval for α is $0.55616 \pm 1.96(0.021502)^{1/2}$, or 0.55616 ± 0.28741, and for θ is $2{,}561.1 \pm 1.96(1{,}045{,}620)^{1/2}$, or $2{,}561.1 \pm 2{,}004.2$.

13.63 The density function is $f(x|\theta) = \theta^{-1}$, $0 \leq x \leq \theta$. The likelihood function is

$$\begin{aligned} L(\theta) &= \theta^{-n}, \; 0 \leq x_1, \ldots, x_n \leq \theta, \\ &= 0, \text{ otherwise.} \end{aligned}$$

As a function of θ, the likelihood function is sometimes zero, and sometimes θ^{-n}. In particular, it is θ^{-n} only when θ is greater than or equal to all the xs. Equivalently, we have

$$\begin{aligned} L(\theta) &= 0, \; \theta < \max(x_1, \ldots, x_n) \\ &= \theta^{-n}, \; \theta \geq \max(x_1, \ldots, x_n). \end{aligned}$$

Therefore, the likelihood function is maximized at $\hat{\theta} = \max(x_1, \ldots, x_n)$. Note that the calculus technique of setting the derivative equal to zero does not work here because the likelihood function is not continuous (and therefore not differentiable) at the maximum. From Examples 10.5 and 10.7 we know that this estimator is asymptotically unbiased and consistent, and we have its variance without recourse to Theorem 13.5. According to Theorem 13.5, we need

$$\begin{aligned} l(\theta) &= -n \ln \theta, \; \theta \geq \max(x_1, \ldots, x_n), \\ l'(\theta) &= -n\theta^{-1}, \; \theta \geq \max(x_1, \ldots, x_n), \\ l''(\theta) &= n\theta^{-2}, \; \theta \geq \max(x_1, \ldots, x_n). \end{aligned}$$

Then $E[l''(\theta)] = n\theta^{-2}$ because with regard to the random variables, $n\theta^{-2}$ is a constant and, therefore, its expected value is itself. The information is then the negative of this number and must be negative.

With regard to assumption (ii) of Theorem 13.5,

$$\int_0^\theta \frac{\partial}{\partial \theta} \frac{1}{\theta} dx = \int_0^\theta -\theta^{-2} dx = -\frac{1}{\theta} \neq 0.$$

13.64 From Exercise 13.62 we have $\hat{\alpha} = 0.55616$, $\hat{\theta} = 2{,}561.1$, and covariance matrix

$$\begin{bmatrix} 0.021503 & -99.0188 \\ -99.0188 & 1{,}045{,}668 \end{bmatrix}.$$

The function to be estimated is $g(\alpha, \theta) = \alpha\theta$ with partial derivatives of θ and α. The approximated variance is

$$\begin{bmatrix} 2{,}561.1 & 0.55616 \end{bmatrix} \begin{bmatrix} 0.021503 & -99.0188 \\ -99.0188 & 1{,}045{,}668 \end{bmatrix} \begin{bmatrix} 2{,}561.1 \\ 0.55616 \end{bmatrix} = 182{,}402.$$

The confidence interval is $1{,}424.4 \pm 1.96\sqrt{182{,}402}$, or $1{,}424.4 \pm 837.1$.

13.65 The partial derivatives of the mean are

$$\frac{\partial e^{\mu + \sigma^2/2}}{\partial \mu} = e^{\mu + \sigma^2/2} = 123.017,$$

$$\frac{\partial e^{\mu + \sigma^2/2}}{\partial \sigma} = \sigma e^{\mu + \sigma^2/2} = 134.458.$$

The estimated variance is then

$$\begin{bmatrix} 123.017 & 134.458 \end{bmatrix} \begin{bmatrix} 0.1195 & 0 \\ 0 & 0.0597 \end{bmatrix} \begin{bmatrix} 123.017 \\ 134.458 \end{bmatrix} = 2{,}887.73.$$

13.66 The first partial derivatives are

$$\frac{\partial l(\alpha, \beta)}{\partial \alpha} = -5\alpha - 3\beta + 50,$$

$$\frac{\partial l(\alpha, \beta)}{\partial \beta} = -3\alpha - 2\beta + 2.$$

The second partial derivatives are

$$\frac{\partial^2 l(\alpha, \beta)}{\partial \alpha^2} = -5,$$

$$\frac{\partial^2 l(\alpha, \beta)}{\partial \beta^2} = -2,$$

$$\frac{\partial^2 l(\alpha, \beta)}{\partial \alpha \partial \beta} = -3,$$

and so the information matrix is

$$\begin{bmatrix} 5 & 3 \\ 3 & 2 \end{bmatrix}.$$

The covariance matrix is the inverse of the information, or

$$\begin{bmatrix} 2 & -3 \\ -3 & 5 \end{bmatrix}.$$

13.67 For the first case, the observed loglikelihood and its derivatives are

$$l(\theta) = 62\ln[1 - e^{-1,000/\theta}] + 38\ln e^{-1,000/\theta},$$

$$l'(\theta) = \frac{-62e^{-1,000/\theta}(1,000/\theta^2)}{1 - e^{-1,000/\theta}} + \frac{38,000}{\theta^2}$$

$$= \frac{-62,000e^{-1,000/\theta}\theta^{-2} + 38,000\theta^{-2} - 38,000e^{-1,000/\theta}\theta^{-2}}{1 - e^{-1,000/\theta}}$$

$$= \frac{38,000e^{1,000/\theta} - 100,000}{\theta^2(e^{1,000/\theta} - 1)},$$

$$l''(\theta) = \frac{-\theta^2(e^{1,000/\theta} - 1)38,000e^{1,000/\theta}1,000\theta^{-2}}{-(38,000e^{1,000/\theta} - 100,000)[2\theta(e^{1,000/\theta} - 1) - \theta^2 e^{1,000/\theta}1,000\theta^{-2}]}{\theta^4(e^{1,000/\theta} - 1)^2}.$$

Evaluating the second derivative at $\hat{\theta} = 1033.50$ and changing the sign give $\hat{I}(\theta) = 0.00005372$. The reciprocal gives the variance estimate of 18,614. Similarly, for the case with more information

$$l(\theta) = -62\ln\theta - 66,140\theta^{-1},$$
$$l'(\theta) = -62\theta^{-1} + 66,140\theta^{-2},$$
$$l''(\theta) = 62\theta^{-2} - 132,280\theta^{-3},$$
$$l''(1,066.77) = -0.000054482.$$

The variance estimate is the negative reciprocal, or 18,355.[2]

13.68 (a) $f(x) = px^{p-1}$, $\ln f(x) = \ln p + (p-1)\ln x$, $\partial^2 \ln f(x)/\partial p^2 = -p^{-2}$, $I(p) = nE(p^{-2}) = np^{-2}$, $\text{Var}(\hat{p}) \doteq p^2/n$.

(b) From Exercise 13.46, $\hat{p} = -n/\Sigma\ln x_j$. The CI is $\hat{p} \pm 1.96\hat{p}/\sqrt{n}$.

(c) $\mu = p/(1+p)$. $\hat{p}/(1+\hat{p})$. $\partial\mu/\partial p = (1+p)^{-2}$. $\text{Var}(\hat{\mu}) \doteq (1+p)^{-4}p^2/n$. The CI is $\hat{p}(1+\hat{p})^{-1} \pm 1.96\hat{p}(1+\hat{p})^{-2}/\sqrt{n}$.

13.69 (a) $\ln f(x) = -\ln\theta - x/\theta$, $\partial^2 \ln f(x)/\partial\theta^2 = \theta^{-2} - 2\theta^{-3}x$, $I(\theta) = nE(-\theta^{-2} + 2\theta^{-3}X) = n\theta^{-2}$, $\text{Var}(\hat{\theta}) \doteq \theta^2/n$.

(b) From Exercise 13.49, $\hat{\theta} = \bar{x}$. The CI is $\bar{x} \pm 1.96\bar{x}/\sqrt{n}$.

(c) $\text{Var}(X) = \theta^2$. $\partial\text{Var}(X)/\partial\theta = 2\theta$. $\widehat{\text{Var}(X)} = \bar{x}^2$. $\text{Var}[\widehat{\text{Var}(X)}] \doteq (2\theta)^2\theta^2/n = 4\theta^4/n$. The CI is $\bar{x}^2 \pm 1.96(2\bar{x}^2)/\sqrt{n}$.

---

[2]Comparing the variances at the same $\hat{\theta}$ value would be more useful.

13.70 $\ln f(x) = -(1/2)\ln(2\pi\theta) - x^2/(2\theta)$, $\partial^2 \ln f(x)/\partial\theta^2 = (2\theta^2)^{-1} - x^2(\theta^3)^{-1}$, and $I(\theta) = nE[-(2\theta^2)^{-1} + X^2(\theta^3)^{-1}] = n(2\theta^2)^{-1}$ since $X \sim N(0,\theta)$. Then $\text{MSE}(\hat{\theta}) \doteq \text{Var}(\hat{\theta}) \doteq 2\theta^2/n \doteq 2\hat{\theta}^2/n = 8/40 = 0.2$.

13.71 The maximum likelihood estimate is $\hat{\theta} = \bar{x} = 1,000$. $\text{Var}(\hat{\theta}) = \text{Var}(\bar{x}) = \theta^2/6$. The quantity to be estimated is $S(\theta) = e^{-1,500/\theta}$, and then

$$S'(\theta) = 1,500\theta^{-2}e^{-1,500/\theta}.$$

From the delta method

$$
\begin{aligned}
\text{Var}[S(\hat{\theta})] &= [S'(\hat{\theta})]^2\text{Var}(\hat{\theta}) \\
&= [1,500(1,000)^{-2}e^{-1,500/1,000}]^2(1,000^2/6) = 0.01867.
\end{aligned}
$$

The standard deviation is 0.13664 and with $S(1,000) = 0.22313$, the confidence interval is $0.22313 \pm 1.96(0.13664)$, or 0.22313 ± 0.26781. An alternative that does not use the delta method is to start with a confidence interval for θ: $1,000 \pm 1.96(1,000)/\sqrt{6}$, which is $1,000 \pm 800.17$. Putting the endpoints into $S(\theta)$ produces the interval 0.00055 to 0.43463.

13.72 (a) $L = F(2)[1 - F(2)]^3$. $F(2) = \int_0^2 2\lambda x e^{-\lambda x^2}dx = -e^{-\lambda x^2}\big|_0^2 = 1 - e^{-4\lambda}$. $l = \ln(1-e^{-4\lambda}) - 12\lambda$. $\partial l/\partial\lambda = (1-e^{-4\lambda})^{-1}4e^{-4\lambda} - 12 = 0$. $e^{-4\lambda} = 3/4$. $\hat{\lambda} = (1/4)\ln(4/3)$.

(b) $P_1(\lambda) = 1 - e^{-4\lambda}$, $P_2(\lambda) = e^{-4\lambda}$, $P_1'(\lambda) = 4e^{-4\lambda}$, $P_2'(\lambda) = -4e^{-4\lambda}$. $I(\lambda) = 4[16e^{-8\lambda}/(1 - e^{-4\lambda}) + 16e^{-8\lambda}/e^{-4\lambda}]$. $\widehat{\text{Var}(\hat{\lambda})} = \{4[16(9/16)/(1/4) + 16(9/16)/(3/4)]\}^{-1} = 1/192$.

13.73 The loglikelihood function is $l = 81.61837(\alpha-1) - 38,000\theta^{-1} - 10\ln\Gamma(\alpha)$ $- 10\alpha\ln\theta$. Also, $\hat{\alpha} = 6.341$ and $\hat{\theta} = 599.3$. Using $v = 4$, we have

$$\frac{\partial^2 l(\alpha,\theta)}{\partial\alpha^2} \doteq \frac{l(6.3416341,599.3) - 2l(6.341,599.3) + l(6.3403659,599.3)}{(0.0006341)^2} = -1.70790,$$

$$\frac{\partial^2 l(\alpha,\theta)}{\partial\alpha\partial\theta} \doteq \frac{\begin{array}{c}l(6.34131705,599.329965) - l(6.34131705,599.270035)\\-l(6.34068295,599.329965) + l(6.34068295,599.270035)\end{array}}{(0.0006341)(.05993)}$$

$$= 0.0166861,$$

$$\frac{\partial^2 l(\alpha,\theta)}{\partial\theta^2} \doteq \frac{l(6.341,599.35993) - 2l(6.341,599.3) + l(6.341,599.25007)}{(0.05993)^2} = -0.000176536,$$

$$I(\hat{\alpha},\hat{\theta}) = \begin{bmatrix} 1.70790 & 0.0166861 \\ 0.0166861 & 0.000176536 \end{bmatrix},$$

and its inverse is

$$\widehat{\text{Var}} = \begin{bmatrix} 7.64976 & -723.055 \\ -723.055 & 74,007.7 \end{bmatrix}.$$

The mean is $\alpha\theta$, and so the derivative vector is $\begin{bmatrix} 599.3 & 6.341 \end{bmatrix}$. The variance of $\widehat{\alpha\theta}$ is estimated as 227,763 and a 95% CI is $3,800 \pm 1.97\sqrt{227,763} = 3,800 \pm 935$.

13.74 $\hat{\alpha} = 3.8629$. $\ln f(x) = \ln\alpha + \alpha\ln\lambda - (\alpha+1)\ln(\lambda+x)$. $\partial^2 \ln f(x)/\partial\alpha^2 = -\alpha^{-2}$. $I(\alpha) = n\alpha^{-2}$. $\mathrm{Var}(\hat{\alpha}) \doteq \alpha^2/n$. Inserting the estimate gives 2.9844.

$$
\begin{aligned}
\mathrm{E}(X \wedge 500) &= \int_0^{500} x\alpha 1{,}000^\alpha (1{,}000 + x)^{-\alpha-1} dx \\
&\quad +500 \int_{500}^\infty \alpha 1{,}000^\alpha (1{,}000 + x)^{-\alpha-1} dx \\
&= \frac{1{,}000}{\alpha - 1} - (2/3)^\alpha \frac{1{,}500}{\alpha - 1}.
\end{aligned}
$$

Evaluated at $\hat{\alpha}$, it is 239.88. The derivative with respect to α is

$$
-\frac{1{,}000}{(\alpha - 1)^2} + \left(\frac{2}{3}\right)^\alpha \frac{1{,}500}{(\alpha - 1)^2} - \left(\frac{2}{3}\right)^\alpha \frac{1{,}500}{\alpha - 1} \ln\left(\frac{2}{3}\right),
$$

which is -39.428 when evaluated at $\hat{\alpha}$. The variance of the LEV estimator is $(-39.4298)^2(2.9844) = 5{,}639.45$, and the CI is 239.88 ± 133.50.

13.75 (a) Let $\theta = \mu/\Gamma(1+\tau^{-1})$. From Appendix A, $\mathrm{E}(X) = \theta\Gamma(1+\tau^{-1}) = \mu$.

(b) The density function is $f(x) = \exp\left\{-\left[\frac{\Gamma(1+\tau^{-1})x}{\mu}\right]^\tau\right\} \frac{\tau}{x}\left[\frac{\Gamma(1+\tau^{-1})x}{\mu}\right]^\tau$, and its logarithm is

$$
\ln f(x) = -\left[\frac{\Gamma(1+\tau^{-1})x}{\mu}\right]^\tau + \ln\tau + \tau\ln\left[\frac{\Gamma(1+\tau^{-1})}{\mu}\right] + (\tau - 1)\ln x.
$$

The loglikelihood function is

$$
l(\mu) = \sum_{j=1}^n \left\{ -\left[\frac{\Gamma(1+\tau^{-1})x_j}{\mu}\right]^\tau + \ln\tau + \tau\ln\left[\frac{\Gamma(1+\tau^{-1})}{\mu}\right] + (\tau - 1)\ln x_j \right\},
$$

and its derivative is

$$
l'(\mu) = \sum_{j=1}^n \left\{ \tau\frac{[\Gamma(1+\tau^{-1})x_j]^\tau}{\mu^{\tau+1}} - \frac{\tau}{\mu} \right\}.
$$

Setting the derivative equal to zero, moving the last term to the right-hand side, multiplying by μ, and dividing by τ produce the equation

$$\sum_{j=1}^{n}\left[\frac{\Gamma(1+\tau^{-1})x_j}{\mu}\right]^{\tau} = n$$

$$\left[\frac{\Gamma(1+\tau^{-1})}{\mu}\right]^{\tau}\sum_{j=1}^{n}x_j^{\tau} = n$$

$$\left[\frac{\Gamma(1+\tau^{-1})}{n^{1/\tau}}\right]^{\tau}\sum_{j=1}^{n}x_j^{\tau} = \mu^{\tau} \tag{13.1}$$

and, finally,

$$\hat{\mu} = \Gamma(1+\tau^{-1})\left(\sum_{j=1}^{n}\frac{x_j^{\tau}}{n}\right)^{1/\tau}.$$

(c) The second derivative of the loglikelihood function is

$$l''(\mu) = \sum_{j=1}^{n}\left\{-\tau(\tau+1)\frac{[\Gamma(1+\tau^{-1})x_j]^{\tau}}{\mu^{\tau+2}} + \frac{\tau}{\mu^2}\right\}$$

$$= \frac{n\tau}{\mu^2} - \tau(\tau+1)\Gamma(1+\tau^{-1})^{\tau}\mu^{-\tau-2}\sum_{j=1}^{n}x_j^{\tau}.$$

From (13.1), $\sum_{j=1}^{n}x_j^{\tau} = \left[\frac{n^{1/\tau}\hat{\mu}^{\tau}}{\Gamma(1+\tau^{-1})}\right]^{\tau}$ and therefore the observed information can be written as

$$l''(\hat{\mu}) = \frac{n\tau}{\hat{\mu}^2} - \tau(\tau+1)\Gamma(1+\tau^{-1})^{\tau}\hat{\mu}^{-\tau-2}\left[\frac{n^{1/\tau}\hat{\mu}^{\tau}}{\Gamma(1+\tau^{-1})}\right]^{\tau}$$

$$= \frac{n\tau}{\hat{\mu}^2} - \frac{\tau(\tau+1)n}{\hat{\mu}^2} = -\frac{\tau^2 n}{\hat{\mu}^2},$$

and the negative reciprocal provides the variance estimate.

(d) The information requires the expected value of X^{τ}. From Appendix A, it is $\theta^{\tau}\Gamma(1+\frac{\tau}{\tau}) = \theta^{\tau} = [\mu/\Gamma(1+\tau^{-1})]^{\tau}$. Then

$$E[l''(\mu)] = \frac{n\tau}{\mu^2} - \tau(\tau+1)\Gamma(1+\tau^{-1})^{\tau}\mu^{-\tau-2}n[\mu/\Gamma(1+\tau^{-1})]^{\tau}$$

$$= \frac{n\tau}{\mu^2} - \frac{\tau(\tau+1)n}{\mu^2} = -\frac{\tau^2 n}{\mu^2}.$$

Changing the sign, inverting, and substituting $\hat{\mu}$ for μ produce the same estimated variance as in part (c).

(e) To obtain the distribution of $\hat{\mu}$, first obtain the distribution of $Y = X^\tau$. We have

$$
\begin{aligned}
S_Y(y) &= \Pr(Y > y) = \Pr(X^\tau > y) \\
&= \Pr(X > y^{1/\tau}) \\
&= \exp\left\{ -\left[\frac{\Gamma(1+\tau^{-1})y^{1/\tau}}{\mu} \right]^\tau \right\} \\
&= \exp\left\{ -\left[\frac{\Gamma(1+\tau^{-1})}{\mu} \right]^\tau y \right\},
\end{aligned}
$$

which is an exponential distribution with mean $[\mu/\Gamma(1+\tau^{-1})]^\tau$. Then $\sum_{j=1}^{n} X_j^\tau$ has a gamma distribution with parameters n and $[\mu/\Gamma(1+\tau^{-1})]^\tau$. Next look at

$$
\frac{\Gamma(1+\tau^{-1})^\tau}{\mu^\tau} \sum_{j=1}^{n} X_j^\tau.
$$

Multiplying by a constant changes the scale parameter, so this variable has a gamma distribution with parameters n and 1. Now raise this expression to the $1/\tau$ power. Then

$$
\frac{\Gamma(1+\tau^{-1})}{\mu} \left(\sum_{j=1}^{n} X_j^\tau \right)^{1/\tau}
$$

has a transformed gamma distribution with parameters $\alpha = n$, $\theta = 1$, and $\tau = \tau$. To create $\hat{\mu}$, this function must be multiplied by $\mu/n^{1/\tau}$, which changes the scale parameter to $\theta = \mu/n^{1/\tau}$. From Appendix A,

$$
E(\hat{\mu}) = \frac{\mu\Gamma(n+\tau^{-1})}{n^{1/\tau}\Gamma(n)}.
$$

A similar argument provides the second moment and then a variance of

$$
\mathrm{Var}(\hat{\mu}) = \frac{\mu^2\Gamma(n+2\tau^{-1})}{n^{2/\tau}\Gamma(n)} - \frac{\mu^2\Gamma(n+\tau^{-1})^2}{n^{2/\tau}\Gamma(n)^2}.
$$

13.4   SECTION 13.4

13.76 The likelihood function is $L(\theta) = \theta^{-20}e^{-28,488/\theta}$. Then $l(\theta) = -20\ln(\theta) - 28,488/\theta$. With $\hat{\theta} = 1{,}424.4$, $l(\hat{\theta}) = -165.23$. A 95% confidence region solves $l(\theta) = -165.23 - 1.92 = -167.15$. The solutions are 946.87 and 2,285.07. Inserting the solutions in $S(200) = e^{-200/\theta}$ produces the interval 0.810 to 0.916. The symmetric interval was 0.816 to 0.922.

13.5   SECTION 13.5

13.77 For the Kaplan–Meier estimates, the variances are (by Greenwood's formula)

$$\text{Vâr}(\hat{q}_{45}) \;=\; (0.750)^2 \left[\frac{1}{8(7)} + \frac{1}{7(6)} \right] = 0.02344,$$

$$\text{Vâr}(\hat{q}_{46}) \;=\; (0.584)^2 \left[\frac{1}{8(7)} + \frac{1}{6(5)} + \frac{1}{5(4)} \right] = 0.03451.$$

For exact exposure, the deaths were 2 and 3 and the exposures 5.9 and 5.5 for the two ages. The estimated variances are

$$\text{Vâr}(\hat{q}_{45}) \;=\; (1 - 0.28751)^2 \frac{2}{5.9^2} = 0.02917,$$

$$\text{Vâr}(\hat{q}_{46}) \;=\; (1 - 0.42042)^2 \frac{3}{5.5^2} = 0.03331.$$

The actuarial exposures are 7.2 for both ages. The estimated variances are

$$\text{Vâr}(\hat{q}_{45}) \;=\; \frac{0.28751(0.71249)}{7.2} = 0.02845,$$

$$\text{Vâr}(\hat{q}_{46}) \;=\; \frac{0.42042(0.57958)}{7.2} = 0.03384.$$

CHAPTER 14

CHAPTER 14

14.1 SECTION 14.7

14.1 (a) $\hat{q} = \bar{X}/m$, $E(\hat{q}) = E(X)/m = mq/m = q$.

(b)
$$\mathrm{Var}(\hat{q}) = \mathrm{Var}(\bar{X})/m^2 = \mathrm{Var}(X)/(nm^2)$$
$$= mq(1-q)/(nm^2) = q(1-q)/(nm).$$

(c)
$$l = \sum_{j=1}^{n} \ln \binom{m}{x_j} + x_j \ln q + (m - x_j) \ln(1 - q),$$

$$l' = \sum_{j=1}^{n} x_j q^{-1} - (m - x_j)(1 - q)^{-1},$$

$$l'' = \sum_{j=1}^{n} -x_j q^{-2} - (m - x_j)(1 - q)^{-2},$$

$$I(q) = E(-l'') = n[mqq^{-2} + (m - mq)(1 - q)^{-2}]$$
$$= nm[q^{-1} + (1 - q)^{-1}].$$

The reciprocal is $(1 - q)q/(nm)$.

Student Solutions Manual to Accompany Loss Models: From Data to Decisions, Fourth **147**
Edition. By Stuart A. Klugman, Harry H. Panjer, Gordon E. Willmot
Copyright © 2012 John Wiley & Sons, Inc.

(d) $\hat{q} \pm z_{\alpha/2} \sqrt{\hat{q}(1 - \hat{q})/(nm)}$.

(e)
$$1 - \alpha = \Pr\left(-z_{\alpha/2} \leq \frac{\hat{q} - q}{\sqrt{q(1 - q)/(nm)}} \leq z_{\alpha/2}\right),$$

and so
$$|\hat{q} - q| \leq z_{\alpha/2} \sqrt{\frac{q(1 - q)}{nm}},$$

which implies
$$nm(\hat{q} - q)^2 \leq z_{\alpha/2}^2 q(1 - q).$$

Then,
$$(nm + z_{\alpha/2}^2)q^2 - (2nm\hat{q} + z_{\alpha/2}^2)q + nm\hat{q}^2 \leq 0.$$

The boundaries of the CI are the roots of this quadratic:
$$\frac{2nm\hat{q} + z_{\alpha/2}^2 \pm z_{\alpha/2}\sqrt{1 + 4nm\hat{q}(1 - \hat{q})}}{2(nm + z_{\alpha/2}^2)}.$$

14.2 Because $r = 1$, $\hat{\beta} = \bar{X}$.

$$\begin{aligned}
\text{Var}(\bar{X}) &= \text{Var}(X)/n = \beta(1 + \beta)/n, \\
l &= \sum_{j=1}^{n} \ln \Pr(N = x_j) = \sum_{j=1}^{n} \ln[\beta^{x_j}(1 + \beta)^{-x_j - 1}] \\
&= \sum_{j=1}^{n} x_j \ln(\beta) - (x_j + 1)\ln(1 + \beta), \\
l'' &= \sum_{j=1}^{n} -x_j\beta^{-2} + (x_j + 1)(1 + \beta)^{-2}, \\
E(l'') &= -n\beta\beta^{-2} + n(\beta + 1)(1 + \beta)^{-2} = n/[\beta(1 + \beta)].
\end{aligned}$$

The reciprocal matches the true variance of the mle.

14.3 (a) The mle is the sample mean, $[905 + 2(45) + 3(2)]/10{,}000 = 0.1001$, and the CI is $0.1001 \pm 1.96\sqrt{0.1001/10{,}000} = 0.1001 \pm 0.0062$, or $(0.0939, 0.1063)$.

(b) The mle is the sample mean, 0.1001. The CI is
$$0.1001 \pm 1.96\sqrt{0.1001(1.1001)/10{,}000} = 0.1001 \pm 0.0065,$$

or $(0.0936, 0.1066)$.

(c) Numerical methods yield $\hat{r} = 56.1856$ and $\hat{\beta} = 0.00178159$.

(d) $\hat{q} = \bar{x}/4 = 0.025025$.

(e) $0.025025 \pm 1.96\sqrt{0.025025(0.974975)/40{,}000} = 0.025025 \pm 0.001531$ and

$$\frac{2(10{,}000)(4)(0.025025) + 1.96^2 \pm 1.96\sqrt{1 + 4(10{,}000)(4)(0.025025(0.974975)}}{2[10{,}000(4) + 1.96^2]},$$

or 0.025071 ± 0.001531.

(f) The likelihood function increases as $m \to \infty$ and $q \to 0$.

14.4 (a) The sample means are underinsured, $109/1{,}000 = 0.109$, and insured, $57/1{,}000 = 0.057$.

(b) The Poisson parameter is the sum of the individual parameters, $0.109 + 0.057 = 0.166$.

14.5 (a) $\hat{\lambda}$ is the sample mean, 0.166.

(b) Let n_{ij} be the number observations of j counts from population i, where $j = 0, 1, \ldots$ and $i = 1, 2$. The individual estimators are $\hat{\lambda}_i = \sum_{j=0}^{\infty} j n_{ij}$. The estimator for the sum is the sum of the estimators, which is $\hat{\lambda} = \sum_{j=0}^{\infty} j(n_{1j} + n_{2j})$, which is also the estimator from the combined sample.

(c) $\hat{\beta} = 0.166$.

(d) Numerical methods yield $\hat{r} = 0.656060$ and $\hat{\beta} = 0.253026$.

(e) $\hat{q} = 0.166/7 = 0.0237143$.

(f) The likelihood function increases as $m \to \infty$ and $q \to 0$.

14.6 (a) $\hat{\lambda} = 15.688$. When writing the likelihood function, a typical term is $(p_4 + p_5 + p_6)^{47}$, and the likelihood must be numerically maximized.

(b) $\hat{\beta} = 19.145$.

(c) $\hat{r} = 0.56418$ and $\hat{\beta} = 37.903$.

14.7 The maximum likelihood estimate is the sample mean, which is 1. The variance of the sample mean is the variance of a single observation divided by the sample size. For the Poisson distribution, the variance equals the mean, so the estimated variance is $1/3{,}000$. The confidence interval is $1 \pm 1.645\sqrt{1/3{,}000} = 1 \pm 0.030$, which is 0.970 to 1.030.

14.8 The estimator is unbiased, so the mean is λ. The variance of the sample mean is the variance divided by the sample size, or λ/n. The coefficient of variation is $\sqrt{\lambda/n}/\lambda = 1/\sqrt{n\lambda}$. The maximum likelihood estimate of λ is the sample mean, 3.9. The estimated coefficient of variation is $1/\sqrt{10(3.9)} = 0.1601$.

CHAPTER 15

CHAPTER 15

15.1 SECTION 15.2

15.1 $f(y) = \frac{12(4.801121)^{12}}{y(0.195951 + \ln y)^{13}}$. Let $W = \ln Y - \ln 100 = \ln(Y/100)$. Then $y = 100e^w$ and $dy = 100e^w dw$. Thus,

$$f(w) = \frac{12(4.801121)^{12}100e^w}{100e^w(0.195951 + w + \ln 100)^{13}} = \frac{12(4.801121)^{12}}{(4.801121 + w)^{13}}, \quad y > 0,$$

which is a Pareto density with $\alpha = 12$ and $\theta = 4.801121$.

15.2
$$\pi(\alpha|\mathbf{x}) \quad \propto \quad \frac{\alpha^{10}100^{10\alpha}}{\prod x_j^{\alpha+1}} \frac{\alpha^{\gamma-1}e^{-\alpha/\theta}}{\theta^\gamma \Gamma(\gamma)}$$

$$\propto \quad \alpha^{10+\gamma-1} \exp[-\alpha(\theta^{-1} - 10\ln 100 + \sum \ln x_j)],$$

which is a gamma distribution with parameters $10 + \gamma$ and $(\theta^{-1} - 10\ln 100 + \sum \ln x_j)^{-1}$. The mean is $\hat{\alpha}_{\text{Bayes}} = (10 + \gamma)(\theta^{-1} - 10\ln 100 + \sum \ln x_j)^{-1}$. For the mle:

$$l = 10\ln\alpha + 10\alpha\ln 100 - (\alpha+1)\sum \ln x_j,$$
$$l' = 10\alpha^{-1} + 10\ln 100 - \sum \ln x_j = 0,$$

Student Solutions Manual to Accompany Loss Models: From Data to Decisions, Fourth Edition. By Stuart A. Klugman, Harry H. Panjer, Gordon E. Willmot
Copyright © 2012 John Wiley & Sons, Inc.

for $\hat{\alpha}_{\text{mle}} = 10(\sum \ln x_j - 10 \ln 100)^{-1}$. The two estimators are equal when $\gamma = 0$ and $\theta = \infty$, which corresponds to $\pi(\alpha) = \alpha^{-1}$, an improper prior.

15.3 (a) $\pi(\mu, \sigma | \mathbf{x}) \propto \sigma^{-n} \exp\left[-\sum \frac{1}{2} \left(\frac{\ln x_j - \mu}{\sigma} \right)^2 \right] \sigma^{-1}$.

(b) Let

$$l = \ln \pi(\mu, \sigma | \mathbf{x}) = -(n+1) \ln \sigma - \frac{1}{2} \sigma^{-2} \sum (\ln x_j - \mu)^2.$$

Then

$$\frac{\partial l}{\partial \mu} = \frac{1}{2} \sigma^{-2} \sum 2(\ln x_j - \mu)(-1) = 0$$

and the solution is $\hat{\mu} = \frac{1}{n} \sum \ln x_j$. Also,

$$\frac{\partial l}{\partial \sigma} = -(n+1)\sigma^{-1} + \sigma^{-3} \sum (\ln x_j - \mu)^2 = 0,$$

and so $\hat{\sigma} = \left[\frac{1}{n+1} \sum (\ln x_j - \hat{\mu})^2 \right]^{1/2}$.

(c)

$$\pi(\mu, \hat{\sigma} | \mathbf{x}) \propto \exp\left[-\sum \frac{1}{2} \left(\frac{\ln x_j - \mu}{\hat{\sigma}} \right)^2 \right]$$

$$= \exp\left(-\frac{1}{2} \frac{n\mu^2 - 2\mu \sum \ln x_j + \sum (\ln x_j)^2}{\hat{\sigma}^2} \right)$$

$$\propto \exp\left(-\frac{1}{2} \frac{\mu^2 - 2\mu\hat{\mu} + \hat{\mu}^2}{\hat{\sigma}^2/n} \right),$$

which is a normal pdf with mean $\hat{\mu}$ and variance $\hat{\sigma}^2/n$. The 95% HPD interval is $\hat{\mu} \pm 1.96 \hat{\sigma}/\sqrt{n}$.

15.4 (a)

$$\pi(\theta | \mathbf{x}) \propto \frac{(\prod x_j) \exp(-\theta^{-1} \sum x_j)}{\theta^{200}} \frac{\exp(-\lambda\theta^{-1})}{\theta^{\beta+1}}$$

$$\propto \frac{\exp[-\theta^{-1}(\lambda + \sum x_j)]}{\theta^{201+\beta}},$$

which is an inverse gamma pdf with parameters $200 + \beta$ and $30,000 + \lambda$.

(b) $E(2\theta | \mathbf{x}) = 2\frac{30,000+\lambda}{200+\beta-1}$. At $\beta = \lambda = 0$, it is $2\frac{30,000}{199} = 301.51$ while at $\beta = 2$ and $\lambda = 250$, it is $2\frac{30,250}{201} = 301.00$. For the first case, the inverse gamma parameters are 200 and 30,000. For the lower limit,

$$0.025 = \Pr(2\theta < a) = F(a/2) = 1 - \Gamma(200; 60,000/a)$$

for $a = 262.41$. Similarly, the upper limit is 346.34. With parameters 202 and 30,250, the interval is (262.14,345.51).

(c) $\text{Var}(2\theta|\mathbf{x}) = 4\,\text{Var}(\theta|\mathbf{x}) = 4\left[\frac{(30,000+\lambda)^2}{(199+\beta)(198+\beta)} - \left(\frac{30,000+\lambda}{199+\beta}\right)^2\right]$. The two variances are 459.13 and 452.99. The two CIs are 301.51 ± 42.00 and 301.00 ± 41.72.

(d) $l = -\theta^{-1}30,000 - 200\ln\theta$. $l' = \theta^{-2}30,000 - 2000\theta^{-1} = 0$. $\hat{\theta} = 150$. For the variance, $l' = \theta^{-2}\sum x_j - 2000\theta^{-1}$, $l'' = -2\theta^{-3}\sum x_j + 2000\theta^{-2}$, $\text{E}(-l'') = 2\theta^{-3}(2000\theta) - 2000\theta^{-2} = 2000\theta^{-2}$ and so $\text{Var}(\hat{\theta}) \doteq \theta^2/200$ and $\text{Var}(2\theta) \doteq \theta^2/50$. An approximate CI is $300 \pm 1.96(150)/\sqrt{50} = 300 \pm 41.58$.

15.5 (a)
$$\begin{aligned}
f(x) &= \int_0^1 \binom{K}{x}\theta^x(1-\theta)^{K-x}\frac{\Gamma(a+b)}{\Gamma(a)\Gamma(b)}\theta^{a-1}(1-\theta)^{b-1}d\theta \\
&= \binom{K}{x}\frac{\Gamma(a+b)}{\Gamma(a)\Gamma(b)}\frac{\Gamma(x+a)\Gamma(K-x+b)}{\Gamma(a+b+K)} \\
&= \frac{K!}{x!(K-x)!}\frac{\Gamma(x+a)}{\Gamma(a)}\frac{\Gamma(K-x+b)}{\Gamma(b)}\frac{\Gamma(a+b)}{\Gamma(a+b+K)} \\
&= \frac{a(a+1)\cdots(x+a-1)\,b(b+1)\cdots(K-x+b-1)}{x!}\frac{1}{(K-x)!} \\
&\quad \times\frac{K!}{(a+b)\cdots(K+a+b-1)} \\
&= \frac{(-1)^x\binom{-a}{x}(-1)^{K-x}\binom{-b}{K-x}}{(-1)^K\binom{-a-b}{K}} = \frac{\binom{-a}{x}\binom{-b}{K-x}}{\binom{-a-b}{K}}.
\end{aligned}$$

Also,
$$\text{E}(X|\theta) = K\theta,\ \text{E}(X) = \text{E}[\text{E}(X|\theta)] = \text{E}(K\theta) = K\frac{a}{a+b}.$$

(b) $\pi(\theta|\mathbf{x}) \propto \theta^{\sum x_j}(1-\theta)^{\sum K_j - x_j}\theta^{a-1}(1-\theta)^{b-1}$, which is a beta density. Therefore, the actual posterior distribution is

$$\pi(\theta|\mathbf{x}) = \frac{\Gamma(a+b+\sum K_j)}{\Gamma(a+\sum x_j)\Gamma(b+\sum K_j+\Sigma x_j)}\theta^{a+\Sigma x_j-1}(1-\theta)^{b+\Sigma K_j-\Sigma x_j-1}$$

with mean
$$\text{E}(\theta|\mathbf{x}) = \frac{a+\sum x_j}{a+b+\sum K_j}.$$

15.6 (a)
$$
\begin{aligned}
f(x) &= \int_0^\infty \theta e^{-\theta x} \frac{\theta^{\alpha-1} e^{-\theta/\beta}}{\Gamma(\alpha)\beta^\alpha} d\theta \\
&= \frac{1}{\Gamma(\alpha)\beta^\alpha} \int_0^\infty \theta^\alpha e^{-\theta(x+\beta^{-1})} d\theta \\
&= \frac{1}{\Gamma(\alpha)\beta^\alpha} \Gamma(\alpha+1)(x+\beta^{-1})^{-\alpha-1} \\
&= \alpha\beta^{-\alpha}(\beta^{-1}+x)^{-\alpha-1}.
\end{aligned}
$$

Using $E(X|\theta) = \theta^{-1}$,

$$
\begin{aligned}
E(X) &= E[E(X|\theta)] = E(\theta^{-1}) \\
&= \int_0^\infty \theta^{-1} \frac{\theta^{\alpha-1} e^{-\theta/\beta}}{\Gamma(\alpha)\beta^\alpha} d\theta = \frac{\Gamma(\alpha-1)\beta^{\alpha-1}}{\Gamma(\alpha)\beta^\alpha} = \frac{1}{\beta(\alpha-1)}.
\end{aligned}
$$

(b) $\pi(\theta|\mathbf{x}) \propto \theta^n e^{-\theta\Sigma x_j} \theta^{\alpha-1} e^{-\theta/\beta} = \theta^{n+\alpha-1} e^{-\theta(\Sigma x_j + \beta^{-1})}$, which is a gamma density. Therefore, the actual posterior distribution is

$$
\pi(\theta|\mathbf{x}) = \frac{\theta^{n+\alpha-1} e^{-\theta(\Sigma x_j + \beta^{-1})}}{\Gamma(n+\alpha)(\sum x_j + \beta^{-1})^{-n-\alpha}},
$$

with mean

$$
E(\theta|\mathbf{x}) = \frac{n+\alpha}{\sum x_j + \beta^{-1}}.
$$

15.7 (a)
$$
\begin{aligned}
f(x) &= \int f(x|\theta)b(\theta)d\theta \\
&= \binom{r+x-1}{x} \frac{\Gamma(a+b)}{\Gamma(a)\Gamma(b)} \int_0^1 \theta^{r+a-1}(1-\theta)^{b+x-1} d\theta \\
&= \binom{r+x-1}{x} \frac{\Gamma(a+b)}{\Gamma(a)\Gamma(b)} \frac{\Gamma(r+a)\Gamma(b+x)}{\Gamma(r+a+b+x)} \\
&= \frac{\Gamma(r+x)}{\Gamma(r)x!} \frac{\Gamma(a+b)}{\Gamma(a)\Gamma(b)} \frac{\Gamma(a+r)\Gamma(b+x)}{\Gamma(a+r+b+x)}.
\end{aligned}
$$

(b)
$$
\begin{aligned}
\pi(\theta|\mathbf{x}) &\propto \prod f(x_j|\theta)b(\theta) \\
&\propto \theta^{nr}(1-\theta)^{\Sigma x_j} \theta^{a-1}(1-\theta)^{b-1} \\
&= \theta^{a+nr-1}(1-\theta)^{b+\Sigma x_j-1}.
\end{aligned}
$$

Hence, $\pi(\theta|\mathbf{x})$ is beta with parameters

$$
\begin{aligned}
a^* &= \alpha + nr, \\
b^* &= b + \sum x_j, \\
E(\theta|\mathbf{x}) &= \frac{a^*}{a^*+b^*} = \frac{a+nr}{a+nr+b+\sum x_j}.
\end{aligned}
$$

15.8 (a)

$$
\begin{aligned}
f(x) &= \int f(x|\theta)b(\theta)d\theta = \int_0^\infty \sqrt{\frac{\theta}{2\pi}} e^{-\frac{\theta}{2}(x-\mu)^2} \frac{\beta^\alpha}{\Gamma(\alpha)} \theta^{\alpha-1} e^{-\beta\theta} d\theta \\
&= \frac{\beta^\alpha}{(2\pi)^{1/2}\Gamma(\alpha)} \int_0^\infty \theta^{\frac{1}{2}+\alpha-1} \exp\left\{-\theta\left[\frac{1}{2}(x-\mu)^2+\beta\right]\right\} d\theta \\
&= \frac{\beta^\alpha}{(2\pi)^{1/2}\Gamma(\alpha)} \frac{\Gamma\left(\alpha+\frac{1}{2}\right)}{\left[\frac{1}{2}(x-\mu)^2+\beta\right]^{\alpha+\frac{1}{2}}} \\
&= \frac{\Gamma\left(\alpha+\frac{1}{2}\right)}{\sqrt{2\pi\beta}\Gamma(\alpha)} \left[1+\frac{1}{2\beta}(x-\mu)^2\right]^{-\alpha-\frac{1}{2}}.
\end{aligned}
$$

(b) $\pi(\theta|\mathbf{x}) \propto \left[\prod f(x_j|\theta)\right] \pi(\theta)$

$$
\begin{aligned}
&\propto \theta^{n/2} \exp\left[-\frac{\theta}{2}\sum(x_j-\mu)^2\right] \theta^{\alpha-1} e^{-\beta\theta} \\
&= \theta^{\frac{n}{2}+\alpha-1} \exp\left\{-\theta\left[\frac{1}{2}\sum(x_j-\mu)^2+\beta\right]\right\} = \theta^{\alpha^*-1} e^{-\theta\beta^*},
\end{aligned}
$$

where $\alpha^* = \alpha + \frac{n}{2}$, $\beta^* = \beta + \frac{1}{2}\sum(x_j-\mu)^2$. Therefore, $b(\theta|\mathbf{x})$ is gamma (α^*, β^*) and $E(\theta|\mathbf{x}) = \frac{\alpha^*}{\beta^*} = \frac{\alpha+\frac{n}{2}}{\beta+\frac{1}{2}\sum(x_j-\mu)^2}$.

15.9 (a) By the convolution formula,

$$
\begin{aligned}
f_{X_j|\Theta}(x_j|\theta) &= \sum_{y=0}^{x_j} f_{Y_{2j}|\Theta}(y|\theta) f_{Y_{1j}|\Theta}(x_j-y|\theta) \\
&= \sum_{y=0}^{x_j} \binom{N}{y} \left(\frac{\theta}{1+\theta}\right)^y \left(\frac{1}{1+\theta}\right)^{N-y} \frac{\theta^{x_j-y}e^{-\theta}}{(x_j-y)!} \\
&= \frac{\theta^{x_j}\left[\sum_{y=0}^{x_j} \binom{N}{y}/(x_j-y)!\right]}{e^\theta(1+\theta)^N}.
\end{aligned}
$$

The pf is of the form (5.6) with $r(\theta) = \ln\theta$, $p(x) = \sum_{y=0}^x \binom{N}{y}/(x-y)!$, and $q(\theta) = e^\theta(1+\theta)^N$.

(b) Theorem 15.18 applies, yielding

$$
\begin{aligned}
\pi(\theta) &= \frac{[q(\theta)]^{-k}e^{\mu k r(\theta)}r'(\theta)}{c(\mu,k)} \\
&= \frac{e^{-k\theta}(1+\theta)^{-Nk}e^{\mu k \ln\theta}\theta^{-1}}{c(\mu,k)} \\
&= \frac{\theta^{\mu k-1}(1+\theta)^{-Nk}e^{-k\theta}}{c(\mu,k)}.
\end{aligned}
$$

Because $\int_0^\infty \pi(\theta)d\theta = 1$,

$$
\begin{aligned}
c(\mu, k) &= \int_0^\infty \theta^{\mu k-1}(1+\theta)^{-Nk}e^{-k\theta}\,d\theta \\
&= \int_0^\infty t^{\mu k-1}(1+t)^{(\mu k-Nk+1)-\mu k-1}e^{-kt}\,dt \\
&= \Gamma(\mu k)\Psi(\mu k, \mu k - Nk + 1, k).
\end{aligned}
$$

15.10 (a) Let N be Poisson(λ).

$$
\begin{aligned}
f(x) &= \sum_{n=x}^\infty \frac{n!}{x!(n-x)!} \frac{p^x(1-p)^{n-x}e^{-\lambda}\lambda^n}{n!} \\
&= \left(\frac{p}{1-p}\right)^x \frac{e^{-\lambda}}{x!} \sum_{n=x}^\infty \frac{[(1-p)\lambda]^n}{(n-x)!} \\
&= \left(\frac{p}{1-p}\right)^x \frac{e^{-\lambda}}{x!} \sum_{n=0}^\infty \frac{[(1-p)\lambda]^{n+x}}{n!} \\
&= \left(\frac{p}{1-p}\right)^x \frac{e^{-\lambda}}{x!}[(1-p)\lambda]^x e^{(1-p)\lambda} \\
&= \frac{e^{-p\lambda}(p\lambda)^x}{x!},
\end{aligned}
$$

a Poisson distribution with parameter $p\lambda$.

(b) Let N be binomial(m, r).

$$
\begin{aligned}
f(x) &= \sum_{n=x}^m \frac{n!}{x!(n-x)!} p^x(1-p)^{n-x} \frac{m!}{n!(m-n)!} r^n(1-r)^{m-n} \\
&= \left(\frac{p}{1-p}\right)^x (1-r)^m \frac{m!}{x!} \sum_{n=x}^m \left(\frac{[1-p]r}{1-r}\right)^n \frac{1}{(n-x)!(m-n)!} \\
&= \left(\frac{p}{1-p}\right)^x (1-r)^m \frac{m!}{x!} \sum_{n=0}^{m-x} \left(\frac{[1-p]r}{1-r}\right)^{n+x} \frac{1}{n!(m-n-x)!}
\end{aligned}
$$

$$= \left(\frac{p}{1-p}\right)^x (1-r)^m \frac{m!}{x!} \left(\frac{[1-p]r}{1-r}\right)^x \frac{1}{(m-x)!}$$

$$\times \sum_{n=0}^{m-x} \left(\frac{[1-p]r}{1-rp}\right)^n \left(\frac{1-r}{1-rp}\right)^{-n} \frac{(m-x)!}{n!(m-n-x)!}$$

$$= \left(\frac{pr}{1-r}\right)^x (1-r)^m \frac{m!}{x!(m-x)!} \left(\frac{1-r}{1-rp}\right)^{-m+x}$$

$$\times \sum_{n=0}^{m-x} \left(\frac{[1-p]r}{1-rp}\right)^n \left(\frac{1-r}{1-rp}\right)^{m-n-x} \frac{(m-x)!}{n!(m-n-x)!}$$

$$= \frac{m!}{x!(m-x)!} (pr)^x (1-rp)^{m-x},$$

which is binomial (m, pr).

(c) Let N be negative binomial (r, β).

$$f(x) = \sum_{n=x}^{\infty} \frac{n!}{x!(n-x)!} p^x (1-p)^{n-x}$$

$$\times \left(\frac{\beta}{1+\beta}\right)^n \left(\frac{1}{1+\beta}\right)^r \frac{r(r+1)\cdots(r+n-1)}{n!}$$

$$= \left(\frac{p}{1-p}\right)^x \left(\frac{1}{1+\beta}\right)^r \frac{1}{x!} \sum_{n=x}^{\infty} \left[\frac{\beta(1-p)}{1+\beta}\right]^n \frac{r(r+1)\cdots(r+n-1)}{(n-x)!}$$

$$= \left(\frac{p}{1-p}\right)^x \left(\frac{1}{1+\beta}\right)^r \frac{1}{x!} \sum_{n=0}^{\infty} \left[\frac{\beta(1-p)}{1+\beta}\right]^{n+x}$$

$$\times \frac{r(r+1)\cdots(r+n+x-1)}{n!}$$

$$= \left(\frac{p\beta}{1+\beta}\right)^x \left(\frac{1}{1+\beta}\right)^r \frac{r(r+1)\cdots(r+x-1)}{x!}$$

$$\times \sum_{n=0}^{\infty} \left[\frac{\beta(1-p)}{1+\beta}\right]^n \frac{(r+x)\cdots(r+n+x-1)}{n!}$$

and the summand is almost a negative binomial density with the term

$$\left[1 - \frac{\beta(1-p)}{1+\beta}\right]^{r+x} = \left(\frac{1+p\beta}{1+\beta}\right)^{r+x}$$

missing. Place this term in the sum so the sum is one and then divide by it to produce

$$f(x) = \left(\frac{1+p\beta}{1+\beta}\right)^{-r-x}$$

$$= \left(\frac{p\beta}{1+p\beta}\right)^x \left(\frac{1}{1+p\beta}\right)^r \frac{r(r+1)\cdots(r+x-1)}{x!},$$

which is negative binomial with parameters r and $p\beta$.

15.11 Let D be the die. Then

$$\Pr(D = 2|2, 3, 4, 1, 4)$$

$$= \frac{\Pr(2, 3, 4, 1, 4|D = 2)\Pr(D = 2)}{\Pr(2, 3, 4, 1, 4|D = 1)\Pr(D = 1) + \Pr(2, 3, 4, 1, 4|D = 2)\Pr(D = 2)}$$

$$= \frac{\frac{1}{6}\frac{1}{6}\frac{3}{6}\frac{1}{6}\frac{3}{6}\frac{1}{2}}{\frac{3}{6}\frac{1}{6}\frac{1}{6}\frac{1}{6}\frac{1}{6}\frac{1}{2} + \frac{1}{6}\frac{1}{6}\frac{3}{6}\frac{1}{6}\frac{3}{6}\frac{1}{2}} = \frac{3}{4}.$$

15.12 (a) $\Pr(Y = 0) = \int_0^1 e^{-\theta}(1)d\theta = 1 - e^{-1} = 0.63212 > 0.35.$

(b) $\Pr(Y = 0) = \int_0^1 \theta^2(1)d\theta = 1/3 < 0.35.$

(c) $\Pr(Y = 0) = \int_0^1 (1 - \theta)^2(1)d\theta = 1/3 < 0.35.$
   Only (a) is possible.

15.13 $\Pr(H = 1/4|d = 1)$

$$= \frac{\Pr(d = 1|H = 1/4)\Pr(H = 1/4)}{\Pr(d = 1|H = 1/4)\Pr(H = 1/4) + \Pr(d = 1|H = 1/2)\Pr(H = 1/2)}$$

$$= \frac{\frac{1}{4}\frac{4}{5}}{\frac{1}{4}\frac{4}{5} + \frac{1}{2}\frac{1}{5}} = \frac{2}{3}.$$

15.14 The equations are $\alpha\theta = 0.14$ and $\alpha\theta^2 = 0.0004$. The solution is $\alpha = 49$ and $\theta = 1/350$. From Example 15.8, the posterior distribution is gamma with $\alpha = 49 + 110 = 159$ and $\theta = (1/350)/[620(1/350) + 1] = 1/970$. The mean is $159/970 = 0.16392$ and the variance is $159/970^2 = 0.00016899$.

15.15 The posterior pdf is proportional to

$$te^{-t5}te^{-t} = t^2e^{-t6},$$

which is a gamma distribution with $\alpha = 3$ and $\beta = 1/6$. The posterior pdf is $\pi(t|x = 5) = 108t^2 e^{-6t}$.

15.16 $S_m|Q \sim \text{bin}(m, Q)$ and $Q \sim \text{beta}(1, 99)$. Then,

$$E(S_m) = E[E(S_m|Q)] = E(mQ) = m\frac{1}{1+99} = 0.01m.$$

For the mean to be at least 50, m must be at least 5,000.

15.17 $\pi(\beta|x) \propto f(x|\beta)\pi(\beta) = \beta^{-1}e^{-x/\beta}100\beta^{-3}e^{-10/\beta} \propto \beta^{-4}e^{-(10+x)/\beta}$. This is an inverse gamma distribution with $\alpha = 3$ and $\theta = 10 + x$. The posterior mean is $\theta/(\alpha - 1) = (10 + x)/2$.

15.18 The likelihood function is

$$
\begin{aligned}
L(\theta) &= \theta^{-1}e^{-1100/\theta}\theta^{-1}e^{-3200/\theta}\theta^{-1}e^{-3300/\theta}\theta^{-1}e^{-3500/\theta}\theta^{-1}e^{-3900/\theta} \\
&\quad \times [e^{-4000/\theta}]^{495} \\
&= \theta^{-5}e^{-1,995,000/\theta}.
\end{aligned}
$$

The posterior density is proportional to

$$\pi(\theta|\mathbf{x}) \propto \theta^{-6}e^{-1,995,000/\theta}.$$

This is an inverse gamma distribution with parameters 5 and 1,995,000. The posterior mean is $1,995,000/4 = 498,750$. The maximum likelihood estimate divides by 5 rather than 4.

15.19 (a)

$$
\begin{aligned}
f(x|\theta_1, \theta_2) &= \sqrt{\frac{\theta_2}{2\pi}}\exp\left[-\frac{\theta_2}{2}(x - \theta_1)^2\right], \\
b(\theta_1|\theta_2) &= \sqrt{\frac{\theta_2}{2\pi\sigma^2}}\exp\left[-\frac{\theta_2}{2\sigma^2}(\theta_1 - \mu)^2\right], \\
b(\theta_2) &= \frac{\beta^\alpha}{\Gamma(\alpha)}\theta_2^{\alpha-1}e^{-\beta\theta_2}.
\end{aligned}
$$

$$\pi\left(\theta_1, \theta_2 | \mathbf{x}\right) \quad \propto \quad \left[\prod_{j=1}^{r} f(x_j | \theta_1, \theta_2)\right] \pi\left(\theta_1 | \theta_2\right) \pi\left(\theta_2\right)$$

$$\propto \quad \theta_2^{n/2} \exp\left[-\frac{\theta_2}{2} \sum (x_j - \theta_1)^2\right] \theta_2^{1/2}$$

$$\times \exp\left[-\frac{\theta_2}{2\sigma_2} (\theta_1 - \mu)^2\right] \theta_2^{\alpha-1} e^{-\beta\theta_2}$$

$$= \quad \theta_2^{\alpha + \frac{n+1}{2} - 1}$$

$$\times \exp\left\{-\theta_2\left[\beta + \frac{1}{2}\left(\frac{\theta_1 - \mu}{\sigma}\right)^2 + \frac{1}{2}\sum (x_j - \theta_1)^2\right]\right\}.$$

$$\pi\left(\theta_1 | \theta_2, \mathbf{x}\right) \quad \propto \quad \pi\left(\theta_1, \theta_2 | \mathbf{x}\right)$$

$$\propto \quad \exp\left[-\frac{\theta_2}{2}\left(\frac{\theta_1^2}{\sigma^2} - \frac{2\mu\theta_1}{\sigma^2} + n\theta_1^2 - 2\theta_1 \sum x_j\right)\right]$$

$$= \quad \exp -\frac{1}{2}\left[\theta_1^2\left(\frac{\theta_2}{\sigma_2} + n\theta_2\right) - 2\theta_1\left(\frac{\mu\theta_2}{\sigma^2} + \theta_2 \sum x_j\right)\right],$$

which is normal with variance $\sigma_*^2 = \left[\frac{\theta_2}{\sigma^2} + n\theta_2\right]^{-1} = \frac{\sigma^2}{\theta_2(1+n\sigma^2)}$ and mean μ_*, which satisfies $\frac{\mu_*}{\sigma_*^2} = \frac{\mu\theta_2}{\sigma^2} + \theta_2 n\bar{x}$. Then, $\mu_* = \frac{\mu}{1+n\sigma^2} + \frac{n\sigma^2\bar{x}}{1+n\sigma^2}$.

For the posterior distribution of θ_2,

$$\pi\left(\theta_2 | \mathbf{x}\right) \quad \propto \quad \int \pi\left(\theta_1, \theta_2 | \mathbf{x}\right) d\theta_1$$

$$= \quad \theta_2^{\alpha + \frac{n+1}{2} - 1} e^{-\theta_2\beta}$$

$$\times \int \exp\left\{-\frac{\theta_2}{2}\left[\left(\frac{\theta_1 - \mu}{\sigma}\right)^2 + \sum (x_j - \theta_1)^2\right]\right\} d\theta_1.$$

Now $\sum (x_j - \theta_1)^2 = \sum (x_j - \bar{x})^2 + n\left(\bar{x} - \theta_1\right)^2$ and, therefore,

$$\pi\left(\theta_2 | \mathbf{x}\right) \quad \propto \quad \theta_2^{\alpha + \frac{n+1}{2} - 1} \exp\left\{-\theta_2\left[\beta + \frac{1}{2}\sum (x_j - \bar{x})^2\right]\right\}$$

$$\times \int \exp\left\{-\frac{\theta_2}{2}\left[\left(\frac{\theta_1 - \mu}{\sigma}\right)^2 + n\left(\bar{x} - \theta_1\right)^2\right]\right\} d\theta_1.$$

To evaluate the integral, complete the square as follows:

$$-\frac{\theta_2}{2}\left[\left(\frac{\theta_1-\mu}{\sigma}\right)^2 + n\left(\bar{x}-\theta_1\right)^2\right]$$

$$= -\frac{\theta_2}{2}\left[\theta_1^2\left(\frac{1}{\sigma^2}+n\right) - 2\theta_1\left(\frac{\mu}{\sigma^2}+n\bar{x}\right) + \frac{\mu}{\sigma^2}+n\bar{x}^2\right]$$

$$= -\frac{1}{2}\theta_2\left(\frac{1}{\sigma^2}+n\right)\left(\theta_1-\frac{\mu+n\sigma^2\bar{x}}{1+n\sigma^2}\right)^2 + \frac{\theta_2}{2}\left[\frac{(\mu+n\sigma^2\bar{x})^2}{\sigma^2(1+n\sigma^2)}-\frac{\mu^2}{\sigma^2}-n\bar{x}\right].$$

The first term is a normal density and integrates to $[\theta_2(1/\sigma^2+n)]^{-1/2}$. The second term does not involve θ_1 and so factors out of the integral. The posterior density contains θ_2 raised to the $\alpha+\frac{n}{2}-1$ power and an exponential term involving θ_2 multiplied by

$$\beta + \frac{1}{2}\sum(x_j-\bar{x})^2 + \frac{1}{2}\left[\frac{(\mu+n\sigma^2\bar{x})^2}{\sigma^2(1+n\sigma^2)}-\frac{\mu^2}{\sigma^2}-n\bar{x}\right]$$

$$= \beta + \frac{1}{2}\sum(x_j-\bar{x})^2 + \frac{n(\bar{x}-\mu)^2}{2(1+n\sigma^2)}.$$

This constitutes a gamma density with the desired parameters.

(b) Because the mean of Θ_1 given Θ_2 and $\mathbf{x}$ does not depend on θ_2, it is also the mean of Θ_1 given just $\mathbf{x}$, which is μ_*. The mean of Θ_2 given $\mathbf{x}$ is the ratio of the parameters, or

$$\frac{\alpha+n/2}{\beta+\frac{1}{2}\sum(x_j-\bar{x})^2+\dfrac{n(\bar{x}-\mu)^2}{2(1+n\sigma^2)}}.$$

15.2   SECTION 15.3

15.20 By Exercise 5.26(a), $S|\Theta$ has pf of the form

$$f_{S|\Theta}(s|\theta) = \frac{p_n(s)e^{r(\theta)s}}{[q(\theta)]^n}.$$

Thus,

$$\pi(\theta|x) \propto f(x|\theta)\pi(\theta) = \left[\prod_{j=1}^n f(x_j|\theta)\right]\pi(\theta) \propto \frac{\exp\left[r(\theta)\sum_{j=1}^n x_j\right]\pi(\theta)}{[q(\theta)]^n},$$

or

$$\pi(\theta|x) \propto \frac{e^{r(\theta)s}\pi(\theta)}{[q(\theta)]^n}.$$

But $\pi(\theta|s) \propto f_{S|\Theta}(s|\theta)\pi(\theta) \propto \frac{e^{r(\theta)s}\pi(\theta)}{[q(\theta)]^n}$ also.

15.21 The posterior pdf is proportional to

$$\frac{e^{-\theta}\theta^0}{0!}e^{-\theta} = e^{-2\theta}.$$

This is an exponential distribution. The pdf is $\pi(\theta|y=0) = 2e^{-2\theta}$.

15.22 The posterior pdf is proportional to

$$\frac{e^{-\theta}\theta^1}{1!}\theta e^{-\theta} = \theta^2 e^{-2\theta}.$$

This is a gamma distribution with parameters 3 and 0.5. The pdf is $\pi(\theta|y = 1) = 4\theta^2 e^{-2\theta}$.

15.23 From Example 15.8, the posterior distribution is gamma with $\alpha = 50 + 177 = 227$ and $\theta = 0.002/[1,850(0.002) + 1] = 1/2,350$. The mean is $\alpha\theta = 0.096596$ and the variance is $\alpha\theta^2 = 0.000041105$. The coefficient of variation is $\sqrt{\alpha\theta^2}/(\alpha\theta) = 1/\sqrt{\alpha} = 0.066372$.

15.24 The posterior pdf is proportional to

$$\binom{3}{1}\theta^1(1 - \theta)^{3-1}6\theta(1 - \theta) \propto \theta^2(1 - \theta)^3.$$

This is a beta distribution with pdf $\pi(\theta|r = 1) = 60\theta^2(1 - \theta)^3$.

15.25 The prior exponential distribution is also a gamma distribution with $\alpha = 1$ and $\theta = 2$. From Example 15.8, the posterior distribution is gamma with $\alpha = 1 + 3 = 4$ and $\theta = 2/[1(2) + 1] = 2/3$. The pdf is $\pi(\lambda|y = 3) = 27\lambda^3 e^{-3\lambda/2}/32$.

15.26 (a) The posterior distribution is proportional to

$$\binom{3}{2}\theta^2(1 - \theta)280\theta^3(1 - \theta)^4 \propto \theta^5(1 - \theta)^5,$$

which is a beta distribution. The pdf is $\pi(\theta|y = 2) = 2772\theta^5(1 - \theta)^5$.

(b) The mean is $6/(6 + 6) = 0.5$.

15.27 The posterior distribution is $\pi(q|2) = 6q^2(1-q)^2 6p(1-q) \propto q^3(1-q)^3$. The mode can be determined by setting the derivative equal to zero. $0 = 3q^2(1-q)^3 - 3q^3(1-q)^2$, which is equivalent to $q = 1 - q$ for $q = 0.5$.

CHAPTER 16

CHAPTER 16 SOLUTIONS

16.1 SECTION 16.3

16.1 For Data Set B truncated at 50, the maximum likelihood parameter estimates are $\hat{\tau} = 0.80990$ and $\hat{\theta} = 675.25$, leading to the graph in Figure 16.1.

For Data Set B censored at 1,000, the estimates are $\hat{\tau} = 0.99984$ and $\hat{\theta} = 718.00$. The graph is in Figure 16.2.

For Data Set C, the parameter estimates are $\hat{\tau} = 0.47936$ and $\hat{\theta} = 11,976$. The plot is given in Figure 16.3.

16.2 For Data Set B truncated at 50, the plot is given in Figure 16.4.

For Data Set B censored at 1,000, the plot is given in Figure 16.5.

16.3 The plot for Data Set B truncated at 50 is given in Figure 16.6.

For Data Set B censored at 1,000, the plot is given in Figure 16.7.

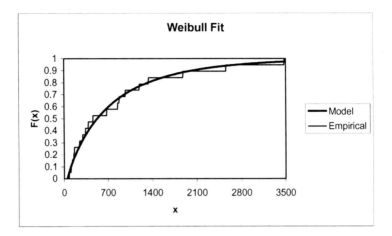

Figure 16.1 Cdf plot for Data Set B truncated at 50.

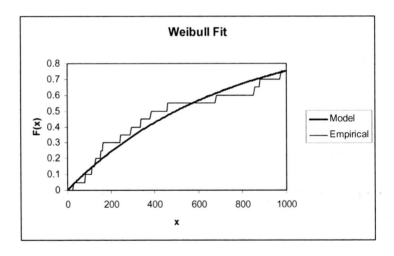

Figure 16.2 Cdf plot for Data Set B censored at 1,000.

16.2 SECTION 16.4

16.4 For Data Set B truncated at 50, the test statistic is 0.0887, while the critical value is unchanged from the example (0.3120). The null hypothesis is not rejected, and it is plausible that the data came from a Weibull population. For Data Set B censored at 1,000, the test statistic is 0.0991, while the critical value is 0.3041. The null hypothesis is not rejected.

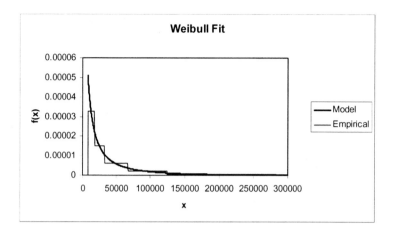

Figure 16.3   Pdf and histogram for Data Set C.

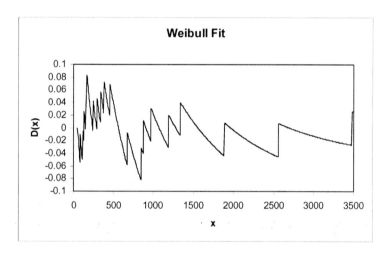

Figure 16.4   Difference plot for Data Set B truncated at 50.

16.5 The first step is to obtain the distribution function. It can be recognized as an inverse exponential distribution or the calculation done as

$$F(x) = \int_0^x 2y^{-2}e^{-2/y}dy = \int_{2/x}^\infty 2(2/z)^{-2}e^{-z}(2z^{-2})dz$$

$$= \int_{2/x}^\infty e^{-z}dz = e^{-2/x}.$$

In the first line, the substitution $z = 2/y$ was used. The calculations are in Table 16.1. The test statistic is the maximum from the final column, or 0.168.

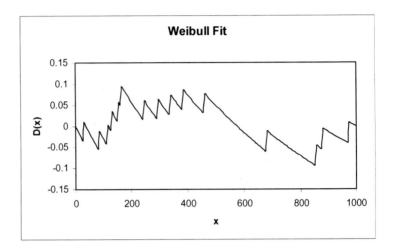

Figure 16.5   Difference plot for Data Set B censored at 1,000.

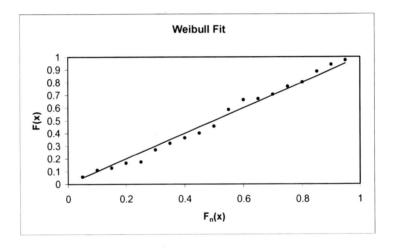

Figure 16.6 p–p plot for Data Set B truncated at 50.

16.6 The distribution function is

$$F(x) = \int_0^x 2(1+y)^{-3}dy = -(1+y)^{-2}\big|_0^x = 1 - (1+x)^{-2}.$$

The calculations are in Table 16.2. The test statistic is the maximum from the final column, 0.189.

16.7 For Data Set B truncated at 50, the test statistic is 0.1631, which is less than the critical value of 2.492, and the null hypothesis is not rejected.

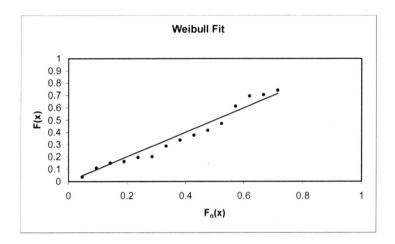

Figure 16.7 p–p plot for Data Set B censored at 1,000.

Table 16.1   Calculations for Exercise 16.5.

x	$F(x)$	Compare to	Max difference
1	0.135	0, 0.2	0.135
2	0.368	0.2, 0.4	0.168
3	0.513	0.4, 0.6	0.113
5	0.670	0.6, 0.8	0.130
13	0.857	0.8, 1	0.143

Table 16.2   Calculations for Exercise 16.6.

x	$F(x)$	Compare to	Max difference
0.1	0.174	0, 0.2	0.174
0.2	0.306	0.2, 0.4	0.106
0.5	0.556	0.4, 0.6	0.156
1.0	0.750	0.6, 0.8	0.150
1.3	0.811	0.8, 1	0.189

For Data Set B censored at 1,000, the test statistic is 0.1712 and the null hypothesis is again not rejected.

16.8 The calculations for Data Set B truncated at 50 are in Table 16.3. The sum is 0.3615. With three degrees of freedom, the critical value is 7.8147 and the Weibull model is not rejected. The p-value is 0.9481.

The calculations for Data Set B censored at 1,000 are in the Table 16.4. The sum is 0.5947. With two degrees of freedom, the critical value is 5.9915 and the Weibull model is not rejected. The p-value is 0.7428.

Table 16.3   Data Set B truncated at 50 for Exercise 16.8.

Range	$\hat{p}$	Expected	Observed	χ^2
50–150	0.1599	3.038	3	0.0005
150–250	0.1181	2.244	3	0.2545
250–500	0.2064	3.922	4	0.0015
500–1,000	0.2299	4.368	4	0.0310
1,000–2,000	0.1842	3.500	3	0.0713
2,000–∞	0.1015	1.928	2	0.0027

Table 16.4   Data Set B censored at 1,000 for Exercise 16.8.

Range	$\hat{p}$	Expected	Observed	χ^2
0–150	0.1886	3.772	4	0.0138
150–250	0.1055	2.110	3	0.3754
250–500	0.2076	4.151	4	0.0055
500–1,000	0.2500	4.999	4	0.1997
1,000–∞	0.2484	4.968	5	0.0002

Table 16.5   Data Set C truncated at 7,500 for Exercise 16.8.

Range	$\hat{p}$	Expected	Observed	χ^2
7,500–17,500	0.3299	42.230	42	0.0013
17,500–32,500	0.2273	29.096	29	0.0003
32,500–67,500	0.2178	27.878	28	0.0005
67,500–125,000	0.1226	15.690	17	0.1094
125,000–300,000	0.0818	10.472	9	0.2070
300,000–∞	0.0206	2.632	3	0.0513

The calculations for Data Set C are in Table 16.5. The sum is 0.3698. With three degrees of freedom, the critical value is 7.8147 and the Weibull model is not rejected. The p-value is 0.9464.

16.9 The calculations are in Table 16.6. For the test, there are three degrees of freedom (four groups less zero estimated parameters less one) and at a 5% significance level, the critical value is 7.81. The null hypothesis is accepted and, therefore, the data may have come from a population with the given survival function.

Table 16.6   Calculations for Exercise 16.9

Interval	Observed	Expected	Chi-square
0 to 1	21	$150F(1) = 150(2/20) = 15$	$\frac{6^2}{15} = 2.40$
1 to 2	27	$150[F(2) - F(1)] = 150(4/20) = 30$	$\frac{3^2}{30} = 0.30$
2 to 3	39	$150[F(3) - F(2)] = 150(6/20) = 45$	$\frac{6^2}{45} = 0.80$
3 to 4	63	$150[F(4) - F(3)] = 150(8/20) = 60$	$\frac{3^2}{60} = 0.15$
Total	150	150	3.65.

Table 16.7   Calculations for Exercise 16.10.

No. of claims	Observed	Expected	Chi-square
0	50	$365e^{-1.6438} = 70.53$	$\frac{20.53^2}{70.53} = 5.98$
1	122	$365(1.6438)e^{-1.6438} = 115.94$	$\frac{6.06^2}{115.94} = 0.32$
2	101	$365(1.6438)^2 e^{-1.6438}/2 = 95.29$	$\frac{5.71^2}{95.29} = 0.34$
3 or more	92	$365 - 70.53 - 115.94 - 95.29 = 83.24$	$\frac{8.76^2}{83.24} = 0.92$

16.10 Either recall that for a Poisson distribution the mle is the sample mean or derive it from

$$L(\lambda) = \left(e^{-\lambda}\right)^{50} \left(\lambda e^{-\lambda}\right)^{122} \left(\frac{\lambda^2 e^{-\lambda}}{2}\right)^{101} \left(\frac{\lambda^3 e^{-\lambda}}{6}\right)^{92} \propto \lambda^{600} e^{-365\lambda},$$

$$\ln L(\lambda) = 600 \ln \lambda - 365\lambda,$$
$$0 = 600\lambda^{-1} - 365,$$
$$\hat{\lambda} = 600/365 = 1.6438.$$

For the goodness-of-fit test, the calculations are in Table 16.7. The last two groups were combined. The total is 7.56. There are two degrees of freedom (four groups less one estimated parameter less one). At a 2.5% significance level, the critical value is 7.38 and, therefore, the null hypothesis is rejected. The Poisson model is not appropriate.

16.11 With 365 observations, the expected count for k accidents is

$$365\Pr(N = k) = \frac{365e^{-0.6}0.6^k}{k!}.$$

The test statistic is calculated in Table 16.8. The total of the last column is the test statistic of 2.85. With three degrees of freedom (four groups less one less zero estimated parameters), the critical value is 7.81 and the null hypothesis of a Poisson distribution cannot be rejected.

Table 16.8 Calculations for Exercise 16.11.

No. of accidents	Observed	Expected	Chi-square
0	209	200.32	0.38
1	111	120.19	0.70
2	33	36.06	0.26
3	7	7.21	1.51[b]
4	3	1.08	
5	2	0.14[a]	

[a]This is 365 less the sum of the other entries to reflect the expected for five or more accidents.
[b]The last three cells are grouped for an observed of 12 and an expected of 8.43.

16.12
$$\chi^2 = \sum_{j=1}^{20} \frac{(O_j - 50)^2}{50} = 0.02 \left[\sum_{j=1}^{20} O_j^2 - 100 \sum_{j=1}^{20} O_j + 20(50)^2 \right]$$
$$= 0.02[51{,}850 - 100(1{,}000) + 50{,}000] = 37.$$

With 19 degrees of freedom, the probability of exceeding 37 is 0.007935.

16.13 The density function and likelihood functions are

$$f(x) = \frac{\alpha \theta^\alpha}{(x + \theta)^{\alpha+1}}, \quad L(\alpha, \theta) = \frac{\alpha^{20} \theta^{20\alpha}}{\prod_{j=1}^{20} (x_j + \theta)^{\alpha+1}}.$$

Then,

$$l(\alpha, \theta) = 20 \ln(\alpha) + 20\alpha \ln(\theta) - (\alpha + 1) \sum_{j=1}^{20} \ln(x_j + \theta).$$

Under the null hypothesis, $\alpha = 2$ and $\theta = 3.1$, the loglikelihood value is -58.7810. Under the alternative hypothesis, $\alpha = 2$ and $\theta = 7.0$, and the loglikelihood value is -55.3307. Twice the difference is 6.901. There is one degree of freedom (no estimated parameters in the null hypothesis versus one in the alternative). The p-value is the probability of exceeding 6.901, which is 0.008615.

16.14
$$L = \prod_{k=1}^{6} \frac{(n_k + e_k + 1) \cdots e_k}{n_k!} \left(\frac{1}{1+\beta} \right)^{e_k} \left(\frac{\beta}{1+\beta} \right)^{n_k}$$
$$\propto \beta^{\Sigma n_k} (1 + \beta)^{-\Sigma(n_k + e_k)}.$$

The logarithm is

$$(\ln \beta) \sum_{k=1}^{6} n_k - [\log(1+\beta)] \sum_{k=1}^{6} (n_k + e_k),$$

and setting the derivative equal to zero yields

$$\beta^{-1} \sum_{k=1}^{6} n_k - (1+\beta)^{-1} \sum_{k=1}^{6} (n_k + e_k) = 0$$

for $\hat{\beta} = \sum_{k=1}^{6} n_k / \sum_{k=1}^{6} e_k = 0.09772$. The expected number is $E_k = \hat{\beta} e_k$, which is exactly the same as for the Poisson model. Because the variance is $e_k \beta (1+\beta)$, the goodness-of-fit test statistic equals the Poisson test statistic divided by $1+\beta$, or $6.19/1.09772 = 5.64$. The geometric model is accepted.

16.15 The null hypothesis is that the data come from a gamma distribution with $\alpha = 1$, that is, from an exponential distribution. The alternative hypothesis is that α has some other value. From Example 13.4, for the exponential distribution, $\hat{\theta} = 1,424.4$ and the loglikelihood value is -165.230. For the gamma distribution, $\hat{\alpha} = 0.55616$ and $\hat{\theta} = 2,561.1$. The loglikelihood at the maximum is $L_0 = -162.293$. The test statistic is $2(-162.293 + 165.230) = 5.874$. The p-value based on one degree of freedom is 0.0154, indicating there is considerable evidence to support the gamma model over the exponential model.

16.16 For the exponential distribution, $\hat{\theta} = 29,721$ and the loglikelihood is -406.027. For the gamma distribution, $\hat{\alpha} = 0.37139$, $\hat{\theta} = 83,020$, and the loglikelihood is -360.496. For the transformed gamma distribution, $\hat{\alpha} = 3.02515$, $\hat{\theta} = 489.97$, $\hat{\tau} = 0.32781$, and the value of the loglikelihood function is -357.535. The models can only be compared in pairs. For exponential (null) versus gamma (alternative), the test statistic is 91.061 and the p-value is essentially zero. The exponential model is convincingly rejected. For gamma (null) versus transformed gamma (alternative), the test statistic is 5.923 with a p-value of 0.015 and there is strong evidence for the transformed gamma model. Exponential versus transformed gamma could also be tested (using two degrees of freedom), but there is no point.

16.17 Poisson expected counts are

$$
\begin{array}{rcl}
0 & : & 10,000(e^{-0.1001}) = 9,047.47, \\
1 & : & 10,000(0.1001e^{-0.1001}) = 905.65, \\
2 & : & 10,000(0.1001^2 e^{-0.1001}/2) = 45.33, \\
3 \text{ or more} & : & 10,000 - 9,047.47 - 905.65 - 45.33 = 1.55.
\end{array}
$$

The test statistic is

$$(9,048 - 9,047.47)^2/9,047.47 + (905 - 905.65)^2/906.65$$
$$+(45 - 45.33)^2/45.33 + (2 - 1.55)^2/1.44 = 0.14.$$

There are two degrees of freedom (four groups less one and less one estimated parameter) and so the 5% critical value is 5.99 and the null hypothesis (and therefore, the Poisson model) is accepted.

Geometric expected counts are 9,090.08, 827.12, 75.26, and 7.54, and the test statistic is 23.77. With two degrees of freedom, the model is rejected.

Negative binomial expected counts are 9,048.28, 904.12, 45.97, and 1.63, and the test statistic is 0.11. With one degree of freedom, the model is accepted.

Binomial ($m = 4$) expected counts are 9,035.95, 927.71, and 36.34 (extra grouping is needed to keep the counts above 1), and the test statistic is 3.70. With one degree of freedom, the model is accepted (critical value is 3.84).

16.18 Poisson expected counts are 847.05, 140.61, and 12.34 (grouping needed to keep expected counts above 1), and the test statistic is 5.56. With one degree of freedom, the model is rejected.

Geometric expected counts are 857.63, 122.10, 17.38, and 2.89, and the test statistic is 2.67. With two degrees of freedom, the model is accepted.

Negative binomial expected counts are 862.45, 114.26, 19.10, and 4.19, and the test statistic is 2.50. With one degree of freedom, the model is accepted.

Binomial ($m = 7$) expected counts are 845.34, 143.74, and 10.92, and test statistic is 8.48. With one degree of freedom, the model is rejected.

16.19 (a) To achieve a reasonable expected count, the first three rows are combined as well as the last two. The test statistic is 16,308. With five degrees of freedom, the model is clearly rejected.

(b) All nine rows can now be used. The test statistic is 146.84. With seven degrees of freedom, the model is clearly rejected.

(c) The test statistic is 30.16. With six degrees of freedom, the model is clearly rejected.

16.20 $\bar{x} = 0.155140$ and $s^2 = 0.179314$. $E(N) = \lambda_1\lambda_2$ and $\text{Var}(N) = \lambda_1(\lambda_2 + \lambda_2^2)$. Solving the equations yields $\hat{\lambda}_1 = 0.995630$ and $\hat{\lambda}_2 = 0.155821$. For the secondary distribution, $f_j = e^{-0.155821}(0.155821)^j/j!$ and then $g_0 = \exp[-0.99563($ $e^{-0.155821})] = 0.866185$. Then,

$$g_k = \sum_{j=1}^{k} \frac{0.99563}{k} j f_j g_{k-j}.$$

For the goodness-of-fit test with two degrees of freedom, see Table 16.9, and the model is clearly rejected.

Table 16.9   Calculations for Exercise 16.20.

Value	Observed	Expected	Chi-square
0	103,704	103,814.9	0.12
1	14,075	13,782.0	6.23
2	1,766	1,988.6	24.92
3	255	238.9	1.09
4+	53	28.6	20.82
Total			53.18

16.21 (a)

$$\chi^2 = \frac{(20,592-20,596.76)^2}{20,596.76} + \frac{(2,651-2,631.03)^2}{2,631.03} + \frac{(297-318.37)^2}{318.37}$$
$$+ \frac{(41-37.81)^2}{37.81} + \frac{(8-5.03)^2}{5.03}$$

$$= 0.0011 + 0.1516 + 1.4344 + 0.2691 + 1.7537 = 3.6099,$$

$$\text{df} = 5 - 2 - 1 = 2, \text{ given } \alpha = 0.05, \Rightarrow$$

$$\chi^2_{2,0.05} = 5.99 > 3.6099 \Rightarrow \text{ fit is acceptable, or}$$
$$p = Pr(x^2_{(2)} > 3.6099) \approx 0.16 \Rightarrow \text{ fit is acceptable.}$$

(b)

$$a = \frac{\beta}{1+\beta}, \quad b = \frac{(r-1)\beta}{1+\beta}, \quad p_n = \left(a + \frac{b}{n}\right)p_{n-1},$$

$$\hat{p}_1 = (\hat{a}+\hat{b})\hat{p}_0 \Leftrightarrow \hat{a}+\hat{b} = \frac{\hat{r}\hat{\beta}}{1+\hat{\beta}} = \frac{\hat{p}_1}{\hat{p}_0} = \frac{2,631.03}{20,596.76} = 0.12774,$$

$$\left(\hat{a}+\frac{\hat{b}}{2}\right) = \frac{(\hat{r}+1)}{2}\frac{\hat{\beta}}{1+\hat{\beta}} = \frac{\hat{p}_2}{\hat{p}_1} = \frac{318.37}{2,631.03} = 0.12101,$$

$$\frac{2\hat{r}}{\hat{r}+1} = \frac{0.12774}{0.12101} = 1.05565 \Rightarrow \hat{r}(2-1.05565) = 1.05565 \Rightarrow$$

$$\hat{r} = 1.11786, \quad \hat{a} = \frac{\hat{\beta}}{1+\hat{\beta}} = \frac{0.12774}{\hat{r}} = 0.11427$$

$$\Rightarrow \hat{\beta} = \frac{0.11427}{1-0.11427} = 0.12901.$$

16.3   SECTION 16.5

16.22 These are discrete data from a discrete population, so the normal and gamma models are not appropriate. There are two ways to distinguish among the three discrete options. One is to look at successive values of kn_k/n_{k-1}.

Table 16.10 Tests for Exercise 16.23.

Criterion	Exponential	Weibull	Trans. gam.
		B truncated at 50	
K–S	0.1340	0.0887	0.0775
A–D	0.4292	0.1631	0.1649
χ^2	1.4034	0.3615	0.5169
p-Value	0.8436	0.9481	0.7723
Loglikelihood	−146.063	−145.683	−145.661
SBC	−147.535	−148.628	−150.078
		B censored at 1,000	
K–S	0.0991	0.0991	N/A
A–D	0.1713	0.1712	N/A
χ^2	0.5951	0.5947	N/A
p-Value	0.8976	0.7428	N/A
Loglikelihood	−113.647	−113.647	N/A
SBC	−115.145	−116.643	N/A
		C	
K–S	N/A	N/A	N/A
A–D	N/A	N/A	N/A
χ^2	61.913	0.3698	0.3148
p-Value	10^{-12}	0.9464	0.8544
Loglikelihood	−214.924	−202.077	−202.077
SBC	−217.350	−206.929	−209.324

They are 2.67, 2.33, 2.01, 1.67, 1.32, and 1.04. The sequence is linear and decreasing, indicating a binomial distribution is appropriate. An alternative is to compute the sample mean and variance. They are 2 and 1.494, respectively. The variance is considerably less than the mean, indicating a binomial model.

16.23 The various tests for the three data sets produce the following results. For Data Set B truncated at 50, the estimates are $\hat{\alpha} = 0.40982$, $\hat{\tau} = 1.24069$, and $\hat{\theta} = 1,642.31$. For Data Set B censored at 1,000, there is no maximum likelihood estimate. For Data Set C, the maximum likelihood estimate is $\hat{\alpha} = 4.50624$, $\hat{\tau} = 0.28154$, and $\hat{\theta} = 71.6242$. The results of the tests are in Table 16.10.

For Data Set B truncated at 50, there is no reason to use a three-parameter distribution. For Data Set C, the transformed gamma distribution does not provide sufficient improvement to drop the Weibull as the model of choice.

16.24 The loglikelihood values for the two models are −385.9 for the Poisson and −382.4 for the negative binomial. The test statistic is $2(-382.4+385.9) =$

7.0. There is one degree of freedom (two parameters minus one parameter), and so the critical value is 3.84. The null hypothesis is rejected, and so the data favors the negative binomial distribution.

16.25 The penalty function subtracts $\ln(100)/2 = 2.3$ for each additional parameter. For the five models, the penalized loglikelihoods are: generalized Pareto: $-219.1 - 6.9 = -226.0$; Burr: $-219.2 - 6.9 = -226.1$; Pareto: $-221.2 - 4.6 = -225.8$; lognormal: $-221.4 - 4.6 = -226.0$; and inverse exponential: $-224.3 - 2.3 = -226.6$. The largest value is for the Pareto distribution.

16.26 The loglikelihood function for an exponential distribution is

$$l(\theta) = \ln \prod_{i=1}^{n} \theta^{-1} e^{-x_i/\theta} = \sum_{i=1}^{n} -\ln \theta - \frac{x_i}{\theta} = -n \ln \theta - \frac{n\bar{x}}{\theta}.$$

Under the null hypothesis that Sylvia's mean is double that of Phil's, the maximum likelihood estimates of the mean are 916.67 for Phil and 1833.33 for Sylvia. The loglikelihood value is

$$
\begin{aligned}
l_{\text{null}} &= -20 \ln 916.67 - 20{,}000/916.67 - 10 \ln 1{,}833.33 - 15{,}000/1833.33 \\
&= -241.55.
\end{aligned}
$$

Under the alternative hypothesis of arbitrary parameters the loglikelihood value is

$$l_{\text{alt}} = -20 \ln 1{,}000 - 20{,}000/1{,}000 - 10 \ln 1{,}500 - 15{,}000/1{,}500 = -241.29.$$

The likelihood ratio test statistic is $2(-241.29 + 241.55) = 0.52$, which is not significant (the critical value is 3.84 with one degree of freedom). To add a parameter, the SBC requires an improvement of $\ln(30)/2 = 1.70$. Both procedures indicate that there is not sufficient evidence in the data to dispute Sylvia's claim.

16.27 The deduction to compute the SBC is $(r/2)\ln(n) = (r/2)\ln(260) = 2.78r$, where r is the number of parameters. The SBC values are -416.78, -417.56, -419.34, -420.12, and -425.68. The largest value is the first one, so that is the model to select.

16.28 Both the Poisson and negative binomial have acceptable p-values (0.93 and 0.74) with the Poisson favored. The Poisson has a higher loglikelihood value than the geometric. The negative binomial improves the loglikelihood by 0.01 over the Poisson, less than the 1.92 required by LRT or the 3.45 required by SBC. The Poisson is acceptable and preferred.

Table 16.11   Calculations for Exercise 16.31.

Model	Parameters	NLL	Chi-square	df
Poisson	$\hat\lambda = 1.74128$	2,532.86	1,080.80	5
Geometric	$\hat\beta = 1.74128$	2,217.71	170.72	7
Negative binomial	$\hat r = .867043,\ \hat\beta = 2.00830$	2,216.07	165.57	6

16.29 Both the geometric and negative binomial have acceptable p-values (0.26 and 0.11), with the geometric favored. The geometric has a higher loglikelihood value than the Poisson. The negative binomial improves the loglikelihood by 0.71 over the geometric, less than the 1.92 required by LRT or the 2.30 required by SBC. The geometric model is acceptable and preferred.

16.30 The negative binomial distribution has the best p-value (0.000037) though it is clearly unacceptable. For the two one-parameter distributions, the geometric distribution is a better loglikelihood and SBC than the Poisson. The negative binomial model improves the loglikelihood by $1132.25 - 1098.64 = 33.61$, more than the 1.92 required by the likelihood ratio test and is more than the $0.5 \ln 503 = 3.11$ required by the SBC. For the three models, the negative binomial is the best, but is not very good. It turns out that zero-modified models should be used.

16.31 (a) For $k = 1, 2, 3, 4, 5, 6, 7$, the values are 0.276, 2.315, 2.432, 2.891, 4.394, 2.828, and 4.268, which, if anything, are increasing. The negative binomial or geometric models may work well.

(b) The values appear in Table 16.11. Because the sample variance exceeds the sample mean, there is no mle for the binomial distribution.

(c) The geometric is better than the Poisson by both likelihood and chi-square measures. The negative binomial distribution is not an improvement over the geometric as the NLL decreases by only 1.64. When doubled, 3.28 does not exceed the critical value of 3.841. The best choice is geometric, but it does not pass the goodness-of-fit test.

16.32 For each data set and model, Table 16.12 first gives the negative loglikelihood and then the chi-square test statistic, degrees of freedom, and p-value. If there are not enough degrees of freedom to do the test, no p-value is given.

For Exercise 14.3, the Poisson is the clear choice. It is the only one-parameter distribution acceptable by the goodness-of-fit test and no two-parameter distribution improves the NLL by more than 0.03.

Table 16.12   Results for Exercise 16.32.

	Ex. 14.3	Ex. 14.5	Ex. 14.6	Ex. 16.31
Poisson	3,339.66	488.241	3,578.58	2,532.86
	.00;1;.9773	5.56;1;.0184	16,308;4;0	1,081;5;0
Geometric	3,353.39	477.171	1,132.25	2,217.71
	23.76;2;0	.28;1;.5987	146.84;7;0	170.72;7;0
Neg. bin.	3,339.65	476.457	1,098.64	2,216.07
	.01;0	1.60;0	30.16;6;0	165.57;6;0
ZM Poisson	3,339.66	480.638	2,388.37	2,134.59
	.00;0	1.76;0	900.42;3;0	37.49;6;0
ZM geometric	3,339.67	476.855	1,083.56	2,200.56
	.00;0	1.12;0	1.52;6;.9581	135.43;6;0
ZM logarithmic	3,339.91	475.175	1,171.13	2,308.82
	.03;0	.66;0	186.05;6;0	361.18;6;0
ZM neg. bin.	3,339.63	473.594	1,083.47	2,132.42
	.00;-1	.05;0	1.32;5;.9331	28.43;5;0

For Exercise 14.5, the geometric is the best one-parameter distribution and is acceptable by the goodness-of-fit test. The best two-parameter distribution is the negative binomial, but the improvement in the NLL is only 0.714, which is not significant. (The test statistic with one degree of freedom is 1.428). The three-parameter ZM negative binomial improves the NLL by 3.577 over the geometric. This is significant (with two degrees of freedom). So an argument could be made for the ZM negative binomial, but the simpler geometric still looks to be a good choice.

For Exercise 14.6, the best one-parameter distribution is the geometric, but it is not acceptable. The best two-parameter distribution is the ZM geometric, which does pass the goodness-of-fit test and has a much lower NLL. The ZM negative binomial lowers the NLL by 0.09 and is not a significant improvement.

For Exercise 16.31, none of the distributions fit well. According to the NLL, the ZM negative binomial is the best choice, but it does not look very promising.

16.33(a) The mle is $\hat{\rho} = 3.0416$ using numerical methods.

(b) The test statistic is 785.18 and with three degrees of freedom the model is clearly not acceptable.

Table 16.13   Results for Exercise 16.34.

	Ex. 14.3	Ex. 14.5	Ex. 14.6	Ex. 16.31
Poisson–Poisson	3,339.65	478.306	1,198.28	2,151.88
	0.01;0	1.35;0	381.25;6;0	51.85;6;0
Polya–Aeppli	3,339.65	477.322	1,084.95	2,183.48
	0.01;0	1.58;0	4.32;6;0.6335	105.95;6;0
Poisson–I.G.	3,339.65	475.241	1,174.82	2,265.34
	0.01;0	1.30;0	206.08;6;0	262.74;6;0
Poisson–ETNB	3,339.65	473.624	1,083.56	did not
	0.01;−1	0.02;−1	1.52;5;0.9112	converge

16.34 Results appear in Table 16.13. The entries are the negative loglikelihood, the chi-square test statistic, degrees of freedom, and the p-value (if the degrees of freedom are positive).

For Exercise 14.3, the Poisson cannot be topped. These four improve the loglikelihood by only 0.01 and all have more parameters.

For Exercise 14.5, both the Poisson–inverse Gaussian and Poisson–ETNB improve the loglikelihood over the geometric. The improvements are 1.93 and 3.547. When doubled, they are slightly (p-values of 0.04945 and 0.0288, respectively, with one and two degrees of freedom) significant. The goodness-of-fit test cannot be done. The geometric model, which easily passed the goodness–of-fit test, still looks good.

For Exercise 14.6, none of the models improved the loglikelihood over the ZM geometric (although the Poisson–ETNB, with one more parameter, tied). As well, the ZM geometric has the highest p-value and is clearly acceptable.

For Exercise 16.31, none of the models have a superior loglikelihood versus the ZM negative binomial. Although this model is not acceptable, it is the best one from among the available choices.

16.35 The coefficient discussed in the section is $\frac{(\mu_3 - 3\sigma^2 + 2\mu)\mu}{(\sigma^2 - \mu)^2}$. For the five data sets, use the empirical estimates. For the last two sets, the final category is for some number or more. For these cases, estimate by assuming the observations were all at that highest value. The five coefficient estimates are (a) −0.85689, (b) −1,817.27, (c) −5.47728, (d) 1.48726, and (e) −0.42125. For all but Data Set (d), it appears that a compound Poisson model will not be appropriate. For Data Set (d), it appears that the Polya–Aeppli model will do well. Table 16.14 summarizes a variety of fits. The entries are the negative loglikelihood, the chi-square test statistic, the degrees of freedom, and the p-value.

Table 16.14   Results for Exercise 16.35.

	(a)	(b)	(c)	(d)	(e)
Poisson	36,188.3	206.107	481.886	1,461.49	841.113
	190.75;2;0	0.06;1;.8021	2.40;2;.3017	267.52;2;0	6.88;6;.3323
Geometric	36,123.6	213.052	494.524	1,309.64	937.975
	41.99;3;0	14.02;2;0	24.03;3;0	80.13;4;0	189.47;9;0
NB	36,104.1	did not	481.054	1,278.59	837.455
	0.09;1;.7631	converge	0.31;1;.5779	1.57;4;.8139	3.46;6;.7963
P–bin.	36,106.9	did not	481.034	1,320.71	837.438
$m = 2$	2.38;1;.1228	converge	0.38;1;.5357	69.74;2;0	3.10;6;.7963
P–bin.	36,106.1	did not	481.034	1,303.00	837.442
$m = 3$	1.20;1;.2728	converge	0.35;1;.5515	63.10;3;0	3.19;6;.7853
Polya–	36,104.6	did not	481.044	1,280.59	837.452
Aeppli	0.15;1;.6966	converge	0.32;1;.5731	6.52;4;.1638	3.37;6;.7615
Ney.–A	36,105.3	did not	481.037	1,288.56	837.448
	0.49;1;.4820	converge	0.33;1;.5642	24.14;3;0	3.28;6;.7736
P–iG	36,103.6	did not	481.079	1,281.90	837.455
	0.57;1;.4487	converge	0.31;1;.5761	8.75;4;.0676	3.63;6;.7260
P–ETNB	36,103.5	did not	did not	1,278.58	did not
	5.43;1;.0198	converge	converge	1.54;3;.6740	converge

(a) All two-parameter distributions are superior to the two one-parameter distributions. The best two-parameter distributions are negative binomial (best loglikelihood) and Poisson–inverse Gaussian (best p-value). The three-parameter Poisson–ETNB is not a significant improvement by the likelihood ratio test. The simpler negative binomial is an excellent choice.

(b) Because the sample variance is less than the sample mean, mles exist only for the Poisson and geometric distributions. The Poisson is clearly acceptable by the goodness-of-fit test.

(c) None of the two-parameter models are significant improvements over the Poisson according to the likelihood ratio test. Even though some have superior p-values, the Poisson is acceptable and should be our choice.

(d) The two-parameter models are better by the likelihood ratio test. The best is negative binomial on all measures. The Poisson–ETNB is not better, and so use the negative binomial, which passes the goodness-of-fit test. The moment analysis supported the Polya–Aeppli, which was acceptable, but not as good as the negative binomial.

(e) The two-parameter models are better by the likelihood ratio test. The best is Poisson–binomial with $m = 2$, though the simpler and more popular negative binomial is a close alternative.

16.36 Excel® solver reports the following mles to four decimals: $\hat{p} = 0.9312$, $\hat{\lambda}_1 = 0.1064$, and $\hat{\lambda}_2 = 0.6560$. The negative loglikelihood is 10,221.9. Rounding these numbers to two decimals produces a negative loglikelihood of 10,223.3 while Tröbliger's solution is superior at 10,222.1. A better two-decimal solution is $(0.94, 0.11, 0.69)$, which gives 10,222.0. The negative binomial distribution was found to have a negative loglikelihood of 10,223.4. The extra parameter for the two-point mixture cannot be justified (using the likelihood ratio test).

CHAPTER 17

CHAPTER 17 SOLUTIONS

17.1 SECTION 17.7

17.1

$$\lambda_0 = (1.96/0.05)^2 = 1{,}536.64,$$

$$E(X) = \int_0^{100} \frac{100x - x^2}{5{,}000}dx = 33\tfrac{1}{3},$$

$$E(X^2) = \int_0^{100} \frac{100x^2 - x^3}{5{,}000}dx = 1{,}666\tfrac{2}{3},$$

$$\mathrm{Var}(X) = 1{,}666\tfrac{2}{3} - (33\tfrac{1}{3})^2 = 555\tfrac{5}{9},$$

$$n\lambda = 1{,}536.64\left[1 + \left(\frac{\sqrt{555\tfrac{5}{9}}}{33\tfrac{1}{3}}\right)^2\right] = 2{,}304.96.$$

2,305 claims are needed.

17.2 $0.81 = n\lambda/\lambda_0$. $0.64 = n\lambda \left[\lambda_0\left(1 + \frac{\alpha\beta^2}{\alpha^2\beta^2}\right)\right]^{-1} = 0.81(1 + \alpha^{-1})^{-1}$, $\alpha = 3.7647$. $\alpha\beta = 100$, $\beta = 26.5625$.

Student Solutions Manual to Accompany Loss Models: From Data to Decisions, Fourth **183**
Edition. By Stuart A. Klugman, Harry H. Panjer, Gordon E. Willmot
Copyright © 2012 John Wiley & Sons, Inc.

17.3 $\lambda_0 = 1{,}082.41$. $\mu = 600$. Estimate the variance as $\sigma^2 = \frac{0^2 + 75^2 + (-75)^2}{2} = 75^2$. The standard for full credibility is $1{,}082.41(75/600)^2 = 16.913$. $Z = \sqrt{3/16.913} = 0.4212$. The credibility pure premium is

$$0.4212(475) + 0.5788(600) = 547.35.$$

17.4 $\mu = s\beta\theta_Y$; $\sigma^2 = s\beta\sigma_Y^2 + s\beta(1 + \beta)\theta_Y^2$; where s is used in place of the customary negative binomial parameter, r. Then

$$1.645 = \frac{r\mu\sqrt{n}}{\sigma} = \frac{0.05\sqrt{n}s\beta\theta_Y}{\sqrt{s\beta\sigma_Y^2 + s\beta(1 + \beta)\theta_Y^2}},$$

and so

$$1{,}082.41 = \frac{ns^2\beta^2\theta_Y^2}{s\beta\sigma_Y^2 + s\beta(1 + \beta)\theta_Y^2} = ns\beta\left(\frac{\theta_Y^2}{\sigma_Y^2 + \theta_Y^2(1 + \beta)}\right).$$

The standard for full credibility is

$$ns\beta = 1{,}082.41\left(1 + \beta + \frac{\sigma_Y^2}{\theta_Y^2}\right).$$

Partial credibility is obtained by taking the square root of the ratio of the number of claims to the standard for full credibility.

17.5 $\lambda_0 = (2.2414/0.03)^2 = 5{,}582.08$, and so 5,583 claims are required. (From the wording of the problem, $\lambda = \lambda_0$.)

17.6
$$E(X) = \int_0^{200{,}000} \frac{x}{200{,}000}\,dx = 100{,}000,$$

$$E(X^2) = \int_0^{200{,}000} \frac{x^2}{200{,}000}\,dx = 13{,}333{,}333{,}333\frac{1}{3},$$

$$\text{Var}(X) = 3{,}333{,}333{,}333\frac{1}{3}.$$

The standard for full credibility is

$$1{,}082.41(1 + 3{,}333{,}333{,}333.33/10{,}000{,}000{,}000) = 1{,}443.21.$$

$Z = \sqrt{1{,}082/1{,}443.21} = 0.86586.$

17.7 $(1.645/0.06)^2(1 + 7{,}500^2/1{,}500^2) = 19{,}543.51$, or 19,544 claims.

17.8 $Z = \sqrt{6{,}000/19{,}543.51} = 0.55408$. The credibility estimate is

$$0.55408(15{,}600{,}000) + 0.44592(16{,}500{,}000) = 16{,}001{,}328.$$

17.9 For the standard for estimating the number of claims, $800 = (y_p/0.05)^2$, and so $y_p = \sqrt{2}$.

$$
\begin{aligned}
\mathrm{E}(X) &= \int_0^{100} 0.0002x(100 - x)dx = 33\frac{1}{3}, \\
\mathrm{E}(X^2) &= \int_0^{100} 0.0002x^2(100 - x)dx = 1{,}666\frac{2}{3}, \\
\mathrm{Var}(X) &= 1{,}666\frac{2}{3} - (33\frac{1}{3})^2 = 555\frac{5}{9}.
\end{aligned}
$$

The standard for full credibility is $(\sqrt{2}/0.1)^2[1 + 555\frac{5}{9}/(33\frac{1}{3})^2] = 300$.

17.10 $1{,}000 = (1.96/0.1)^2(1 + c^2)$. The solution is the coefficient of variation, 1.2661.

17.11 $Z = \sqrt{10{,}000/17{,}500} = 0.75593$. The credibility estimate is

$$0.75593(25{,}000{,}000) + 0.24407(20{,}000{,}000) = 23{,}779{,}650.$$

17.12 The standard for estimating claim numbers is $(2.326/0.05)^2 = 2{,}164.11$. For estimating the amount of claims, we have $\mathrm{E}(X) = \int_1^{\infty} 2.5x^{-2.5}dx = 5/3$, $\mathrm{E}(X^2) = \int_1^{\infty} 2.5x^{-1.5}dx = 5$, and $\mathrm{Var}(X) = 5 - (5/3)^2 = 20/9$. Then $2164.11 = (1.96/K)^2[1 + (20/9)/(25/9)]$, and so $K = 0.056527$

17.13 $\mathrm{E}(X) = 0.5(1) + 0.3(2) + 0.2(10) = 3.1$, $\mathrm{E}(X^2) = 0.5(1) + 0.3(4) + 0.2(100) = 21.7$, $\mathrm{Var}(X) = 21.7 - 3.1^2 = 12.09$. The standard for full credibility is $(1.645/.1)^2(1 + 12.09/3.1^2) = 611.04$, and so 612 claims are needed.

17.14 $3{,}415 = (1.96/k)^2(1 + 4)$, $k = 0.075$, or 7.5%.

17.15 $Z = \sqrt{n/F}$, $R = ZO + (1 - Z)P$, $Z = (R - P)/(O - P) = \sqrt{n/F}$. $n/F = (R - P)^2/(O - P)^2$. $n = \frac{F(R-P)^2}{(O-P)^2}$.

17.16 For the severity distribution, the mean is 5,000 and the variance is $10{,}000^2/12$. For credibility based on accuracy with regard to the number of claims,

$$2{,}000 = \left(\frac{z}{0.03}\right)^2, \quad z^2 = 1.8,$$

where z is the appropriate value from the standard normal distribution. For credibility based on accuracy with regard to the total cost of claims, the number of claims needed is

$$\frac{z^2}{0.05^2}\left(1 + \frac{10,000^2/12}{5,000^2}\right) = 960.$$

CHAPTER 18

CHAPTER 18

18.1 SECTION 18.9

18.1 The conditional distribution of X given that $Y = y$ is

$$
\begin{aligned}
f_{X|Y}(x|y) &= \frac{f_{X,Y}(x,y)}{f_Y(y)} = \frac{P_r(X = x, Y = y)}{P_r(Y = y)} \\
&= \frac{P_r(X = x, Z = y - x)}{P_r(Y = y)} \\
&= \frac{P_r(X = x)P_r(Z = y - x)}{P_r(Y = y)} = \frac{\frac{\lambda_1^x e^{-\lambda_1}}{x!} \frac{\lambda_2^{y-x} e^{-\lambda_2}}{(y-x)!}}{\frac{(\lambda_1 + \lambda_2)^y e^{-\lambda_1 - \lambda_2}}{y!}} \\
&= \frac{y!}{x!(y-x)!} \left(\frac{\lambda_1}{\lambda_1 + \lambda_2} \right)^x \left(\frac{\lambda_2}{\lambda_1 + \lambda_2} \right)^{y-x}
\end{aligned}
$$

for $x = 0, 1, 2, \ldots, y$. This is a binomial distribution with parameters $m = y$ and $q = \lambda_1/(\lambda_1 + \lambda_2)$.

18.2
$$f(x|y) = \frac{f(x,y)}{f(y)} = \frac{\Pr(X = x,\ Z = y - x)}{\Pr(Y = y)}$$
$$= \frac{\binom{n_1}{x}p^x(1-p)^{n_1-x}\binom{n_2}{y-x}p^{y-x}(1-p)^{n_2-y+x}}{\binom{n_1+n_2}{y}p^y(1-p)^{n_1+n_2-y}}$$
$$= \frac{\binom{n_1}{x}\binom{n_2}{y-x}}{\binom{n_1+n_2}{y}}.$$

This is the hypergeometric distribution.

18.3 Using (18.3) and conditioning on N yields

$$E(X) = E[E(X|N)] = E[NE(Y_i)] = E[\mu_Y N] = \mu_Y E(N) = \lambda\mu_Y.$$

For the variance, use (18.6) to obtain

$$\begin{aligned}
\text{Var}(X) &= E[\text{Var}(X|N)] + \text{Var}[E(X|N)] \\
&= E[N\text{Var}(Y_i)] + \text{Var}[NE(Y_i)] \\
&= E[\sigma_Y^2 N] + \text{Var}[\mu_Y N] \\
&= \sigma_Y^2 E(N) + \mu_Y^2 \text{Var}(N) \\
&= \lambda(\mu_Y^2 + \sigma_Y^2) \\
&= \lambda E[Y_i^2].
\end{aligned}$$

18.4(a) $f_X(0) = 0.3,\ f_X(1) = 0.4,\ f_X(2) = 0.3.$
$f_Y(0) = 0.25,\ f_Y(1) = 0.3,\ f_Y(2) = 0.45.$

(b) The following array presents the values for $x = 0, 1, 2$:

$$\begin{aligned}
f(x|Y=0) &= 0.2/0.25 = 4/5,\ 0/0.25 = 0,\ 0.05/0.25 = 1/5, \\
f(x|Y=1) &= 0/0.3 = 0,\ 0.15/0.3 = 1.2,\ 0.15/0.3 = 1/2, \\
f(x|Y=2) &= 0.1/0.45 = 2/9,\ 0.25/0.45 = 5/9,\ 0.1/0.45 = 2/9.
\end{aligned}$$

(c)
$$\begin{aligned}
E(X|Y=0) &= 0(4/5) + 1(0) + 2(1/5) = 2/5, \\
E(X|Y=1) &= 0(0) + 1(1/2) + 2(1/2) = 3/2, \\
E(X|Y=2) &= 0(2/9) + 1(5/9) + 2(2/9) = 1, \\
E(X^2|Y=0) &= 0(4/5) + 1(0) + 4(1/5) = 4/5, \\
E(X^2|Y=1) &= 0(0) + 1(1/2) + 4(1/2) = 5/2, \\
E(X^2|Y=2) &= 0(2/9) + 1(5/9) + 4(2/9) = 13/9, \\
\text{Var}(X|Y=0) &= 4/5 - (2/5)^2 = 16/25, \\
\text{Var}(X|Y=1) &= 5/2 - (3/2)^2 = 1/4, \\
\text{Var}(X|Y=2) &= 13/9 - 1^2 = 4/9.
\end{aligned}$$

$$\text{(d)} \quad \begin{aligned} E(X) &= (2/5)(0.25) + (3/2)(0.3) + 1(0.45) = 1, \\ E[\text{Var}(X|Y)] &= (16/25)(0.25) + (1/4)(0.3) + (4/9)(0.45) = 0.435, \\ \text{Var}[E(X|Y)] &= (2/5)^2(0.25) + (3/2)^2(0.3) + 1^2(0.45) - 1^2 = 0.165, \\ \text{Var}(X) &= 0.435 + 0.165 = 0.6. \end{aligned}$$

18.5 (a)

$$f(x,y) \propto \exp\left\{-\frac{1}{2(1-\rho^2)}\left[\left(\frac{x-\mu_1}{\sigma_1}\right)^2 - 2\rho\left(\frac{x-\mu_1}{\sigma_1}\right)\left(\frac{y-\mu_2}{\sigma_2}\right)\right]\right\}$$

$$\propto \exp\left\{-\frac{1}{2(1-\rho^2)}\left[\frac{x^2}{\sigma_1^2} - 2x\left(\frac{\mu_1}{\sigma_1^2} + \rho\frac{y-u_2}{\sigma_1\sigma_2}\right)\right]\right\}.$$

Now a normal density $N(\mu, \sigma^2)$ has pdf $f(x) \propto \exp\left[-\frac{1}{2\sigma^2}(x^2 - 2\mu x)\right]$. Then $f_{X|Y}(x|y) \propto f(x,y)$ is $N\left[\mu_1 + \rho\frac{\sigma_1}{\sigma_2}(y - \mu_2), (1-\rho^2)\sigma_1^2\right].$

(b)

$$\begin{aligned} f_X(x) &= \int f(x,y)dy \\ &\propto \int \exp\left\{-\frac{1}{2(1-\rho^2)}\left[\left(\frac{x-\mu_1}{\sigma_1}\right)^2 - 2\rho\left(\frac{x-\mu_1}{\sigma_1}\right)\left(\frac{y-\mu_2}{\sigma_2}\right)\right.\right. \\ &\qquad\qquad \left.\left. + \left(\frac{y-\mu_2}{\sigma_2}\right)^2\right]\right\} dy \\ &= \exp\left[-\frac{1}{2}\left(\frac{x-\mu_1}{\sigma_1}\right)^2\right] \\ &\qquad \times \int \exp\left[-\frac{1}{2}\left(\frac{y-\mu_2-\rho\frac{\sigma_2}{\sigma_1}(x-\mu_1)}{\sigma_2\sqrt{1-\rho^2}}\right)^2\right] dy \\ &= \exp\left[-\frac{1}{2}\left(\frac{x-\mu_1}{\sigma_1}\right)^2\right]\sqrt{2\pi\sigma_2\sqrt{1-\rho^2}} \\ &\propto \exp\left[-\frac{1}{2}\left(\frac{x-\mu_1}{\sigma_1}\right)^2\right]. \end{aligned}$$

Since the normal density is $\frac{1}{\sqrt{2\pi}\sigma}\exp\left[-\frac{1}{2}\left(\frac{x-\mu}{\sigma}\right)^2\right]$, in general, we have

$$f_X(x) = \frac{1}{\sqrt{2\pi}\sigma_1}\exp\left[-\frac{1}{2}\left(\frac{x-\mu_1}{\sigma_1}\right)^2\right] \sim N\left(\mu_1, \sigma_1^2\right).$$

(c) Suppose $f_X(x)f_Y(y) = f_{X,Y}(x,y)$. Then $f_X(x)f_Y(y) = f_{X,Y}(x,y) = f_{X|Y}(x|y)f_Y(y)$. Therefore, $f_X(x) = f_{X|Y}(x|y)$. From the results of (a) and (b), $\rho = 0$.

Then

$$f_{X,Y}(x,y) \propto \exp\left\{-\frac{1}{2}\left[\left(\frac{x-\mu_1}{\sigma_1}\right)^2 + \left(\frac{y-\mu_2}{\sigma_2}\right)^2\right]\right\} \propto f_X(x)f_Y(x).$$

Therefore, $f_{X,Y}(x,y) = f_X(x)f_Y(y)$.

18.6 (a)
$$
\begin{aligned}
\mathrm{E}(X) &= \mathrm{E}[\mathrm{E}(X|\Theta_1,\Theta_2)] = \mathrm{E}(\Theta_1) \\
\mathrm{Var}(X) &= \mathrm{E}[\mathrm{Var}(X|\Theta_1,\Theta_2)] + \mathrm{Var}[\mathrm{E}(X|\Theta_1,\Theta_2)] \\
&= \mathrm{E}(\Theta_2) + \mathrm{Var}(\Theta_1).
\end{aligned}
$$

(b) $f_{X|\Theta_1,\Theta_2}(x|\theta_1,\theta_2) = (2\pi\theta_2^2)^{-1/2}\exp\left[-\frac{1}{2\theta_2}(x-\theta_1)^2\right].$

$$
\begin{aligned}
f_X(x) &= \int\int (2\pi\theta_2^2)^{-1/2}\exp\left[-\frac{1}{2\theta_2}(x-\theta_1)^2\right]\pi(\theta_1,\theta_2)\,d\theta_1 d\theta_2 \\
&= \int\int (2\pi\theta_2^2)^{-1/2}\exp\left[-\frac{1}{2\theta_2}(x-\theta_1)^2\right]\pi_1(\theta_1)\pi_2(\theta_2)\,d\theta_1 d\theta_2.
\end{aligned}
$$

We are also given, $f_{Y|\Theta_2}(y|\theta_2) = (2\pi\theta_2^2)^{-1/2}\exp\left(-\frac{1}{2\theta_2}y^2\right)$. Let $Z = Y + \Theta_1$. Then

$$f_{Z,|\Theta_2}(z|\theta_2) = \int f_{Y|\theta_2}(z-\theta_1|\theta_2)\pi_1(\theta_1)d\theta_1$$

and

$$
\begin{aligned}
f_Z(z) &= \int f_{Z,|\Theta_2}(z|\theta_2)\pi_2(\theta_2)d\theta_2 \\
&= \int\int f_{Y|\theta_2}(z-\theta_1|\theta_2)\pi_1(\theta_1)d\theta_1\pi_2(\theta_2)d\theta_2 \\
&= \int\int (2\pi\theta_2^2)^{-1/2}\exp\left[-\frac{1}{2\theta_2}(z-\theta_1)^2\right]\pi_1(\theta_1)d\theta_1\pi_2(\theta_2)d\theta_2 \\
&= f_X(x).
\end{aligned}
$$

18.7
$$
\begin{aligned}
f_X(x) &= \int \frac{e^{-\theta}\theta^x}{x!}\pi_1(\theta)d\theta = \int \frac{e^{-\theta}\theta^x}{x!}\pi(\theta-x)d\theta, \\
f_Y(y) &= \frac{e^{-\alpha}\alpha^y}{y!}, \\
f_Z(z) &= \int \frac{e^{-\theta}\theta^z}{z!}\pi(\theta)d\theta.
\end{aligned}
$$

Let $W = Y + Z$. Then

$$
\begin{aligned}
f_W(w) &= \sum_{y=0}^{w} f_Y(y) f_Z(w-y) \\
&= \sum_{y=0}^{w} \frac{e^{-\alpha}\alpha^y}{y!} \int \frac{e^{-\theta}\theta^{(w-y)}}{(w-y)!}\pi(\theta)d\theta \\
&= \int \frac{e^{-(\alpha+\theta)}(\alpha+\theta)^w}{w!} \sum_{y=0}^{w} \binom{w}{y} \left(\frac{\alpha}{\alpha+\theta}\right)^y \left(\frac{\theta}{\alpha+\theta}\right)^{w-y} \pi(\theta)d\theta \\
&= \int \frac{e^{-(\alpha+\theta)}(\alpha+\theta)^w}{w!}\pi(\theta)d\theta,
\end{aligned}
$$

with the last line following because the sum contains binomial probabilities. Let $r = \alpha + \theta$ and so

$$
\begin{aligned}
f_W(w) &= \int \frac{e^{-r}r^w}{w!}\pi(r-\alpha)dr \\
&= f_X(x).
\end{aligned}
$$

18.8 (a) $\pi(\theta_{ij}) = 1/6$ for die i and spinner j.

(b)(c) The calculations are in Table 18.1.

Table 18.1   Calculations for Exercise 18.8(b) and (c).

i	j	$\Pr(X=0|\theta_{ij})$	$\Pr(X=3|\theta_{ij})$	$\Pr(X=8|\theta_{ij})$	$\mu(\theta_{ij})$	$v(\theta_{ij})$
1	1	25/30	1/30	4/30	35/30	6,725/900
1	2	25/30	2/30	3/30	30/30	5,400/900
1	3	25/30	4/30	1/30	20/30	2,600/900
2	1	10/30	4/30	16/30	140/30	12,200/900
2	2	10/30	8/30	12/30	120/30	10,800/900
2	3	10/30	16/30	4/30	80/30	5,600/900

(d) $\Pr(X_1 = 3) = (1 + 2 + 4 + 4 + 8 + 16)/(30 \cdot 6) = 35/180.$

(e) The calculations are in Table 18.2.

(f) The calculations are in Table 18.3.

Table 18.2 Calculations for Exercise 18.8(e).

i	j	$\Pr(X_1 = 3\|\theta_{ij})$	$\Pr(\Theta = \theta_{ij}\|X_1 = 3) = \dfrac{\Pr(X_1=3\|\theta_{ij})(1/6)}{35/180}$
1	1	1/30	1/35
1	2	2/30	2/35
1	3	4/30	4/35
2	1	4/30	4/35
2	2	8/30	8/35
2	3	16/30	16/35

Table 18.3 Calculations for Exercise 18.8(f).

x_2	$\Pr(X_2 = x_2\|X_1 = 3) = \sum \Pr(X_2 = x_2\|\Theta = \theta_{ij})\Pr(\Theta = \theta_{ij}\|X_1 = 3)$
0	$\frac{1}{30}\frac{1}{35}[25(1) + 25(2) + 25(4) + 10(4) + 10(8) + 10(16)] = 455/1{,}050$
3	$\frac{1}{30}\frac{1}{35}[1(1) + 2(2) + 4(4) + 4(4) + 8(8) + 16(16)] = 357/1{,}050$
8	$\frac{1}{30}\frac{1}{35}[4(1) + 3(2) + 1(4) + 16(4) + 12(8) + 4(16)] = 238/1{,}050$

(g)

$$
\begin{aligned}
E(X_2|X_1 = 3) &= \frac{1}{30}\frac{1}{35}[35(1) + 30(2) + 20(4) + 140(4) + 120(8) + 80(16)] \\
&= \frac{2{,}975}{1{,}050}.
\end{aligned}
$$

(h)
$$
\begin{aligned}
\Pr(X_2 = 0,\ X_1 = 3) &= \frac{1}{6}\left[\frac{25(1)}{900} + \frac{25(2)}{900} + \frac{25(4)}{900}\right. \\
&\quad \left. + \frac{10(4)}{900} + \frac{10(8)}{900} + \frac{10(16)}{900}\right] = \frac{455}{5{,}400}.
\end{aligned}
$$

$\Pr(X_2 = 3|X_1 = 3) = \frac{357}{5{,}400}$. $\Pr(X_2 = 8|X_1 = 3) = \frac{238}{5{,}400}$.

(i) Divide answers to (h) by $\Pr(X_1 = 3) = 35/180$ to obtain the answers to (f).

(j) $E(X_2|X_1 = 3) = 0\frac{455}{1{,}050} + 3\frac{357}{1{,}050} + 8\frac{238}{1{,}050} = \frac{2{,}975}{1{,}050}$.

(k)
$$
\begin{aligned}
\mu &= \frac{1}{6}\frac{1}{30}(35 + 30 + 20 + 140 + 120 + 80) = \frac{425}{180}, \\
v &= \frac{1}{6}\frac{1}{900}(5{,}725 + 5{,}400 + 2{,}600 + 12{,}200 + 10{,}800 + 5{,}600) = \frac{43{,}325}{5{,}400}, \\
a &= \frac{1}{6}\frac{1}{900}(35^2 + 30^2 + 20^2 + 140^2 + 120^2 + 80^2) - \left(\frac{425}{180}\right)^2 = \frac{76{,}925}{32{,}400}.
\end{aligned}
$$

(1)
$$Z = \left(1 + \frac{43{,}425/5{,}400}{76{,}925/32{,}400}\right)^{-1}$$
$$= 0.228349.$$
$$P_c = 0.228349(3) + 0.771651(425/180)$$
$$= 2.507.$$

18.9 (a) $\pi(\theta_i) = 1/3$, $i = 1, 2, 3$.

(b)(c) The calculations appear in Table 18.4.

Table 18.4   Calculations for Exercise 18.9(b) and (c).

i	1	2	3
$\Pr(X = 0\vert\theta_i)$	0.1600	0.0625	0.2500
$\Pr(X = 1\vert\theta_i)$	0.2800	0.0500	0.1500
$\Pr(X = 2\vert\theta_i)$	0.3225	0.3350	0.3725
$\Pr(X = 3\vert\theta_i)$	0.1750	0.1300	0.1050
$\Pr(X = 4\vert\theta_i)$	0.0625	0.4225	0.1225
$\mu(\theta_i)$	1.7	2.8	1.7
$v(\theta_i)$	1.255	1.480	1.655

(d) $\Pr(X_1 = 2) = \frac{1}{3}(0.3225 + 0.335 + 0.3725) = 0.34333.$

(e) The calculations appear in Table 18.5.

Table 18.5   Calculations for Exercise 18.9(e).

i	$\Pr(X_1 = 2\vert\theta_i)$	$\Pr(\Theta = \theta_i\vert X_1 = 2) = \frac{\Pr(X_1=2\vert\theta_i)(1/3)}{.34333}$
1	0.3225	0.313107
2	0.3350	0.325243
3	0.3725	0.361650

(f) The calculations appear in Table 18.6.

(g) $E(X_2\vert X_1 = 2) = 1.7(0.313107) + 2.8(0.325243) + 1.7(0.361650)$
$$= 2.057767.$$

Table 18.6   Calculations for Exercise 18.9(f).

x_2	$\Pr(X_2 = x_2 \vert X_1 = 2) = \sum \Pr(X_2 = x_2 \vert \Theta = \theta_i) \Pr(\Theta = \theta_i \vert X_1 = 2)$
0	$0.16(0.313107) + 0.0625(0.325243) + 0.25(0.361650) = 0.160837$
1	$0.28(0.313107) + 0.05(0.325243) + 0.15(0.361650) = 0.158180$
2	$0.3225(0.313107) + 0.335(0.325243) + 0.3725(0.361650) = 0.344648$
3	$0.175(0.313107) + 0.13(0.325243) + 0.105(0.361650) = 0.135049$
4	$0.0625(0.313107) + 0.4225(0.325243) + 0.1225(0.361650) = 0.201286$

(h)
$$\begin{aligned}
\Pr(X_2 = 0,\ X_1 = 2) &= [0.16(0.3225) + 0.0625(0.335) + 0.25(0.3725)]/3 \\
&= 0.055221,
\end{aligned}$$

$$\Pr(X_2 = 1, X_1 = 2) = 0.054308.\ \Pr(X_2 = 2, X_1 = 2) = 0.118329,$$
$$\Pr(X_2 = 3, X_1 = 2) = 0.046367.\ \Pr(X_2 = 4, X_1 = 2) = 0.069108.$$

(i) Divide answers to (h) by $\Pr(X_1 = 2) = 0.343333$ to obtain the answers to (f).

(j)
$$\begin{aligned}
\mathrm{E}(X_2 \vert X_1 = 2) &= 0(0.160837) + 1(0.158180) + 2(0.344648) \\
&\quad + 3(0.135049) + 4(0.201286) = 2.057767.
\end{aligned}$$

(k)
$$\begin{aligned}
\mu &= \tfrac{1}{3}(1.7 + 2.8 + 1.7) = 2.06667, \\
v &= \tfrac{1}{3}(1.255 + 1.48 + 1.655) = 1.463333, \\
a &= \tfrac{1}{3}(1.7^2 + 2.8^2 + 1.7^2) - 2.06667^2 = 0.268889.
\end{aligned}$$

(l)
$$\begin{aligned}
Z &= \left(1 + \frac{1.463333}{.267779}\right)^{-1} \\
&= 0.155228, \\
P_c &= 0.155228(2) + 0.844772(2.06667) \\
&= 2.056321.
\end{aligned}$$

(m) Table 18.4 becomes Table 18.7 and the quantities become $\mu = 1.033333$, $v = 0.731667$, $\alpha = 0.067222$. $Z = \frac{2}{2 + .731667/0.067222} = 0.155228$.

Table 18.7   Calculations for Exercise 18.9(m).

i	$\Pr(X = 0\vert\theta_i)$	$\Pr(X = 1\vert\theta_i)$	$\Pr(X = 2\vert\theta_i)$	$\mu(\theta_i)$	$v(\theta_i)$
1	0.40	0.35	0.25	0.85	0.6275
2	0.25	0.10	0.65	1.40	0.7400
3	0.50	0.15	0.35	0.85	0.8275

18.10

$$\begin{aligned}
\mathrm{E}\,(S|\theta_A) &= \mathrm{E}\,(N|\theta_A)\,\mathrm{E}\,(X|\theta_A) = 0.2(200) = 40, \\
\mathrm{E}\,(S|\theta_B) &= 0.7(100) = 70, \\
\mathrm{Var}\,(S|\theta_A) &= \mathrm{E}\,(N|\theta_A)\,\mathrm{Var}\,(X|\theta_A) + \mathrm{Var}\,(N|\theta_A)\,[\mathrm{E}\,(X|\theta_A)]^2 \\
&= 0.2(400) + 0.2(40,000) = 8,800, \\
\mathrm{Var}\,(S|\theta_B) &= 0.7(1500) + 0.3(10,000) = 4,050, \\
\mu_S &= \tfrac{2}{3}40 + \tfrac{1}{3}70 = 50, \\
v_S &= \tfrac{2}{3}8,800 + \tfrac{1}{3}4,050 = 7,216.67, \\
a_S &= \mathrm{Var}[\mu(\theta)] = \tfrac{2}{3}40^2 + \tfrac{1}{3}70^2 - 50^2 = 200, \\
k &= \frac{v_S}{a_S} = 36.083, \\
Z &= \frac{4}{4 + 36.083} = 0.10, \\
P_c &= 0.10(125) + 0.90(50) = 57.50.
\end{aligned}$$

18.11 Let S denote total claims. Then $\mu_S = \mu_N \mu_Y = 0.1(100) = 10$.

$$\begin{aligned}
v_S &= \mathrm{E}\{\mathrm{E}\,(N|\theta_1)\,\mathrm{Var}\,(Y|\theta_2) + \mathrm{Var}\,(N|\theta_1)\,\mathrm{E}[(Y|\theta_2)]^2\} \\
&= \mathrm{E}[\mathrm{E}\,(N|\theta_1)]\mathrm{E}[\mathrm{Var}\,(Y|\theta_2)] + \mathrm{E}[\mathrm{Var}\,(N|\theta_1)]\mathrm{E}\{[\mathrm{E}\,(Y|\theta_2)]^2\} \\
&= \mu_N v_Y + v_N \mathrm{E}\{[\mathrm{E}(Y|\theta_2)]^2\}.
\end{aligned}$$

Since $a_Y = \mathrm{Var}[\mu_Y(\theta)] = \mathrm{E}\{[\mu_Y(\theta)]^2\} - \{\mathrm{E}[\mu_Y(\theta)]\}^2$, $v_S = \mu_N v_Y + v_N(a_Y + \mu_Y^2)$. Then $a_Y = \mathrm{Var}[\mathrm{E}(Y|\theta_2)] = \mathrm{Var}(\theta_2)$ since Y is exponentially distributed. But, again using the exponential distribution,

$$\begin{aligned}
\mathrm{Var}(\theta_2) &= \mathrm{E}\,(\theta_2^2) - [\mathrm{E}(\theta_2)]^2 = \mathrm{E}[\mathrm{Var}(Y|\theta_2)] - \{\mathrm{E}[\mathrm{E}(Y|\theta_2)]\}^2 \\
&= v_Y - \mu_Y^2,
\end{aligned}$$

from which $a_Y + \mu_Y^2 = v_Y$. Then

$$\begin{aligned}
v_S &= \mu_N v_Y + v_N(v_Y - \mu_Y^2 + \mu_Y^2) = \mu_N v_Y + v_N v_Y \\
&= 0.1(25,000) + 0.1(25,000) = 5,000.
\end{aligned}$$

Also,

$$\begin{aligned}
a_S &= \mathrm{Var}[\mu_S(\theta_1,\theta_2)] = \mathrm{E}\{[\mu_S(\theta_1,\theta_2)]^2\} - \{\mathrm{E}[\mu_S(\theta_1,\theta_2)]\}^2 \\
&= \mathrm{E}\{[\mu_N(\theta_1)]^2\}\mathrm{E}\{[(\mu_Y(\theta_2)]^2\} - \mu_N^2 \mu_Y^2 \\
&= (a_N + \mu_N^2)(a_Y + \mu_Y^2) - \mu_N^2 \mu_Y^2 \\
&= [0.05 + (0.01)^2](25,000) - (0.1)^2(100)^2 = 1,400.
\end{aligned}$$

Therefore, $k = v_S/a_S = 5,000/1,400 = 3.5714$, $Z = \frac{3}{3+3.5714} = 0.4565$, and $P_c = 0.4565\left(\frac{200}{3}\right) + 0.5435(10) = 35.87$.

18.12 (a) $E(X_j) = E[E(X_j|\Theta)] = E[\beta_j\mu(\Theta)] = \beta_j E[\mu(\Theta)] = \beta_j\mu.$

$$
\begin{aligned}
\mathrm{Var}(X_j) &= E[\mathrm{Var}(X_j|\Theta)] + \mathrm{Var}[E(X_j|\Theta)] \\
&= E[\tau_j(\Theta) + \psi_j v(\Theta)] + \mathrm{Var}[\beta_j\mu(\Theta)] \\
&= \tau_j + \psi_j v + \beta_j^2 a.
\end{aligned}
$$

$$
\begin{aligned}
\mathrm{Cov}(X_i, X_j) &= E(X_i X_j) - E(X_i)E(X_j) \\
&= E[E(X_i X_j|\Theta)] - \beta_i\beta_j\mu^2 \\
&= E[E(X_i|\Theta) E(X_j|\Theta)] - \beta_i\beta_j\mu^2 \\
&= E\{\beta_i\beta_j[\mu(\Theta)]^2\} - \beta_i\beta_j\mu^2 \\
&= \beta_i\beta_j(E\{[\mu(\Theta)]^2\} - \{E[\mu(\Theta)]\}^2) \\
&= \beta_i\beta_j a.
\end{aligned}
$$

(b) The normal equations are

$$
E(X_{n+1}) = \tilde{\alpha}_0 + \sum_{j=1}^{n} \tilde{\alpha}_j E(X_j),
$$

$$
\mathrm{Cov}\,(X_i, X_{n+1}) = \sum_{j=1}^{n} \tilde{\alpha}_j \,\mathrm{Cov}(X_i, X_j),
$$

where $E(X_{n+1}) = \beta_{n+1}\mu$, $E(X_j) = \beta_j\mu$ and $\mathrm{Cov}(X_i, X_{n+1}) = \beta_i\beta_{n+1}a$, and $\mathrm{Cov}(X_i, X_i) = \mathrm{Var}\,(X_i) = \tau_j + \psi_j v + \beta_j^2 a$. On substitution,

$$
\beta_{n+1}\mu = \tilde{\alpha}_0 + \sum_{j=1}^{n} \tilde{\alpha}_j \beta_j\mu
$$

and

$$
\begin{aligned}
\beta_i\beta_{n+1}a &= \sum_{j=1}^{n} \tilde{\alpha}_j \beta_i\beta_j a + \tilde{\alpha}_1(\tau_i + \psi_i v) \\
&= \left(\beta_{n+1} - \frac{\tilde{\alpha}_0}{\mu}\right)\beta_i a + \tilde{\alpha}_i(\tau_i + \psi_i v).
\end{aligned}
$$

Hence,

$$
\frac{\tilde{\alpha}_0}{\mu}\beta_i a = \tilde{\alpha}_i(\tau_i + \psi_i v),
$$

yielding

$$
\tilde{\alpha}_i = \frac{\tilde{\alpha}_0}{\mu}\beta_i a (\tau_i + \psi_i v)^{-1}.
$$

Then

$$
\sum_{i=1}^{n} \tilde{\alpha}_i = \frac{\tilde{\alpha}_0}{\mu} a \sum_{i=1}^{n} (\tau_i + \psi_i v)^{-1}.
$$

Thus,

$$\tilde{\alpha}_0 = \beta_{n+1}\mu - \sum_{j=1}^{n} \tilde{\alpha}_j \beta_j \mu = \beta_{n+1}\mu - \tilde{\alpha}_0 a \sum_{j=1}^{n} \frac{\beta_j^2}{\tau_j + \psi_j v},$$

which gives

$$\tilde{\alpha}_0 = \frac{\beta_{n+1}\mu}{1 + a \sum_{j=1}^{n} \frac{\beta_j^2}{\tau_j + \psi_j v}} = \frac{\beta_{n+1}\mu}{1 + a \sum_{j=1}^{n} m_j} = \frac{\beta_{n+1}\mu}{1 + am}$$

and

$$\tilde{\alpha}_i = \frac{\beta_i \beta_{n+1}}{1 + am} \frac{a}{\tau_i + \psi_i v}.$$

The credibility premium is

$$
\begin{aligned}
\tilde{\alpha}_0 + \sum_{j=1}^{n} \tilde{\alpha}_j X_j &= \frac{\beta_{n+1}\mu}{1 + am} + \frac{\beta_{n+1} a}{1 + am} \sum_{j=1}^{n} \frac{\beta_j}{\tau_j + \psi_j v} X_j \\
&= \frac{E(X_{n+1})}{1 + am} + \frac{\beta_{n+1} a}{1 + am} \sum_{j=1}^{n} \frac{m_j}{\beta_j} X_j \\
&= \frac{E(X_{n+1})}{1 + am} + \frac{\beta_{n+1} am}{1 + am} \overline{X} \\
&= (1 - Z)E(X_{n+1}) + Z\beta_{n+1}\overline{X}.
\end{aligned}
$$

18.13 The posterior distribution is

$$
\begin{aligned}
\pi(\theta|\mathbf{x}) &\propto \left[\prod_{j=1}^{n} f(x_j|\theta) \right] \pi(\theta) \propto \prod_{j=1}^{n} \left[\theta^{x_j}(1-\theta)^{K_j - x_j} \right] \theta^{a-1}(1-\theta)^{b-1} \\
&= \theta^{\Sigma x_j + a - 1}(1-\theta)^{\Sigma(K_j - x_j) + b - 1} \\
&= \theta^{a_*}(1-\theta)^{b_*},
\end{aligned}
$$

which is the kernel of the beta distribution with parameters $a_* = \sum x_j + a$ and $b_* = \sum(K_j - x_j) + b$. So

$$\begin{aligned}
\mathrm{E}(X_{n+1}|\mathbf{x}) &= \int_0^1 \mu_{n+1}(\theta)\pi(\theta|x)d\theta \\
&= \int_0^1 K_{n+1}\theta \frac{\Gamma(a_* + b_*)}{\Gamma(a_*)\Gamma(b_*)}\theta^{a_*-1}(1-\theta)^{b_*-1}d\theta \\
&= K_{n+1}\frac{\Gamma(a_* + b_*)}{\Gamma(a_*)\Gamma(b_*)}\int_0^1 \theta^{a_*+1-1}(1-\theta)^{b_*-1}d\theta \\
&= K_{n+1}\frac{\Gamma(a_* + b_*)}{\Gamma(a_*)\Gamma(b_*)}\frac{\Gamma(a_* + 1)\Gamma(b_*)}{\Gamma(a_* + 1 + b_*)} \\
&= K_{n+1}\frac{a_*}{a_* + b_*} \\
&= K_{n+1}\frac{\sum x_j + a}{\sum x_j + a + \sum(K_j - x_j) + b} \\
&= K_{n+1}\left(\frac{\sum x_j}{\sum K_j + a + b}\frac{\sum K_j}{\sum K_j} + \frac{a}{\sum K_j + a + b}\frac{a+b}{a+b}\right) \\
&= K_{n+1}\left(\frac{\sum x_j}{\sum K_j}\frac{\sum K_j}{\sum K_j + a + b} + \frac{a}{a+b}\frac{a+b}{\sum K_j + a + b}\right).
\end{aligned}$$

Let

$$Z = \frac{\sum K_j}{\sum K_j + a + b}, \quad \overline{X} = \frac{\sum X_j}{\sum K_j}, \quad \mu = \frac{a}{a+b}.$$

Then $\mathrm{E}(X_{n+1}|\mathbf{x}) = K_{n+1}[Z\overline{X} + (1-Z)\mu]$. Normalizing, $\mathrm{E}\left(\frac{X_{n+1}}{K_{n+1}}\middle|\mathbf{x}\right) = Z\overline{X} + (1-Z)\mu$, the credibility premium.

18.14 (a) $f_{X_j|\Theta}(x_j|\theta) = p(x_j)e^{r(\theta)x_j}/q(\theta)$, where

$$p(x) = \Gamma(\alpha + x)/[\Gamma(\alpha)x!], r(\theta) = \ln(\theta)$$

and $q(\theta) = (1-\theta)^{-\alpha}$. Thus for $0 < \theta < 1$, $\pi(\theta) \propto (1-\theta)^{\alpha k}\theta^{\mu k}(1/\theta)$, which is the kernel of a beta pdf (Appendix A) with parameters $a = \mu k$ and $b = \alpha k + 1$. As $a > 0$ and $b > 0$, the result follows.

$$\mu(\theta) = q'(\theta)/[r'(\theta)q(\theta)] = \alpha\theta/(1-\theta),$$

(b)
and thus

$$\begin{aligned}
\mathrm{E}[\mu(\Theta)] &= \int_0^1 \frac{\alpha\theta}{1-\theta}\pi(\theta)d\theta \\
&= \frac{\alpha\Gamma(\mu k + \alpha k + 1)}{\Gamma(\mu k)\Gamma(\alpha k + 1)}\int_0^1 \theta^{\mu k}(1-\theta)^{\alpha k - 1}d\theta,
\end{aligned}$$

which is infinite if $\alpha k < 0$ (or $k < 0$ because $\alpha > 0$). If $\alpha k > 0$,

$$\mathrm{E}[\mu(\Theta)] = \frac{\alpha\Gamma(\mu k + \alpha k + 1)}{\Gamma(\mu k)\Gamma(\alpha k + 1)}\frac{\Gamma(\mu k + 1)\Gamma(\alpha k)}{\Gamma(\mu k + \alpha k + 1)} = \mu.$$

Alternatively, because

$$\frac{\pi(\theta)}{kr'(\theta)} = \frac{\Gamma(\mu k + \alpha k + 1)}{k\Gamma(\mu k)\Gamma(\alpha k + 1)} \theta^{\mu k}(1 - \theta)^{\alpha k}$$

equals zero for $\theta = 0$ and $\theta = 1$ unless $k < 0$ (in which case it equals $-\infty$ for $\theta = 1$), the result follows directly from (18.38).

(c) $$v(\theta) = \frac{\mu'(\theta)}{r'(\theta)} = \alpha \left[\frac{d}{d\theta} \left(\frac{1}{1 - \theta} - 1 \right) \right] / \theta^{-1} = \frac{\alpha\theta}{(1 - \theta)^2}$$

and

$$E[v(\Theta)] = \frac{\alpha\Gamma(\mu k + \alpha k + 1)}{\Gamma(\mu k)\Gamma(\alpha k + 1)} \int_0^1 \theta^{\mu k}(1 - \theta)^{\alpha k - 2} d\theta.$$

As in (b), $E[v(\Theta)] = \infty$ if $\alpha k \leq 1$, whereas if $\alpha k > 1$,

$$
\begin{aligned}
E[v(\Theta)] &= \frac{\alpha\Gamma(\mu k + \alpha k + 1)}{\Gamma(\mu k)\Gamma(\alpha k + 1)} \frac{\Gamma(\mu k + 1)\Gamma(\alpha k - 1)}{\Gamma(\mu k + \alpha k)} \\
&= \frac{\alpha(\mu k + \alpha k)\mu k}{\alpha k(\alpha k - 1)} \\
&= \frac{\mu k(\mu + \alpha)}{\alpha k - 1}.
\end{aligned}
$$

Similarly, $[\mu(\theta)]^2 = \alpha^2\theta^2/(1 - \theta)^2$ and

$$E\{[\mu(\Theta)]^2\} = \frac{\alpha^2\Gamma(\mu k + \alpha k + 1)}{\Gamma(\mu k)\Gamma(\alpha k + 1)} \int_0^1 \theta^{\mu k + 1}(1 - \theta)^{\alpha k - 2} d\theta,$$

which is infinite for $\alpha k \leq 1$, whereas if $\alpha k > 1$,

$$
\begin{aligned}
E\{[\mu(\Theta)]^2\} &= \frac{\alpha^2\Gamma(\mu k + \alpha k + 1)}{\Gamma(\mu k)\Gamma(\alpha k + 1)} \frac{\Gamma(\mu k + 2)\Gamma(\alpha k - 1)}{\Gamma(\mu k + \alpha k + 1)} \\
&= \frac{\alpha^2(\mu k)(\mu k + 1)}{(\alpha k)(\alpha k - 1)} \\
&= \alpha\mu \left(\frac{\mu k + 1}{\alpha k - 1} \right).
\end{aligned}
$$

As $k > 1/\alpha > 0$, $E[\mu(\Theta)] = \mu$ from (b), and thus

$$
\begin{aligned}
\text{Var}[\mu(\Theta)] &= E\{[\mu(\Theta)]^2\} - \{E[\mu(\Theta)]\}^2 \\
&= \frac{(\alpha\mu)(\mu k + 1)}{\alpha k - 1} - \mu^2 \\
&= \frac{\mu^2(\alpha k) + \alpha\mu - \mu^2(\alpha k - 1)}{\alpha k - 1} \\
&= \frac{\mu(\alpha + \mu)}{\alpha k - 1}.
\end{aligned}
$$

Clearly, $E[v(\Theta)] = k \, \text{Var}[\mu(\Theta)]$.

Alternatively, because $k > 1/\alpha > 0$, $\pi(\theta)/[kr'(\theta)] = 0$ for $\theta = 0$ and $\theta = 1$, implying that (18.52) holds. Furthermore,

$$\frac{\mu(\theta)\pi(\theta)}{r'(\theta)} = \frac{\alpha\Gamma(\mu k + \alpha k + 1)}{\Gamma(\mu k)\Gamma(\alpha k + 1)}\theta^{\mu k+1}(1-\theta)^{\alpha k-1},$$

which equals zero for $\theta = 0$ and $\theta = 1$ if $k > 1/\alpha$, implying, in turn, that (18.52) reduces to $k = E[v(\Theta)]/\text{Var}[\mu(\Theta)]$.

(d)
$$\pi(\theta|\mathbf{x}) \propto \left[\prod_{j=1}^{n}(1-\theta)^{\alpha}\theta^{x_j}\right]\theta^{\mu k-1}(1-\theta)^{\alpha k}$$
$$= \theta^{\mu k+n\bar{x}-1}(1-\theta)^{\alpha(k+n)}$$
$$= \theta^{\mu_* k_*-1}(1-\theta)^{\alpha k_*},$$

with $k_* = k + n$ and $\mu_* = (\mu k + n\bar{x})/(k+n)$. As shown in (b),

$$E(X_{n+1}|\mathbf{X}=\mathbf{x}) = E[\mu(\Theta)|X=\mathbf{x}] = \mu_*$$

if $k_* > 0$ and is infinite if $-1/\alpha < k_* < 0$. But $k_* = k + n$, and $k_* > 0$ if and only if $k > -n$. But $k_* > -1/\alpha$ is the same as $k > -n - 1/\alpha$, which is clearly satisfied because $k > -1/\alpha$. Also, $k_* < 0$ is the same as $k < -n$. Therefore, if $n < 1/\alpha$, it is possible to have $-1/\alpha < k < -n$, or $n - 1/\alpha < k_* < 0$, in which case the Bayesian premium is infinite. If $k = n$, then $k_* = 0$, and

$$\pi(\theta|\mathbf{x}) \propto \theta^{-1}, \quad 0 < \theta < 1,$$

which is impossible, that is, there is no posterior pdf in this case.

(e) If $k > 1/\alpha$, then the credibility premium exists from (b), and the Bayesian premium is a linear function of the x_js from (d). Hence, they must be equal.

18.15 (a) The posterior distribution is

$$\pi(\theta|\mathbf{x}) \propto \left\{\prod_{j=1}^{n}\frac{\exp(-m\theta x_j)}{[q(\theta)]^m}\right\}[q(\theta)]^{-k}\exp(-\theta\mu k)$$
$$= [q(\theta)]^{-k-mn}\exp\left[-\theta(m\sum x_j + \mu k)\right].$$

This is the same form as the prior distribution, with

$$k_* = k + mn$$

and

$$\mu_* = \frac{m\sum x_j + \mu k}{mn + k}.$$

The Bayesian premium is clearly given by (18.44), but with these new defini-
tions of k_* and μ_*, because the derivation of (18.44) from (18.41) is completely
analogous to that of (18.38) from (18.36).

(b) Because the Bayesian premium is linear in the x_js as long as (18.45) holds,
the credibility premium must be given by μ_* as defined in (a).

(c) The inverse Gaussian distribution can be written as

$$f(x) = \left(\frac{\theta}{2\pi x^3}\right)^{\frac{1}{2}} \exp\left(-\frac{\theta x}{2\mu^2} + \frac{\theta}{\mu} - \frac{\theta}{2x}\right).$$

Replace θ with m and μ with $(2\theta)^{-\frac{1}{2}}$ to obtain

$$f(x) = \left(\frac{m}{2\pi x^3}\right)^{\frac{1}{2}} \exp\left[-m\theta x + m(2\theta)^{\frac{1}{2}} - \frac{m}{2x}\right].$$

Now let $p(m,x) = \sqrt{\frac{m}{2\pi x^3}} \exp(-\frac{m}{2x}), r(\theta) = \theta$, and $q(\theta) = \exp(-\sqrt{2\theta})$ to see
that $f(x)$ has the desired form.

18.16 (a) They are true when $X_1, X_2,...$ represent values in successive years
and τ is an inflation factor for each year.

(b) This is a special case of Exercise 18.12 with $\beta_j = \tau^j$, $\tau_j(\theta) = 0$, $\psi_j = \tau^{2j}/m_j$ for $j = 1, \ldots, n$.

(c) From Exercise 18.12(b)

$$\tilde{\alpha}_0 + \sum_{j=1}^{n} \tilde{\alpha}_j X_j = (1 - Z)E(X_{n+1}) + Z\tau^{n+1}\bar{X},$$

where

$$\bar{X} = \sum_{j=1}^{n} \frac{\tau^{2j}}{\tau^{2j}} \frac{X_j}{\tau^j} \Bigg/ \left[\sum_{j=1}^{n} \frac{\tau^{2j}}{\tau^{2j}}\right]$$

$$= \sum_{j=1}^{n} \frac{m_j X_j}{\tau^j} \Bigg/ \sum_{j=1}^{n} m_j = \sum_{j=1}^{n} \frac{m_j X_j}{m\tau^j}$$

and

$$Z = \frac{a\sum_{j=1}^{n} \frac{m_j}{v}}{1 + a\sum_{j=1}^{n} \frac{m_j}{v}} = \frac{m}{k + m}.$$

Then,

$$\tilde{\alpha}_0 + \sum_{j=1}^{n} \tilde{\alpha}_j X_j \quad = \quad \frac{k}{k+m} E(X_{n+1}) + \frac{m}{k+m} \tau^{n+1} \bar{X}$$

$$= \quad \frac{k}{k+m} \tau^{n+1} \mu + \frac{m}{k+m} \sum_{j=1}^{n} \frac{m_j}{m} \tau^{n-1-j} \bar{X}_j.$$

(d) This is the usual Bühlmann–Straub credibility premium updated with inflation to next year's dollars.

(e) $\ln f_{X_j|\Theta}(x_j|\theta) = m_j \tau^{-j} x_j r(\theta) - m_j \ln q(\theta) + \ln p(x_j, m_j, \tau).$

$$\frac{\partial}{\partial \theta} f_{X_j|\Theta}(x_j|\theta) \quad = \quad \left[m_j \tau^{-j} x_j r'(\theta) - m_j \frac{q'(\theta)}{q(\theta)} \right] f_{X_j|\Theta}(x_j|\theta)$$

$$= \quad m_j r'(\theta) [\tau^{-j} x_j - \mu(\theta)] f_{X_j|\Theta}(x_j|\theta).$$

Integrate over all x_j and use Liebniz's rule to obtain

$$0 = m_j r'(\theta) \tau^{-j} E(X_j|\Theta = \theta) - m_j r'(\theta) \mu(\theta)(1),$$

that is,

$$E(X_j|\Theta) = \tau^j \mu(\Theta).$$

Also,

$$\frac{\partial^2}{\partial \theta^2} f_{X_j|\Theta}(x_j|\theta) \quad = \quad m_j r''(\theta) [\tau^{-j} x_j - \mu(\theta)] f_{X_j|\Theta}(x_j|\theta)$$

$$-m_j r'(\theta) \mu'(\theta) f_{X_j|\Theta}(x_j|\theta)$$

$$+m_j^2 [r'(\theta)]^2 [\tau^{-j} x_j - \mu(\theta)]^2 f_{X_j|\Theta}(x_j|\theta) .$$

Again integrating over all x yields

$$0 = 0 - m_j r'(\theta) \mu'(\theta) + m_j^2 \tau^{-2j} [r'(\theta)]^2 \text{Var}(X_j|\Theta = \theta),$$

and solving for $\text{Var}(X_j|\Theta)$ yields $\text{Var}(X_j|\Theta) = \frac{\tau^{2j} \mu'(\Theta)}{m_j r'(\Theta)} = \frac{\tau^{2j} v(\Theta)}{m_j}.$

(f)

$$\pi(\theta|\mathbf{x}) \quad \propto \quad \left[\sum_{j=1}^{n} f(x_j|\theta) \right] \pi(\theta)$$

$$\propto \quad [q(\theta)]^{-k-m} \exp \left[\mu k r(\theta) + \tau^{-j} r(\theta) \sum_{j=1}^{n} m_j x_j \right] r'(\theta)$$

$$= \quad [q(\theta)]^{-k-m} \exp \left[r(\theta) \left(\mu k + \tau^{-j} \sum_{j=1}^{n} m_j x_j \right) \right] r'(\theta)$$

$$= \quad [q(\theta)]^{-k_*} e^{\mu_* k_* r(\theta)} r'(\theta),$$

where $k_* = k + m$ and

$$\mu_* = \frac{\mu k + \tau^{-j} \sum_{j=1}^{n} m_j x_j}{k + m}.$$

Thus, $\pi(\theta|\mathbf{x})$ is the same as (18.41), and from (18.44)

$$E[\mu(\Theta)|\mathbf{X} = \mathbf{x}] = \mu_* + \frac{\pi(\theta_0|\mathbf{x})}{k_* r'(\theta_0)} - \frac{\pi(\theta_1|\mathbf{x})}{k_* r'(\theta_1)}.$$

But from (e) and (18.13), the Bayesian premium is

$$\begin{aligned}
E(X_{n+1}|\mathbf{X} = \mathbf{x}) &= E_{\Theta|\mathbf{X}=\mathbf{x}}[E(X_{n+1}|\Theta)] \\
&= E_{\Theta|\mathbf{X}=\mathbf{x}}[\tau^{n+1}\mu(\Theta)] \\
&= \tau^{n+1} E[\mu(\Theta)|\mathbf{X} = \mathbf{x}].
\end{aligned}$$

18.17 (a) The Poisson pgf of each X_j is $P_{X_j}(z|\theta) = e^{\theta(z-1)}$, and so the pgf of S is $P_S(z|\theta) = e^{n\theta(z-1)}$, which is Poisson with mean $n\theta$. Hence,

$$f_{S|\theta}(s|\theta) = \frac{(n\theta)^s e^{-n\theta}}{s!}$$

and so

$$f_S(s) = \int \frac{(n\theta)^s e^{-n\theta}}{s!} \pi(\theta) d\theta.$$

(b) $\mu(\theta) = E(X|\theta) = \theta$ and $\pi(\theta|\mathbf{x}) = \left[\prod_{j=1}^{n} f(x_j|\theta)\right] \pi(\theta)/f(x)$. We have

$$\begin{aligned}
f(x) &= \int \left[\prod_{j=1}^{n} f(x_j|\theta)\right] \pi(\theta) d\theta \\
&= \frac{\int \theta^{\Sigma x_j} e^{-n\theta} \pi(\theta) d\theta}{\prod_{j=1}^{n} x_j!}.
\end{aligned}$$

Therefore,

$$\pi(\theta|\mathbf{x}) = \frac{\theta^{\Sigma x_j} e^{-n\theta} \pi(\theta)}{\int_0^\infty \theta^{\Sigma x_j} e^{-n\theta} \pi(\theta) d\theta}.$$

The Bayesian premium is

$$E(X_{n+1}|\mathbf{x}) = \int_0^\infty \mu(\theta)\pi(\theta|\mathbf{x}) d\theta = \frac{\int_0^\infty \theta^{\Sigma x_j + 1} e^{-n\theta} \pi(\theta) d\theta}{\int_0^\infty \theta^{\Sigma x_j} e^{-n\theta} \pi(\theta) d\theta}$$

$$= \frac{\frac{(s+1)!}{n^{s+1}} \int_0^\infty \frac{n^{s+1}}{(s+1)!} \theta^{s+1} e^{-n\theta} \pi(\theta) d\theta}{\frac{s!}{n^s} \int_0^\infty \frac{n^s}{s!} \theta^s e^{-n\theta} \pi(\theta) d\theta} = \frac{s+1}{n} \frac{f_S(s+1)}{f_S(s)}.$$

(c)

$$f_S(s) = \int_0^\infty \frac{(n\theta)^s e^{-n\theta}}{s!} \frac{\beta^{-\alpha}}{\Gamma(\alpha)} \theta^{\alpha-1} e^{-\theta/\beta} d\theta$$

$$= \frac{n^s}{s!} \frac{\beta^{-\alpha}}{\Gamma(\alpha)} \int_0^\infty \theta^{s+\alpha-1} e^{-(n+\beta^{-1})\theta} d\theta$$

$$= \frac{n^s}{s!} \frac{\beta^{-\alpha}}{\Gamma(\alpha)} \frac{\Gamma(s+\alpha)}{(n+\beta^{-1})^{s+\alpha}}$$

$$= \frac{\Gamma(s+\alpha)}{\Gamma(s+1)\Gamma(\alpha)} \left(\frac{1}{1+n\beta}\right)^\alpha \left(\frac{n\beta}{1+n\beta}\right)^s$$

$$= \binom{r+s-1}{s} \left(\frac{1}{1+\beta_*}\right)^r \left(\frac{\beta_*}{1+\beta_*}\right)^s,$$

where $\beta_* = n\beta$ and $r = \alpha$. This is a negative binomial distribution.

18.18 (a) Clearly,

$$\pi_{\Theta|\mathbf{X}}(\theta|\mathbf{x}) \propto \theta^{n\bar{x}} e^{-n\theta} \pi(\theta)$$

$$\propto \theta^{n\bar{x}} e^{-n\theta} \left(\theta^{-\frac{3}{2}} e^{-\frac{\gamma}{2\mu^2}\theta - \frac{\gamma}{2\theta}}\right)$$

$$= \theta^{n\bar{x}-\frac{3}{2}} e^{-\alpha(n)\theta - \frac{\gamma}{2\theta}}.$$

From Exercise 5.20(g) with $m = n\bar{x}$ (a nonnegative integer because of the Poisson assumption) and θ replaced by γ yields the normalizing constant

$$\int_0^\infty \theta^{n\bar{x}-\frac{3}{2}} e^{-\alpha(n)\theta - \frac{\gamma}{2\theta}} d\theta = 2 \left[\frac{\gamma}{2\alpha(n)}\right]^{\frac{n\bar{x}}{2}-\frac{1}{4}} K_{n\bar{x}-\frac{1}{2}}\left[\sqrt{2\alpha(n)\gamma}\right].$$

(b)

$$f_{X_{n+1}|\mathbf{X}}(x_{n+1}|\mathbf{x}) = \int_0^\infty f_{X_{n+1}|\Theta}(x_{n+1}|\theta)\pi_{\Theta|\mathbf{X}}(\theta|\mathbf{x}) d\theta$$

$$= \int_0^\infty \frac{\theta^{x_{n+1}} e^{-\theta}}{x_{n+1}!} \left\{ \frac{\left[\frac{2\alpha(n)}{\gamma}\right]^{\frac{n\bar{x}}{2}-\frac{1}{4}} \theta^{n\bar{x}-\frac{3}{2}} e^{-\alpha(n)\theta - \frac{\gamma}{2\theta}}}{2K_{n\bar{x}-\frac{1}{2}}\left[\sqrt{2\alpha(n)\gamma}\right]} \right\} d\theta$$

$$= \frac{\left[\frac{2\alpha(n)}{\gamma}\right]^{\frac{n\bar{x}}{2}-\frac{1}{4}}}{2(x_{n+1}!)K_{n\bar{x}-\frac{1}{2}}\left[\sqrt{2\alpha(n)\gamma}\right]}$$

$$\times \int_0^\infty \theta^{x_{n+1}+n\bar{x}-\frac{3}{2}} e^{-\alpha(n+1)\theta - \frac{\gamma}{2\theta}} d\theta.$$

Again using Exercise 5.20(g) yields

$$f_{X_{n+1}|\mathbf{X}}(x_{n+1}|\mathbf{x})$$

$$= \frac{\left[\dfrac{2\alpha(n)}{\gamma}\right]^{\frac{n\bar{x}}{2}-\frac{1}{4}} \left[\dfrac{\gamma}{2\alpha(n+1)}\right]^{\frac{x_{n+1}+n\bar{x}}{2}-\frac{1}{4}} K_{x_{n+1}+n\bar{x}-\frac{1}{2}}\left[\sqrt{2\alpha(n+1)\gamma}\right]}{(x_{n+1}!)K_{n\bar{x}-\frac{1}{2}}\left[\sqrt{2\alpha(n)\gamma}\right]}$$

$$= \frac{\left[\dfrac{\gamma}{2\alpha(n+1)}\right]^{\frac{x_{n+1}}{2}} \left[\dfrac{\alpha(n)}{\alpha(n+1)}\right]^{\frac{n\bar{x}}{2}-\frac{1}{4}} K_{x_{n+1}+n\bar{x}-\frac{1}{2}}\left[\sqrt{2\alpha(n+1)\gamma}\right]}{(x_{n+1}!)K_{n\bar{x}-\frac{1}{2}}\left[\sqrt{2\alpha(n)\gamma}\right]}.$$

(c) Let $x = n\theta$, and so $\theta = x/n$ and $d\theta = (dx)/n$. Thus,

$$f_S(s) = \int_0^\infty \frac{x^s e^{-x}}{s!}\left[\frac{1}{n}\pi\left(\frac{x}{n}\right)\right]dx.$$

But

$$\begin{aligned}
\frac{1}{n}\pi\left(\frac{x}{n}\right) &= \frac{1}{n}\sqrt{\frac{\gamma}{2\pi(x/n)^3}}\exp\left[-\frac{\gamma}{2(x/n)}\left(\frac{\frac{x}{n}-\mu}{\mu}\right)^2\right]\\
&= \sqrt{\frac{\gamma n}{2\pi x^3}}\exp\left[-\frac{n\gamma}{2x}\left(\frac{x-n\mu}{n\mu}\right)^2\right],
\end{aligned}$$

which is the pdf of the inverse Gaussian distribution with parameters γ and μ replaced by $n\gamma$ and $n\mu$, respectively. As in Example 7.17, let $\mu_* = n\mu$ and $\beta_* = n\mu^2/\gamma$, which implies that $n\gamma = n^2\mu^2/\beta_* = \mu_*^2/\beta_*$. Then

$$\begin{aligned}
\frac{1}{n}\pi\left(\frac{x}{n}\right) &= \sqrt{\frac{\mu_*^2}{2\pi\beta_* x^3}}\exp\left[-\frac{\mu_*^2}{2\beta_* x}\left(\frac{x-\mu_*}{\mu_*}\right)^2\right]\\
&= \frac{\mu_*}{\sqrt{2\pi\beta_* x^3}}\exp\left[-\frac{(x-\mu_*)^2}{2\beta_* x}\right].
\end{aligned}$$

Therefore, S has a Poisson–inverse Gaussian distribution [or, equivalently, a compound Poisson distribution with ETNB ($r = -\frac{1}{2}$) secondary distribution]. with parameters $\mu_* = n\mu$ and $\beta_* = n\mu^2/\gamma$, and the pf $f_S(s)$ can be computed recursively. As shown in Exercise 18.17(b), the Bayesian premium is then given by

$$E(X_{n+1}|\mathbf{X} = \mathbf{x}) = \frac{1+n\bar{x}}{n}\frac{f_S(1+n\bar{x})}{f_S(n\bar{x})}.$$

18.19 The posterior distribution is

$$
\pi(\theta|\mathbf{x}) \quad \propto \quad \left\{ \prod_{j=1}^{n} \exp\left[-\frac{1}{2v}(x_j - \theta)^2\right] \right\} \exp\left[-\frac{1}{2a}(\theta - \mu)^2\right]
$$

$$
= \quad \exp\left[(2v)^{-1}\left(-\sum x_j^2 + 2\theta n\bar{x} - n\theta^2\right) - (2a)^{-1}(\theta^2 - 2\theta\mu + \mu^2)\right]
$$

$$
\propto \quad \exp\left[-\theta^2\left(\frac{n}{2v} + \frac{1}{2a}\right) + 2\theta\left(\frac{n\bar{x}}{2v} + \frac{\mu}{2a}\right)\right].
$$

Let $p = \frac{n}{2v} + \frac{1}{2a}$ and $q = \frac{n\bar{x}}{2v} + \frac{\mu}{2a}$, and then note that $-p\theta^2 + 2q\theta = -(p^{1/2}\theta - qp^{-1/2})^2 - q^2p^{-1}$. Then

$$
\pi(\theta|\mathbf{x}) \quad \propto \quad \exp\left[-(p^{1/2}\theta - qp^{-1/2})^2\right]
$$

$$
= \quad \exp\left[-\frac{1}{2}\left(\frac{\theta - qp^{-1}}{(2p)^{-1/2}}\right)^2\right],
$$

and the posterior distribution is normal with mean

$$
\mu_* = qp^{-1} = \frac{\dfrac{n\bar{x}}{v} + \dfrac{\mu}{a}}{\dfrac{n}{v} + \dfrac{1}{a}}
$$

and variance

$$
a_* = \frac{1}{2p} = \left(\frac{n}{v} + \frac{1}{a}\right)^{-1}.
$$

Then (18.10) implies that $X_{n+1}|\mathbf{x}$ is a mixture with $X_{n+1}|\Theta$ having a normal distribution with mean Θ, and $\Theta|\mathbf{x}$ is normal with mean μ_* and variance a_*. From Example 5.5, $X_{n+1}|\mathbf{x}$ is normally distributed with mean μ_* and variance $a_* + v$, that is,

$$
f_{X_{n+1}|\mathbf{X}}(x_{n+1}|\mathbf{x}) = [2\pi(a_* + v)]^{-1/2} \exp\left[-\frac{(x_{n+1} - \mu_*)^2}{2(a_* + v)}\right], \quad -\infty < x_{n+1} < \infty.
$$

The Bayesian estimate is the mean of the predictive distribution μ_*, which can be written as $Z\bar{x} + (1 - Z)\mu$, where

$$
Z = \frac{n/v}{n/v + 1/a} = \frac{na}{na + v} = \frac{n}{n + v/a}.
$$

Because the Bayesian estimate is a linear function of the data, it must be the Bühlmann estimate as well. To see this directly,

$$
\begin{aligned}
\mu(\Theta) &= \Theta, \ \mu = \mathrm{E}(\Theta) = \mu, \\
v(\Theta) &= v \ (\text{not random}), \ v = \mathrm{E}(v) = v, \\
a &= \mathrm{Var}(\Theta) = a,
\end{aligned}
$$

thus indicating that the quantities in the question were chosen to align with the text. Then, $k = v/a$ and $Z = n/(n+k)$.

18.20 (a) Let Θ represent the selected urn. Then, $f_X(x|\Theta = 1) = \frac{1}{4}$, $x = 1, 2, 3, 4$ and $f_X(x|\Theta = 2) = \frac{1}{6}$, $x = 1, 2, \ldots, 6$. Then, $\mu(1) = \mathrm{E}(X|\Theta = 1) = 2.5$ and $\mu(2) = \mathrm{E}(X|\theta = 2) = 3.5$.

For the Bayesian solution, the marginal probability of drawing a 4 is $f_X(4) = \frac{1}{2} \times \frac{1}{4} + \frac{1}{2} \times \frac{1}{6} = \frac{5}{24}$, and the posterior probability for urn 1 is

$$\pi(\theta = 1|X = 4) = \frac{f_{X|\Theta}(4|1)\pi(1)}{f_X(4)} = \frac{\frac{1}{4}\frac{1}{2}}{\frac{5}{24}} = \frac{3}{5}$$

and for urn 2 is

$$\pi(\theta = 2|X = 4) = 1 - \frac{3}{5} = \frac{2}{5}.$$

The expected value of the next observation is

$$\mathrm{E}(X_2|X_1 = 4) = 2.5\left(\frac{3}{5}\right) + 3.5\left(\frac{2}{5}\right) = 2.9.$$

(b) Using Bühlmann credibility,

$$
\begin{aligned}
\mu &= \tfrac{1}{2}(2.5 + 3.5) = 3, \\
v(1) &= \tfrac{1}{4}(1^2 + 2^2 + 3^2 + 4^2) - (2.5)^2 = 1.25, \\
v(2) &= \tfrac{1}{6}(1^2 + \cdots + 6^2) - (3.5)^2 = 2.917, \\
v &= \tfrac{1}{2}v(1) + \tfrac{1}{2}v(2) = 2.0835, \\
a &= \mathrm{Var}[\mu(\theta)] = \mathrm{E}\{[\mu(\theta)]^2\} - \{\mathrm{E}[\mu(\theta)]\}^2 = \tfrac{1}{2}[2.5^2 + 3.5^2] - 3^2 \\
&= 0.25, \\
k &= \frac{v}{a} = \frac{2.0835}{0.25} = 8.334, \\
Z &= \frac{1}{1 + 8.334} = 0.1071352.
\end{aligned}
$$

The credibility premium is $P_c = Z\bar{x} + (1 - Z)\mu = 0.1071352(4) + 0.8927648(3) = 3.10709$.

18.21 (a)
$$
\begin{aligned}
\mu(\theta) &= \theta, v(\theta) = \theta, \\
\mu &= \mathrm{E}(\theta) = \int_1^\infty 3\theta^{-3}\,d\theta = 1.5, \\
v &= \mathrm{E}(\theta) = 1.5, \\
a &= \mathrm{Var}(\theta) = \int_1^\infty 3\theta^{-2}\,d\theta - 2.25 = 0.75, \\
k &= 1.5/0.75 = 2, \\
Z &= \frac{2}{2 + 2} = 0.5, \\
P_c &= 0.5(10) + 0.5(1.5) = 5.75.
\end{aligned}
$$

(b) Because the support of the prior distribution is $\theta > 1$, that is also the support of the posterior distribution. Therefore, the posterior distribution is not gamma. $\pi(\theta|N_1 + N_2 = 20) \propto e^{-2\theta}\theta^{20}\theta^{-4} = e^{-2\theta}\theta^{16}$. The required constant is

$$\int_1^\infty e^{-2\theta}\theta^{16}d\theta = e^{-2}\left[\frac{1}{2} + \frac{17}{4} + \frac{17(16)}{8} + \cdots + \frac{16!}{2^{17}}\right] = 1,179,501,863e^{-2},$$

and the posterior distribution is $\pi(\theta|N_1+N_2 = 20) = e^{-2\theta}\theta^{16}/1,179,501,863e^{-2}$. The posterior mean is

$$\frac{\int_1^\infty \theta e^{-2\theta}\theta^{16}d\theta}{1,179,501,863e^{-2}} = 8.5.$$

The mean is actually slightly less than 8.5 (which would be the exact answer if integrals from zero to infinity were used to create a gamma posterior).

18.22 $Z = \frac{0.5}{0.5+k} = 0.5$, $k = 0.5$, $Z = \frac{3}{3+0.5} = 6/7$.

18.23 (a)

$$
\begin{aligned}
\Pr(X_1 = 1|A) &= 3(0.1^2)(0.9) = 0.027, \\
\Pr(X_1 = 1|B) &= 3(0.6^2)(0.4) = 0.432, \\
\Pr(X_1 = 1|C) &= 3(0.8^2)(0.2) = 0.384, \\
\Pr(A|X_1 = 1) &= 0.027/(0.027 + 0.432 + 0.384) = 27/843 = 9/281, \\
\Pr(B|X_1 = 1) &= 144/281, \\
\Pr(C|X_1 = 1) &= 128/281, \\
\mu(A) &= 3(0.9) = 2.7, \\
\mu(B) &= 3(0.4) = 1.2, \\
\mu(C) &= 3(0.2) = 0.6, \\
E(X_2|X_1 = 1) &= [9(2.7) + 144(1.2) + 128(0.6)]/281 = 0.97473.
\end{aligned}
$$

(b)
$$
\begin{aligned}
\mu &= (2.7 + 1.2 + 0.6)/3 = 1.5, \\
a &= (2.7^2 + 1.2^2 + 0.6^2)/3 - 2.25 = 0.78, \\
v(A) &= 3(0.9)(0.1) = 0.27, \; v(B) = 0.72, \; v(C) = 0.48, \\
v &= (0.27 + 0.72 + 0.48)/3 = 0.49, \\
k &= 49/78, \; Z = (1 + 49/78)^{-1} = 78/127, \\
P_c &= \frac{78}{127}(1) + \frac{49}{127}(1.5) = 1.19291.
\end{aligned}
$$

18.24 (a) $\quad \mu(\lambda) \;=\; \lambda,\; v(\lambda) = \lambda,$

$$\mu \;=\; E(\lambda) = \int_1^\infty 4\lambda^{-4}d\lambda = 4/3,$$

$$v \;=\; E(\lambda) = 4/3,$$

$$a \;=\; \text{Var}(\lambda) = \int_1^\infty 4\lambda^{-3}d\lambda - 16/9 = 2/9,$$

$$k \;=\; (4/3)/(2/9) = 6,\; Z = \frac{3}{3+6} = 1/3,$$

$$P_c \;=\; (1/3)(1) + (2/3)(4/3) = 11/9.$$

(b)

$$\mu \;=\; \int_0^1 \lambda d\lambda = 1/2,$$

$$v \;=\; \mu = 1/2,$$

$$a \;=\; \int_0^1 \lambda^2 d\lambda - 1/4 = 1/12,$$

$$k \;=\; (1/2)/(1/12) = 6,\; Z = \frac{3}{3+6} = 1/3,$$

$$P_c \;=\; (1/3)(1) + (2/3)(1/2) = 2/3.$$

18.25 $\mu(h) = h,\; \mu = E(h) = 2,\; v(h) = h,\; v = E(h) = 2,\; a = \text{Var}(h) = 2,$ $k = 2/2 = 1,\; Z = \frac{1}{1+1} = 1/2.$

18.26 (a) $r \sim \text{bin}(3, \theta),\; \pi(\theta) = 6\theta(1-\theta).$

$$\pi(\theta|X=1) \propto 3\theta(1-\theta)^2 6\theta(1-\theta) \propto \theta^2(1-\theta)^3,$$

and so the posterior distribution is beta with parameters 3 and 4. Then the expected next observation is $E(3\theta|X=1) = 3(3/7) = 9/7.$

(b) $\quad \mu(\theta) \;=\; 3\theta,\; v(\theta) = 3\theta(1-\theta),$

$$\mu \;=\; E(3\theta) = 3\int_0^1 \theta 6\theta(1-\theta)d\theta = 1.5,$$

$$v \;=\; E[3\theta(1-\theta)] = 3\int_0^1 \theta(1-\theta)6\theta(1-\theta)d\theta = 0.6,$$

$$a \;=\; \text{Var}(3\theta) = 9\int_0^1 \theta^2 6\theta(1-\theta)d\theta - 2.25 = 0.45,$$

$$k \;=\; 0.6/0.45 = 4/3,\; Z = (1+4/3)^{-1} = 3/7,$$

$$P_c \;=\; (3/7)(1) + (4/7)(1.5) = 9/7.$$

18.27 (a)

$$
\begin{aligned}
\mu(A) &= 20,\ \mu(B) = 12,\ \mu(C) = 10, \\
v(A) &= 416,\ v(B) = 288,\ v(C) = 308, \\
\mu &= (20 + 12 + 10)/3 = 14, \\
v &= (416 + 288 + 308)/3 = 337\tfrac{1}{3}, \\
a &= (20^2 + 12^2 + 10^2)/3 - 14^2 = 18\tfrac{2}{3}, \\
k &= 337\tfrac{1}{3}/18\tfrac{2}{3} = 18\tfrac{1}{14}, \\
Z &= (1 + 18\tfrac{1}{14})^{-1} = 14/267, \\
P_c &= (14/267)(0) + (253/267)(14) = 13.2659.
\end{aligned}
$$

(b)

$$
\begin{aligned}
\pi(A|X=0) &= 2/(2+3+4) = 2/9, \\
\pi(B|X=0) &= 3/9,\ \pi(C|X=0) = 4/9, \\
E(X_2|X_1=0) &= (2/9)20 + (3/9)12 + (4/9)10 = 12\tfrac{8}{9}.
\end{aligned}
$$

18.28 (a) $\Pr(N=0) = \int_1^3 e^{-\lambda}(0.5)d\lambda = (e^{-1} - e^{-3})/2 = 0.159046.$

(b)

$$
\begin{aligned}
\mu = v &= E(\lambda) = \int_1^3 \lambda(0.5)d\lambda = 2, \\
a &= \mathrm{Var}(\lambda) = \int_1^3 \lambda^2(0.5)d\lambda - 4 = 1/3, \\
k &= 2/(1/3) = 6,\ Z = \frac{1}{1+6} = 1/7, \\
P_c &= (1/7)(1) + (6/7)(2) = 13/7.
\end{aligned}
$$

(c) $\pi(\lambda|X_1=1) = e^{-\lambda}\lambda(.5)/\int_1^3 e^{-\lambda}\lambda(.5)d\lambda = e^{-\lambda}\lambda/(2e^{-1} - 4e^{-3}),$

$$
\begin{aligned}
E(\lambda|X_1=1) &= \int_1^3 e^{-\lambda}\lambda^2 d\lambda/(2e^{-1} - 4e^{-3}) \\
&= (5e^{-1} - 17e^{-3})/(2e^{-1} - 4e^{-3}) = 1.8505.
\end{aligned}
$$

18.29 (a)

$$
\begin{aligned}
\mu(A) &= (1/6)(4) = 2/3,\ \mu(B) = (5/6)(2) = 5/3, \\
v(A) &= (1/6)(20) + (5/36)(16) = 50/9, \\
v(B) &= (5/6)(5) + (5/36)(4) = 85/18, \\
\mu &= [(2/3) + (5/3)]/2 = 7/6, \\
v &= [(50/9) + (85/18)]/2 = 185/36, \\
a &= [(2/3)^2 + (4/3)^2]/2 - 49/36 = 1/4, \\
k &= (185/36)/(1/4) = 185/9, \\
Z &= \frac{4}{4 + 185/9} = 36/221.
\end{aligned}
$$

(b) $(36/221)(0.25) + (185/221)(7/6) = 1{,}349/1{,}326 = 1.01735.$

18.30
$$\begin{aligned} E(X_2) &= (1 + 8 + 12)/3 = 7 \\ &= E[E(X_2|X_1)] \\ &= [2.6 + 7.8 + E(X_2|X_1 = 12)]/3. \\ E(X_2|X_1 = 12) &= 10.6. \end{aligned}$$

18.31 (a) $X \sim \text{Poisson}(\lambda)$, $\pi(\lambda) = e^{-\lambda/2}/2$. The posterior distribution with three claims is proportional to $e^{-\lambda}\lambda^3 e^{-\lambda/2} = \lambda^3 e^{-1.5\lambda}$, which is gamma with parameters 4 and $1/1.5$. The mean is $4/1.5 = 2\frac{2}{3}$.

(b)
$$\begin{aligned} \mu(\lambda) &= v(\lambda) = \lambda, \\ \mu &= v = E(\lambda) = 2, \\ a &= \text{Var}(\lambda) = 4, \\ k &= 2/4 = 0.5, \ Z = \frac{1}{1 + 0.5} = \frac{2}{3}, \\ P_c &= \frac{2}{3}(3) + \frac{1}{3}(2) = \frac{8}{3} = 2\frac{2}{3}. \end{aligned}$$

18.32 (a) $r \sim \text{bin}(3, \theta)$, $\pi(\theta) = 2800\theta^3(1 - \theta)^4$, which is beta(4,5).
$$\pi(\theta|X = 2) \propto 3\theta^2(1 - \theta)2800\theta^3(1 - \theta)^4 \propto \theta^5(1 - \theta)^5,$$

and so the posterior distribution is beta with parameters 6 and 6. Then the expected next observation is $E(3\theta|X = 2) = 3(6/12) = 1.5.$

(b)
$$\begin{aligned} \mu(\theta) &= 3\theta, \ v(\theta) = 3\theta(1 - \theta), \\ \mu &= E(3\theta) = 3(4/9) = 4/3, \\ v &= E[3\theta(1 - \theta)] = 3 \int_0^1 \theta(1 - \theta)2800\theta^3(1 - \theta)^4 d\theta \\ &= 840\frac{\Gamma(5)\Gamma(6)}{\Gamma(11)} = 2/3, \\ a &= \text{Var}(3\theta) = 9 \int_0^1 \theta^2 2800\theta^3(1 - \theta)^4 d\theta - 16/9 \\ &= 2{,}520\frac{\Gamma(6)\Gamma(5)}{\Gamma(11)} - 16/9 = 2/9, \\ k &= (2/3)/(2/9) = 3, \\ Z &= (1 + 3)^{-1} = 1/4, \\ P_c &= (1/4)(2) + (3/4)(4/3) = 1.5. \end{aligned}$$

18.33 (a)

$$
\begin{aligned}
\mu(A_1) &= 0.15,\ \mu(A_2) = 0.05, \\
v(A_1) &= 0.1275,\ v(A_2) = 0.0475, \\
\mu &= (0.15 + 0.05)/2 = 0.1, \\
v &= (0.1275 + 0.0475)/2 = 0.0875, \\
a &= (0.15^2 + 0.05^2)/2 - 0.1^2 = 0.0025, \\
k &= 0.0875/0.0025 = 35, \\
Z &= \frac{3}{3 + 35} = 3/38.
\end{aligned}
$$

Thus, the estimated frequency is $(3/38)(1/3) + (35/38)(0.1) = 9/76$.

$$
\begin{aligned}
\mu(B_1) &= 24,\ \mu(B_2) = 34, \\
v(B_1) &= 64,\ v(B_2) = 84, \\
\mu &= (24 + 34)/2 = 29, \\
v &= (64 + 84)/2 = 74, \\
a &= (24^2 + 34^2)/2 - 29^2 = 25, \\
k &= 74/25, \\
Z &= \frac{1}{1 + 74/25} = 25/99.
\end{aligned}
$$

Thus, the estimated severity is $(25/99)(20) + (74/99)(29) = 294/11$.
The estimated total is $(9/76)(294/11) = 1323/418 = 3.1651$.

(b) Information about the various spinner combinations is given in Table 18.8

Table 18.8   Calculations for Exercise 18.33.

Spinners	μ	v
A_1, B_1	3.6	83.04
A_1, B_2	5.1	159.99
A_2, B_1	1.2	30.56
A_2, B_2	1.7	59.11

$$
\begin{aligned}
\mu &= (3.6 + 5.1 + 1.2 + 1.7)/4 = 2.9, \\
v &= (83.04 + 159.99 + 30.56 + 59.11)/4 = 83.175, \\
a &= (3.6^2 + 5.1^2 + 1.2^2 + 1.7^2)/4 - 2.9^2 = 2.415, \\
k &= 83.175/2.415 = 34.441,\ Z = \frac{3}{3 + 34.441} = 0.080126.
\end{aligned}
$$

Thus, the estimated total is $(0.080126)(20/3) + 0.919874(2.9) = 3.2018$.

(c) For part (a),

$$
\begin{aligned}
\Pr(1|A_1) &= 3(0.15)(0.85)^2 = 0.325125, \\
\Pr(1|A_2) &= 3(0.05)(0.95)^2 = 0.135375, \\
\Pr(A_1|1) &= \frac{0.325125}{0.325125 + 0.135375} = 0.706026, \\
\Pr(A_2|1) &= 1 - 0.706026 = 0.293974.
\end{aligned}
$$

Thus, the estimated frequency is $0.706026(0.15) + 0.293974(0.05) = 0.120603$.

$$
\begin{aligned}
\Pr(20|B_1) &= 0.8, \\
\Pr(20|B_2) &= 0.3, \\
\Pr(B_1|20) &= \frac{0.8}{0.8 + 0.3} = 8/11, \\
\Pr(B_2|20) &= 3/11.
\end{aligned}
$$

Thus, the estimated severity is $(8/11)(24) + (3/11)(34) = 26.727272$.
The estimated total is $0.120603(26.727272) = 3.2234$.
For part (b),

$$
\begin{aligned}
\Pr(0, 20, 0|A_1, B_1) &= (0.85)^2(0.12) = 0.0867, \\
\Pr(0, 20, 0|A_1, B_2) &= (0.85)^2(0.045) = 0.0325125, \\
\Pr(0, 20, 0|A_2, B_1) &= (0.95)^2(0.04) = 0.0361, \\
\Pr(0, 20, 0|A_2, B_2) &= (0.95)^2(0.015) = 0.0135375.
\end{aligned}
$$

The posterior probabilities are 0.51347, 0.19255, 0.21380, 0.08017, and the estimated total is

$$
0.51347(3.6) + 0.19255(5.1) + 0.21380(1.2) + 0.08017(1.7) = 3.2234.
$$

(d)

$$
\begin{aligned}
\Pr(X_1 = 0, \ldots, X_{n-1} = 0|A_1, B_1) &= (0.85)^{n-1}, \\
\Pr(X_1 = 0, \ldots, X_{n-1} = 0|A_1, B_2) &= (0.85)^{n-1}, \\
\Pr(X_1 = 0, \ldots, X_{n-1} = 0|A_2, B_1) &= (0.95)^{n-1}, \\
\Pr(X_1 = 0, \ldots, X_{n-1} = 0|A_2, B_2) &= (0.95)^{n-1}.
\end{aligned}
$$

$$
\begin{aligned}
&E(X_n|X_1 = 0, \ldots, X_{n-1} = 0) \\
&= \frac{(0.85)^{n-1}(3.6) + (0.85)^{n-1}(5.1) + (0.95)^{n-1}(1.2) + (0.95)^{n-1}(1.7)}{(0.85)^{n-1} + (0.85)^{n-1} + (0.95)^{n-1} + (0.95)^{n-1}} \\
&= \frac{2.9 + 8.7(0.85/0.95)^{n-1}}{2 + 2(0.85/0.95)^{n-1}},
\end{aligned}
$$

and the limit as $n \to \infty$ is $2.9/2 = 1.45$.

18.34
$$\Pr(X = 0.12|A) = \frac{1}{\sqrt{2\pi}(0.03)} \exp\left[-\frac{(0.12 - 0.1)^2}{2(0.0009)}\right] = 10.6483,$$

$\Pr(X = 0.12|B) = (X = 0.12|C) = 0$ (actually, just very close to zero), so $\Pr(A|X = 0.12) = 1$. The Bayesian estimate is $\mu(A) = 0.1$.

18.35 $E(X|X_1 = 4) = 2 = Z(4) + (1 - Z)(1)$, $Z = 1/3 = \frac{1}{1+k}$, $k = 2 = v/a = 3/a$, $a = 1.5$.

18.36 $v = E(v) = 8$, $a = \text{Var}(\mu) = 4$, $k = 8/4 = 2$, $Z = \frac{3}{3+2} = 0.6$.

18.37 (a)

$$f(y) = \int_0^\infty \lambda^{-1}e^{-y/\lambda}400\lambda^{-3}e^{-20/\lambda}d\lambda = 400\int_0^\infty \lambda^{-4}e^{-(20+y)/\lambda}d\lambda.$$

Let $\theta = (20 + y)/\lambda$, $\lambda = (20 + y)/\theta$, $d\lambda = -(20 + y)/\theta^2 d\theta$, and so

$$f(y) = 400\int_0^\infty (20 + y)^{-3}\theta^2 e^{-\theta}d\theta = 800(20 + y)^{-3},$$

which is Pareto with parameters 2 and 20, and so the mean is $20/(2-1) = 20$.

(b) $\mu(\lambda) = \lambda$, $v(\lambda) = \lambda^2$. The distribution of λ is inverse gamma with $\alpha = 2$ and $\theta = 20$. Then $\mu = E(\lambda) = 20/(2 - 1) = 20$ and $v = E(\lambda^2)$, which does not exist. The Bühlmann estimate does not exist.

(c) $\pi(\lambda|15, 25) \propto \lambda^{-1}e^{-15/\lambda}\lambda^{-1}e^{-25/\lambda}400\lambda^{-3}e^{-20/\lambda} \propto \lambda^{-5}e^{-60/\lambda}$, which is inverse gamma with $\alpha = 4$ and $\theta = 60$. The posterior mean is $60/(4-1) = 20$.

18.38
$$\begin{aligned}
\mu(\theta) &= \theta, \; v(\theta) = \theta(1 - \theta), \\
a &= \text{Var}(\theta) = 0.07, \\
v &= E(\theta - \theta^2) = E(\theta) - \text{Var}(\theta) - [E(\theta)]^2 \\
&= 0.25 - 0.07 - (0.25)^2 = 0.1175, \\
k &= 0.1175/0.07 = 1.67857, \\
Z &= \frac{1}{1 + 1.67857} = 0.37333.
\end{aligned}$$

18.39 (a) Means are 0, 2, 4, and 6 while the variances are all 9. Thus

$$
\begin{aligned}
\mu &= (0+2+4+6)/4 = 3, \\
v &= 9, \ a = (0+4+16+36)/4 - 3^2 = 5, \\
Z &= \frac{1}{1+9/5} = 5/14 = 0.35714.
\end{aligned}
$$

(b)(i) $v = 9$, $a = 20$, $Z = \frac{1}{1+9/20} = 20/29 = 0.68966$.

(b)(ii) $v = 3.24$, $a = 5$, $Z = \frac{1}{1+3.24/5} = 5/8.24 = 0.60680$.

(b)(iii) $v = 9$, $a = (4+4+100+100)/4 - 36 = 16$, $Z = \frac{1}{1+9/16} = 16/25 = 0.64$.

(b)(iv) $Z = \frac{3}{3+9/5} = 15/24 = 0.625$.

(b)(v) $a = 5$, $v = (9+9+2.25+2.25)/4 = 5.625$, $Z = \frac{2}{2+5.625/5} = 10/15.625 = 0.64$.
The answer is (i).

18.40 (a) Preliminary calculations are given in Table 18.9.

Table 18.9   Calculations for Exercise 18.40.

Risk	100	1,000	20,000	μ	v
1	0.5	0.3	0.2	4,350	61,382,500
2	0.7	0.2	0.1	2,270	35,054,100

$$
\begin{aligned}
\Pr(100|1) &= 0.5, \ \Pr(100|2) = 0.7, \\
\Pr(1|100) &= \frac{0.5(2/3)}{0.5(2/3) + 0.7(1/3)} = 10/17, \ \Pr(2|100) = 7/17.
\end{aligned}
$$

Expected value is $(10/17)(4350) + (7/17)(2,270) = 3,493.53$.

(b)
$$
\begin{aligned}
\mu &= (2/3)(4,350) + (1/3)(2,270) = 3,656.33, \\
v &= (2/3)(61,382,500) + (1/3)(35,054,100) = 52,606,366.67, \\
a &= (2/3)(4,350)^2 + (1/3)(2,270)^2 - 3,656.33^2 = 963,859.91, \\
k &= 54.579, \ Z = 1/55.579 = 0.017992.
\end{aligned}
$$

Estimate is $0.017992(100) + 0.982008(3,656.33) = 3,592.34$.

18.41 (a)
$$v(\mu, \lambda) = \mu(2\lambda^2) = 2\mu\lambda^2,$$
$$v = 2E(\mu\lambda^2) = 2E(\mu)[\mathrm{Var}(\lambda) + E(\lambda)^2]$$
$$= 2(0.1)(640{,}000 + 1{,}000^2)$$
$$= 328{,}000.$$

(b)
$$\mu(\mu, \lambda) = \mu\lambda,$$
$$a = \mathrm{Var}(\mu\lambda) = E(\mu^2\lambda^2) - E(\mu)^2 E(\lambda)^2$$
$$= [\mathrm{Var}(\mu) + E(\mu)^2][\mathrm{Var}(\lambda) + E(\lambda)^2] - E(\mu)^2 E(\lambda)^2$$
$$= (0.0025 + 0.1^2)(640{,}000 + 1{,}000^2) - 0.1^2 1{,}000^2$$
$$= 10{,}500.$$

18.42 For the Bayesian estimate,

$$\Pr(\lambda = 1 | X_1 = r) = \frac{\Pr(X_1 = r | \lambda = 1)\Pr(\lambda = 1)}{\begin{array}{l}\Pr(X_1 = r | \lambda + 1)\Pr(\lambda = 1)\\ + \Pr(X_1 = r | \lambda = 3)\Pr(\lambda = 3)\end{array}}$$

$$= \frac{\frac{e^{-1}}{r!}(0.75)}{\frac{e^{-1}}{r!}(0.75) + \frac{e^{-3}3^r}{r!}(0.25)} = \frac{0.2759}{0.2759 + 0.1245(3^r)}.$$

Then,

$$2.98 = \frac{0.2759}{0.2759 + 0.1245(3^r)}(1) + \frac{0.1245(3^r)}{0.2759 + 0.1245(3^r)}(3).$$

The solution is $r = 7$.

Because the risks are Poisson,

$$\mu = v = E(\lambda) = 0.75(1) + 0.25(3) = 1.5,$$
$$a = \mathrm{Var}(\lambda) = 0.75(1) + 0.25(9) - 2.25 = 0.75,$$
$$Z = \frac{1}{1 + 1.5/0.75} = 1/3,$$

and the estimate is $(1/3)(7) + (2/3)(1.5) = 3.33$.

18.43 For the Bayesian estimate,

$$\Pr(\theta = 8 | X_1 = 5)$$
$$= \frac{\Pr(X_1 = 5 | \theta = 8)\Pr(\theta = 8)}{\Pr(X_1 = 5 | \theta = 8)\Pr(\theta = 8) + \Pr(X_1 = 5 | \theta = 2)\Pr(\theta = 2)}$$
$$= \frac{(1/8)e^{-5/8}(0.8)}{(1/8)e^{-5/8}(0.8) + (1/2)e^{-5/2}(0.2)} = 0.867035.$$

Then,

$$E(X_2|X_1 = 5) = E(\theta|X_1 = 5) = 0.867035(8) + 0.132965(2) = 7.202.$$

For the Bühlmann estimate,

$$
\begin{aligned}
\mu &= 0.8(8) + 0.2(2) = 6.8, \\
v &= 0.8(64) + 0.2(4) = 52.8, \\
a &= 0.8(64) + 0.2(4) - 6.8^2 = 6.56, \\
Z &= \frac{1}{1 + 52.8/6.56} = 0.110512,
\end{aligned}
$$

and the estimate is $0.110512(5) + 0.889488(6.8) = 6.601$.

18.44 The posterior distribution is

$$\pi(\lambda|\mathbf{x}) \propto (e^{-\lambda})^{90}(\lambda e^{-\lambda})^7(\lambda^2 e^{-\lambda})^2(\lambda^3 e^{-\lambda})\lambda^3 e^{-50\lambda} = \lambda^{17} e^{-150\lambda}.$$

This is a gamma distribution with $\alpha = 18$ and $\theta = 150$. The estimate for one risk is the mean, $18(1/150) = 3/25$ and for 100 risks, it is $300/25 = 12$.

Because a Poisson model with a gamma prior is a case where the Bayes and Bühlmann estimates are the same, the Bühlmann estimate is also 12.

18.45 We have

$$
\begin{aligned}
\mu &= 0.6(2,000) + 0.3(3,000) + 0.1(4,000) = 2,500, \\
v &= 1,000^2, \\
a &= 0.6(2,000)^2 + 0.3(3,000)^2 + 0.1(4,000)^2 - 2,500^2 = 450,000, \\
Z &= \frac{80}{80 + \frac{1,000,000}{450,000}} = 0.97297, \\
\bar{x} &= \frac{24,000 + 36,000 + 28,000}{80} = 1,100,
\end{aligned}
$$

and the estimate is $0.97297(1,100) + 0.02703(2,500) = 1,137.84$.

18.46 For one year,

$$\pi(q|x_1) \propto q^{x_1}(1-q)^{8-x_1}q^{a-1}(1-q)^8 = q^{x_1+a-1}(1-q)^{16-x_1},$$

which is a beta distribution with parameters $x_1 + a$ and $17 - x_1$. The mean is the Bayesian estimate of q, and 8 times that value is the estimate of the expected number of claims in year 2. Then, $x_1 = 2$ implies

$$2.4344 = 8\frac{2+a}{17+a}$$

for $a = 5$. For two years,

$$\pi(q|x_1 = 2, x_2 = k) \propto q^2(1-q)^6 q^k (1-q)^{8-k} q^4 (1-q)^8 = q^{6+k}(1-q)^{22-k}.$$

Then,

$$3.73333 = 8\frac{7+k}{30}$$

for $k = 7$.

18.47 If $\rho = 0$, then the claims from successive years are uncorrelated, and hence the past data $\mathbf{x} = (X_1, \ldots, X_n)$ are of no value in helping to predict X_{n+1} so more reliance should be placed on μ. (Unlike most models in this chapter, here we get to know μ as opposed to only knowing a probability distribution concerning μ.) Conversely, if $\rho = 1$, then X_{n+1} is a perfect linear function of $\mathbf{x}$. Thus, no reliance need be placed on μ.

18.48 (a)

$$\begin{aligned}
\mathrm{E}\{[X_{n+1} - g(\mathbf{X})]^2\} &= \mathrm{E}\{[X_{n+1} - \mathrm{E}(X_{n+1}|\mathbf{X}) + \mathrm{E}(X_{n+1}|\mathbf{X}) - g(\mathbf{X})]^2\} \\
&= \mathrm{E}\{[X_{n+1} - \mathrm{E}(X_{n+1}|\mathbf{X})]^2\} \\
&\quad + \mathrm{E}\{[\mathrm{E}(X_{n+1}|\mathbf{X}) - g(\mathbf{X})]^2\} \\
&\quad + 2\mathrm{E}\{[X_{n+1} - \mathrm{E}(X_{n+1}|\mathbf{X})][\mathrm{E}(X_{n+1}|\mathbf{X}) - g(\mathbf{X})]\}.
\end{aligned}$$

The third term is

$$\begin{aligned}
2\mathrm{E}\{[X_{n+1} &- \mathrm{E}(X_{n+1}|\mathbf{X})][\mathrm{E}(X_{n+1}|\mathbf{X}) - g(\mathbf{X})]\} \\
&= 2\mathrm{E}(\mathrm{E}\{[X_{n+1} - \mathrm{E}(X_{n+1}|\mathbf{X})][\mathrm{E}(X_{n+1}|\mathbf{X}) - g(\mathbf{X})]|\mathbf{X}\}) \\
&= 2\mathrm{E}\{[\mathrm{E}(X_{n+1}|\mathbf{X}) - \mathrm{E}(X_{n+1}|\mathbf{X})][\mathrm{E}(X_{n+1}|\mathbf{X}) - g(\mathbf{X})]\} \\
&= 0,
\end{aligned}$$

completing the proof.

(b) The objective function is minimized when $\mathrm{E}\{[\mathrm{E}(X_{n+1}|\mathbf{X}) - g(\mathbf{X})]^2\}$ is minimized. If $g(\mathbf{X})$ is set equal to $\mathrm{E}(X_{n+1}|\mathbf{X})$, the expectation is of a random variable that is identically zero, and so is zero. Because an expected square cannot be negative, this is the minimum. But this is the Bayesian premium.

(c) Inserting a linear function, the mean-squared error to minimize is

$$\mathrm{E}\{[\mathrm{E}(X_{n+1}|\mathbf{X}) - \alpha_0 - \sum_{j=1}^{n} \alpha_j X_j]^2\}.$$

But this is (18.19), which is minimized by the linear credibility premium.

CHAPTER 19

19.1 SECTION 19.5

19.1

$$\bar{X}_1 = 733\tfrac{1}{3},\ \bar{X}_2 = 633\tfrac{1}{3},\ \bar{X}_3 = 900,\ \bar{X} = 755\tfrac{5}{9},$$

$$\hat{v}_1 = (16\tfrac{2}{3}^2 + 66\tfrac{2}{3}^2 + 83\tfrac{1}{3}^2)/2 = 5{,}833\tfrac{1}{3},$$

$$\hat{v}_2 = (8\tfrac{1}{3}^2 + 33\tfrac{1}{3}^2 + 41\tfrac{2}{3}^2)/2 = 1{,}458\tfrac{1}{3},$$

$$\hat{v}_3 = (0^2 + 50^2 + 50^2)/2 = 2{,}500,$$

$$\hat{v} = 3{,}263\tfrac{8}{9},$$

$$\hat{a} = \frac{1}{2}(22\tfrac{2}{9}^2 + 122\tfrac{2}{9}^2 + 144\tfrac{4}{9}^2) - 3{,}263\tfrac{8}{9}/3 = 17{,}060\tfrac{5}{27},$$

$$\hat{k} = 3{,}263\tfrac{8}{9}/17{,}060\tfrac{5}{27} = 0.191316,$$

$$Z = 3/(3 + 0.191316) = 0.94005.$$

The three estimates are

$$0.94005(733\tfrac{1}{3}) + 0.05995(755\tfrac{5}{9}) = 734.67,$$
$$0.94005(633\tfrac{1}{3}) + 0.05995(755\tfrac{5}{9}) = 640.66,$$
$$0.94005(900) + 0.05995(755\tfrac{5}{9}) = 891.34.$$

19.2
$$\begin{aligned}
\bar{X}_1 &= 45{,}000/220 = 204.55, \\
\bar{X}_2 &= 54{,}000/235 = 229.79, \\
\bar{X}_3 &= 91{,}000/505 = 180.20, \\
\hat{\mu} &= \bar{X} = 190{,}000/960 = 197.91.
\end{aligned}$$

$$\begin{aligned}
\hat{v} &= [100(4.55)^2 + 120(3.78)^2 + 90(18.68)^2 + 75(10.21)^2 + 70(13.07)^2 \\
&\quad +150(6.87)^2 + 175(8.77)^2 + 180(14.24)^2/(1+2+2) \\
&= 22{,}401, \\
\hat{a} &= \frac{\begin{array}{c}220(204.55 - 197.91)^2 + 235(229.79 - 197.91)^2 \\ +505(180.20 - 197.91)^2 - 22{,}401(2)\end{array}}{960 - (220^2 + 235^2 + 505^2)/960} = 617.54, \\
\hat{k} &= 36.27, Z_1 = 0.8585, Z_2 = 0.8663, Z_3 = 0.9330.
\end{aligned}$$

The estimates are

$$\begin{aligned}
0.8585(204.55) + 0.1415(197.91) &= 203.61, \\
0.8663(229.79) + 0.1337(197.91) &= 225.53, \\
0.9330(180.20) + 0.0670(197.91) &= 181.39.
\end{aligned}$$

Using the alternative method,

$$\hat{\mu} = \frac{0.8585(204.55) + 0.8663(229.79) + 0.9330(180.20)}{0.8585 + 0.8663 + 0.9330} = 204.32,$$

and the estimates are

$$\begin{aligned}
0.8585(204.55) + 0.1415(204.32) &= 204.50, \\
0.8663(229.79) + 0.1337(204.32) &= 226.37, \\
0.9330(180.20) + 0.0670(204.32) &= 181.81.
\end{aligned}$$

19.3 $\bar{X} = 475$, $\hat{v} = (0^2 + 75^2 + 75^2)/2 = 5{,}625$. With μ known to be 600, $\tilde{a} = (475 - 600)^2 - 5{,}625/3 = 13{,}750$, $\hat{k} = 5{,}625/13{,}750 = 0.4091$, $Z = 3/3.4091 = 0.8800$. The premium is $0.88(475) + 0.12(600) = 490$.

19.4 (a)
$$\begin{aligned}
\text{Var}(X_{ij}) &= \text{E}[\text{Var}(X_{ij}|\Theta_i)] + \text{Var}[\text{E}(X_{ij}|\Theta_i)] \\
&= \text{E}[v(\Theta_i) + \text{Var}[\mu(\Theta_i)] = v + a.
\end{aligned}$$

(b) This follows from (19.6).

(c)

$$\sum_{i=1}^{r}\sum_{j=1}^{n}(X_{ij}-\bar{X})^2 = \sum_{i=1}^{r}\sum_{j=1}^{n}(X_{ij}-\bar{X}_i+\bar{X}_i-\bar{X})^2$$

$$= \sum_{i=1}^{r}\sum_{j=1}^{n}(X_{ij}-\bar{X}_i)^2 + 2\sum_{i=1}^{r}\sum_{j=1}^{n}(X_{ij}-\bar{X}_i)(\bar{X}_i-\bar{X})$$

$$+ \sum_{i=1}^{r}\sum_{j=1}^{n}(\bar{X}_i-\bar{X})^2$$

$$= \sum_{i=1}^{r}\sum_{j=1}^{n}(X_{ij}-\bar{X}_i)^2 + 2\sum_{i=1}^{r}(\bar{X}_i-\bar{X})\sum_{j=1}^{n}(X_{ij}-\bar{X}_i)$$

$$+ n\sum_{i=1}^{r}(\bar{X}_i-\bar{X})^2$$

$$= \sum_{i=1}^{r}\sum_{j=1}^{n}(X_{ij}-\bar{X}_i)^2 + n\sum_{i=1}^{r}(\bar{X}_i-\bar{X})^2.$$

The middle term is zero because $\sum_{j=1}^{n}(X_{ij}-\bar{X}_i)=\sum_{j=1}^{n}X_{ij}-n\bar{X}_i=0$.

(d)

$$\mathrm{E}\left[\frac{1}{nr-1}\sum_{i=1}^{r}\sum_{j=1}^{n}(X_{ij}-\bar{X})^2\right]$$

$$= \mathrm{E}\left[\frac{1}{nr-1}\sum_{i=1}^{r}\sum_{j=1}^{n}(X_{ij}-\bar{X}_i)^2 + \frac{n}{nr-1}\sum_{i=1}^{r}(\bar{X}_i-\bar{X})^2\right].$$

We know that $\frac{1}{n-1}\sum_{j=1}^{n}(X_{ij}-\bar{X}_i)^2$ is an unbiased estimator of $v(\theta_i)$, and so the expected value of the first term is

$$\mathrm{E}\left[\frac{1}{nr-1}\sum_{i=1}^{r}\sum_{j=1}^{n}(X_{ij}-\bar{X}_i)^2\right]$$

$$= \mathrm{E}\left\{\mathrm{E}\left[\frac{1}{nr-1}\sum_{i=1}^{r}\sum_{j=1}^{n}(X_{ij}-\bar{X}_i)^2|\Theta_i\right]\right\}$$

$$= \mathrm{E}\left[\frac{n-1}{nr-1}\sum_{i=1}^{r}v(\Theta_i)\right] = \frac{r(n-1)}{nr-1}v.$$

For the second term note that $\mathrm{Var}(\bar{X}_i)=\mathrm{E}[v(\Theta_i)/n]+\mathrm{Var}[\mu(\Theta_i)]=v/n+a$ and $\frac{1}{r-1}\sum_{i=1}^{r}(\bar{X}_i-\bar{X})^2$ is an unbiased estimator of $v/n+a$. Then, for the second term,

$$
E\left[\frac{n}{nr-1}\sum_{i=1}^{r}(\bar{X}_i - \bar{X})^2\right] = \frac{n(r-1)}{nr-1}\left(\frac{v}{n}+a\right).
$$

Then the total is

$$
\frac{r(n-1)}{nr-1}v + \frac{n(r-1)}{nr-1}\left(\frac{v}{n}+a\right) = v + a - \frac{n-1}{nr-1}a.
$$

(e) Unconditionally, all of the X_{ij}s are assumed to have the same mean when in fact they do not. They also have a conditional variance that is smaller, and so the variance from $\bar{X}$ is not as great as it appears from (b).

19.5

$$
\begin{aligned}
E\left[\sum b_j(Y_j - \bar{Y})^2\right] &= E\left[\sum b_j(Y_j - \gamma + \gamma - \bar{Y})^2\right] \\
&= E\left[\sum b_j(Y_j - \gamma)^2 + \sum b_j(\gamma - \bar{Y})^2 \right. \\
&\quad \left. +2\sum b_j(Y_j - \gamma)(\gamma - \bar{Y})\right] \\
&= \sum b_j(a_j + \sigma^2/b_j) + b\operatorname{Var}(\bar{Y}) \\
&\quad +2E\left[\gamma\sum b_j Y_j - b\gamma^2 + b\gamma\bar{Y} - \bar{Y}\sum b_j Y_j\right].
\end{aligned}
$$

$$
\begin{aligned}
E\left[\gamma\sum b_j Y_j - b\gamma^2 + b\gamma\bar{Y} - \bar{Y}\sum b_j Y_j\right] &= E[\gamma b\bar{Y} - b\gamma^2 + b\gamma\bar{Y} - b\bar{Y}^2] \\
&= -E[b(\bar{Y} - \gamma)^2] \\
&= -b\operatorname{Var}(\bar{Y}).
\end{aligned}
$$

$$
\begin{aligned}
\operatorname{Var}(\bar{Y}) &= \frac{1}{b^2}\sum b_j^2 \operatorname{Var}(Y_j) = \frac{1}{b^2}\sum b_j^2(a_j + \sigma^2/b_j) \\
&= \frac{1}{b^2}\sum b_j^2 a_j + \frac{1}{b}\sigma^2.
\end{aligned}
$$

$$
\begin{aligned}
E\left[\sum b_j(Y_j - \bar{Y})^2\right] &= \sum b_j(a_j + \sigma^2/b_j) - b\operatorname{Var}(\bar{Y}) \\
&= \sum b_j(a_j + \sigma^2/b_j) - \frac{1}{b}\sum b_j^2 a_j - \sigma^2 \\
&= \sum a_j(b_j - b_j^2/b) + (n-1)\sigma^2.
\end{aligned}
$$

19.6 $\bar{X} = 333/2{,}787 = 0.11948 = \hat{v}$. The sample variance is $447/2{,}787 - 0.11948^2 = 0.14611$, and so $\hat{a} = 0.14611 - 0.11948 = 0.02663$. Then, $\hat{k} = 0.11948/0.02663 = 4.4867$ and $Z = 1/5.4867 = 0.18226$. The premiums are given in Table 19.1.

Table 19.1   Calculations for Exercise 19.6.

No. of claims	Premium
0	$0.18226(0) + 0.81774(0.11948) = 0.09770$
1	$0.18226(1) + 0.81774(0.11948) = 0.27996$
2	$0.18226(2) + 0.81774(0.11948) = 0.46222$
3	$0.18226(3) + 0.81774(0.11948) = 0.64448$
4	$0.18226(4) + 0.81774(0.11948) = 0.82674$

19.7 (a) See Appendix B.

(b)
$$a = \mathrm{Var}[\mu(\Theta)] = \mathrm{Var}(\Theta),$$
$$v = \mathrm{E}[v(\Theta)] = \mathrm{E}[\Theta(1+\Theta)],$$
$$\mu = \mathrm{E}[\mu(\Theta)] = \mathrm{E}(\Theta),$$
$$v - \mu - \mu^2 = \mathrm{E}(\Theta) - \mathrm{E}(\Theta^2) - \mathrm{E}(\Theta) - \mathrm{E}(\Theta)^2 = \mathrm{Var}(\Theta) = a.$$

(c)
$$\hat{\mu} = \bar{X} = 0.11948,$$
$$\hat{a} + \hat{v} = 0.14611,$$
$$\hat{a} = \hat{v} - 0.11948 - 0.11948^2,$$
$$\hat{a} - \hat{v} = -0.133755.$$

The solution is $\hat{a} = 0.0061775$ and $\hat{v} = 0.1399325$. Then

$$\hat{k} = 0.1399325/0.0061775 = 22.652$$

and $Z = 1/23.652 = 0.04228$. The premiums are given in Table 19.2

Table 19.2   Calculations for Exercise 19.7.

No. of claims	Premium
0	$0.04228(0) + 0.95772(0.11948) = 0.11443$
1	$0.04228(1) + 0.95772(0.11948) = 0.15671$
2	$0.04228(2) + 0.95772(0.11948) = 0.19899$
3	$0.04228(3) + 0.95772(0.11948) = 0.24127$
4	$0.04228(4) + 0.95772(0.11948) = 0.28355$

19.8

$$f_{\mathbf{x}_i}(\mathbf{x}_i) = \int_0^\infty \prod_{j=1}^{n_i} \left[\frac{(m_{ij}\theta_i)^{t_{ij}} e^{-m_{ij}\theta_i}}{t_{ij}!} \right] \frac{1}{\mu} e^{-\theta_i/\mu} d\theta_i$$

$$= \frac{1}{\mu} \left(\prod_{j=1}^{n_i} \frac{m_{ij}^{t_{ij}}}{t_{ij}!} \right) \int_0^\infty e^{-\theta_i(\mu^{-1}+m_i)} \theta_i^{t_i} d\theta_i$$

$$= \frac{1}{\mu} \left(\prod_{j=1}^{n_i} \frac{m_{ij}^{t_{ij}}}{t_{ij}!} \right) \frac{t_i!}{(\mu^{-1}+m_i)^{t_i+1}} \propto \mu^{-1}(\mu^{-1}+m_i)^{-t_i-1},$$

where $t_i = \sum_{j=1}^{n_i} t_{ij}$. Then the likelihood function is

$$L(\mu) \propto \mu^{-r} \prod_{i=1}^{r} (\mu^{-1} + m_i)^{-t_i - 1}$$

and the logarithm is

$$l(\mu) = -r \ln(\mu) - \sum_{i=1}^{r} (t_i + 1) \ln(\mu^{-1} + m_i)$$

and

$$l'(\mu) = -r\mu^{-1} - \sum_{i=1}^{r} (t_i + 1)(\mu^{-1} + m_i)^{-1}(-\mu^{-2}) = 0.$$

The equation to be solved is

$$r\mu = \sum_{i=1}^{r} \frac{t_i + 1}{\mu^{-1} + m_i}.$$

19.9 (a)

$$
\begin{aligned}
\sum_{i=1}^{r} \sum_{j=1}^{n_i} m_{ij}(X_{ij} - \bar{X})^2 &= \sum_{i=1}^{r} \sum_{j=1}^{n_i} m_{ij}(X_{ij} - \bar{X}_i + \bar{X}_i - \bar{X})^2 \\
&= \sum_{i=1}^{r} \sum_{j=1}^{n_i} m_{ij}(X_{ij} - \bar{X}_i)^2 \\
&\quad + 2 \sum_{i=1}^{r} \sum_{j=1}^{n_i} m_{ij}(X_{ij} - \bar{X}_i)(\bar{X}_i - \bar{X}) \\
&\quad + \sum_{i=1}^{r} \sum_{j=1}^{n_i} m_{ij}(\bar{X}_i - \bar{X})^2 \\
&= \sum_{i=1}^{r} \sum_{j=1}^{n_i} m_{ij}(X_{ij} - \bar{X}_i)^2 + \sum_{i=1}^{r} m_i(\bar{X}_i - \bar{X})^2.
\end{aligned}
$$

The middle term vanishes because $\sum_{j=1}^{n_i} m_{ij}(X_{ij} - \bar{X}_i) = 0$ from the definition of $\bar{X}_i$.

(b)
$$
\hat{a} = (m - m^{-1} \sum_{i=1}^{r} m_i^2)^{-1} \left[\sum_{i=1}^{r} \sum_{j=1}^{n_i} m_{ij}(X_{ij} - \bar{X})^2 \right.
$$

$$
\left. - \sum_{i=1}^{r} \sum_{j=1}^{n_i} m_{ij}(X_{ij} - \bar{X}_i)^2 - (r-1)\hat{v} \right]
$$

$$
= (m - m^{-1} \sum_{i=1}^{r} m_i^2)^{-1} \left[\sum_{i=1}^{r} \sum_{j=1}^{n_i} m_{ij}(X_{ij} - \bar{X})^2 \right.
$$

$$
\left. - \hat{v} \sum_{i=1}^{r} (n_i - 1) - (r-1)\hat{v} \right].
$$

Also

$$
m_* = \frac{\sum_{i=1}^{r} m_i \left(1 - \dfrac{m_i}{m} \right)}{\sum_{i=1}^{r} n_i - 1} = \frac{m - m^{-1} \sum_{i=1}^{r} m_i^2}{\sum_{i=1}^{r} n_i - 1}.
$$

Then

$$
\hat{a} = \frac{m_*^{-1}}{\sum_{i=1}^{r} n_i - 1} \left[\sum_{i=1}^{r} \sum_{j=1}^{n_i} m_{ij}(X_{ij} - \bar{X})^2 - \hat{v} \left(\sum_{i=1}^{r} n_i - 1 \right) \right]
$$

$$
= m_*^{-1} \left[\frac{\sum_{i=1}^{r} \sum_{j=1}^{n_i} m_{ij}(X_{ij} - \bar{X})^2}{\sum_{i=1}^{r} n_i - 1} - \hat{v} \right].
$$

19.10 The sample mean is $21/34$ and the sample variance is $370/340 - (21/34)^2 = 817/1{,}156$. Then, $\hat{v} = 21/34$ and $\hat{a} = 817/1{,}156 - 21/34 = 103/1{,}156$. $\hat{k} = (21/34)/(103/1{,}156) = 714/103$ and $Z = 1/(1 + 714/103) = 103/817$. The estimate is $(103/817)(2) + (714/817)(21/34) = 0.79192$.

19.11 The sample means for the three policyholders are 3, 5, and 4, and the overall mean is $\hat{\mu} = 4$. The other estimates are

$$
\hat{v} = \frac{1^2 + 0^2 + 0^2 + 1^2 + 0^2 + 0^2 + 1^2 + 1^2 + 1^2 + 1^2 + 1^2 + 1^2}{3(4-1)} = \frac{8}{9},
$$

$$
\hat{a} = \frac{(3-4)^2 + (5-4)^2 + (4-4)^2}{3-1} - \frac{8/9}{4} = \frac{7}{9},
$$

$$
Z = \frac{4}{4 + (8/9)/(7/9)} = \frac{7}{9}.
$$

The three estimates are $(7/9)(3)+(2/9)(4) = 29/9$, $(7/9)(5)+(2/9)(4) = 43/9$, and $(7/9)(4) + (2/9)(4) = 4$.

19.12 The estimate of the overall mean, μ, is the sample mean, per vehicle, which is $7/10 = 0.7$. With the Poisson assumption, this is also the estimate of v. Then,

$$\hat{a} = \frac{5(0.4 - 0.7)^2 + 5(1.0 - 0.7)^2 - (2 - 1)(0.7)}{10 - \frac{(5^2 + 5^2)}{10}} = 0.04,$$

$$Z = \frac{5}{5 + 0.7/0.04} = 2/9.$$

For insured A, the estimate is $(2/9)(0.4)+(7/9)(0.7) = 0.6333$, and for insured B, it is $(2/9)(1.0) + (7/9)(0.7) = 0.7667$.

19.13

$$\hat{\mu} = \hat{v} = \bar{x} = \frac{46(0) + 34(1) + 13(2) + 5(3) + 2(4)}{100} = 0.83,$$

$$s^2 = \frac{46(-0.83)^2 + 34(0.17)^2 + 13(1.17)^2 + 5(2.17)^2 + 2(3.17)^2}{99} = 0.95061,$$

$$\hat{a} = 0.95061 - 0.83 = 0.12061,$$

$$Z = \frac{1}{1 + 0.83/0.12061} = 0.12688.$$

The estimated number of claims in five years for this policyholder is $0.12688(3)+ 0.87312(0.83) = 1.10533$. For one year, the estimate is $1.10533/5 = 0.221$.

CHAPTER 20

CHAPTER 20 SOLUTIONS

20.1 SECTION 20.1

20.1 The first seven values of the cumulative distribution function for a Poisson(3) variable are 0.0498, 0.1991, 0.4232, 0.6472, 0.8153, 0.9161, and 0.9665. With $0.0498 \leq 0.1247 < 0.1991$, the first simulated value is $x = 1$. With $0.9161 \leq 0.9321 < 0.9665$, the second simulated value is $x = 6$. With $0.6472 \leq 0.6873 < 0.8153$, the third simulated value is $x = 4$.

20.2 The cumulative distribution function is

$$
F_X(x) = \begin{cases} 0.25x, & 0 \leq x < 2, \\ 0.5, & 2 \leq x < 4, \\ 0.1x + 0.1, & 4 \leq x < 9. \end{cases}
$$

For $u = 0.2$, solve $0.2 = 0.25x$ for $x = 0.8$. The function is constant at 0.5 from 2 to 4, so the second simulated value is $x = 4$. For the third value, solve $0.7 = 0.1x + 0.1$ for $x = 6$.

20.2   SECTION 20.2

20.3 Because $0.372 < 0.4$, the first value is from the Pareto distribution. Solve $0.693 = 1 - \left(\frac{100}{100+x}\right)^3$ for $x = 100\left[(1-0.693)^{-1/3} - 1\right] = 48.24$. Because $0.702 \geq 0.4$, the second value is from the inverse Weibull distribution. Solve $0.284 = e^{-(200/x)^2}$ for $x = 200[-\ln(0.284)]^{-1/2} = 178.26$.

20.4 For the first year, the number who remain employees is $\text{bin}(200, 0.90)$ and the inversion method produces a simulated value of 175. The number alive but no longer employed is $\text{bin}(25, 0.08/0.10 = 0.80)$ and the simulated value is 22. The remaning 3 employees die during the year. For year 2, the number who remain employed is $\text{bin}(175, 0.90)$ and the simulated value is 155. The number of them who are alive but no longer employed is $\text{bin}(20, 0.80)$ and the simulated value is 17, leaving 3 deaths. For the 22 who began the year alive but no longer employed, the number who remain alive is $\text{bin}(22, 0.95)$ and the simulated value is 21. At the end of year 2 there are 155 alive and employed, $17 + 21 = 38$ are alive but no longer employed, and $3 + 3 + 1 = 7$ have died. The normal approximation produces the same values in all cases. Also note that because the number in each state at time 1 was not required, an alternative is to determine the theoretical probabilities for time 2, given employed at time 0, as 0.81, 0.148, and 0.042 and then do a single simulation from this trinomial distribution.

$$
\begin{aligned}
\textbf{20.5}\, d &= \ln(0.3) = -1.204, \quad c = -3(-1.204) = 3.612, \\
\lambda_0 &= 3.612, \quad t_0 = -\ln(0.857)/3.612 = 0.0427, \\
\lambda_1 &= 3.612 - 1.204(1) = 2.408, \quad s_1 = -\ln(0.704)/2.408 = 0.1458, \\
t_1 &= 0.0427 + 0.1458 = 0.1885, \quad \lambda_2 = 3.612 - 1.204(2) = 1.204, \\
s_2 &= -\ln(0.997)/1.204 = 0.0025, \quad t_2 = 0.1885 + 0.0025 = 0.1910.
\end{aligned}
$$

Because $t_{m-1} = t_2 < 2$, the simulated value is $m = 3$.

$$
\begin{aligned}
\textbf{20.6} \quad x_1 &= 2(0.942) - 1 = 0.884, \quad x_2 = 2(0.108) - 1 = -0.784, \\
w &= (0.884)^2 + (-0.784)^2 = 1.396 \geq 1,
\end{aligned}
$$

and so these values cannot be used. Moving to the next pair,

$$
\begin{aligned}
x_1 &= 2(0.217) - 1 = -0.566, \quad x_2 = 2(0.841) - 1 = 0.682, \\
w &= (-0.566)^2 + (0.682)^2 = 0.78548 < 1.
\end{aligned}
$$

These values can be used. Then,

$$
\begin{aligned}
y &= \sqrt{-2\ln(0.78548)/0.78548} = 0.78410, \\
z_1 &= -0.566(0.78410) = -0.44380, \\
z_2 &= 0.682(0.78410) = 0.53476.
\end{aligned}
$$

The simulated lognormal values are $\exp[5+1.5(-0.44380)] = 76.27$ and $\exp[5+1.5(0.53476)] = 331.01$.

20.3 SECTION 20.3

20.7 The requested probability is the same as the probability that at least a of the observations are at or below $\pi_{0.9}$ and at most b are at or below $\pi_{0.9}$. The number of such observations has a binomial distribution with a sample size of n and a success probability of $\Pr(X \leq \pi_{0.9}) = 0.9$. Let N be this binomial variable. We want $0.95 = \Pr(a \leq N \leq b)$. From the central limit theorem,

$$0.95 = \Pr\left[\frac{a - 0.9n}{\sqrt{0.09n}} \leq Z \leq \frac{b - 0.9n}{\sqrt{0.09n}}\right],$$

and a symmetric interval implies

$$-1.96 = \frac{a - 0.9n}{\sqrt{0.09n}},$$

giving $a = 0.9n - 1.96\sqrt{0.9(0.1)n}$. Because a must be an integer, the result should be rounded down. A similar calculation can be done for b.

20.8 The mean and standard deviation are both 100. The analog of (20.1) is

$$\frac{0.02\mu}{\sigma/\sqrt{n}} = 1.645.$$

Substituting the mean and standard deviation produces $n = (1.645/0.02)^2 = 6{,}766$, where the answer has been rounded up for safety. For the probability at 200, the true value is $F(200) = 1 - \exp(-2) = 0.8647$. The equation to solve is

$$\frac{0.02(0.8647)}{\sqrt{0.8647(0.1353)/n}} = 1.645$$

for $n = 1{,}059$. When doing these simulations, the goal should be achieved 90% of the time.

20.9 The answer depends on the particular simulation.

20.10 The sample variance for the five observations is

$$\frac{(1-3)^2 + (2-3)^2 + (3-3)^2 + (4-3)^2 + (5-3)^2}{4} = 2.5.$$

The estimate is the sample mean and its standard deviation is $\sigma/\sqrt{n}$, which is approximated by $\sqrt{2.5/n}$. Setting this equal to the goal of 0.05 gives the answer, $n = 1000$.

20.4   SECTION 20.4

20.11 The inversion method requires a solution to $u = \Phi\left(\frac{x-15,000}{2,000}\right)$, where $\Phi(x)$ is the standard normal cdf. For $u = 0.5398$, the equation to solve is $\frac{x-15,000}{2,000} = 0.1$ for $x = 15,200$. After the deductible is applied, the insurer's cost for the first month is 5,200. The next equation is $-1.2 = \frac{x-15,000}{2,000}$ for $x = 12,600$ and a cost of 2,600. The third month's equation is $-3.0 = \frac{x-15,000}{2,000}$ for $x = 9,000$ and a cost of zero. The final month uses $0.8 = \frac{x-15,000}{2,000}$ for $x = 16,600$ and a cost of 6,600. The total cost is 14,400.

20.12 The equation to solve for the inversion method is $u = \Phi\left(\frac{\ln x - 0.01}{0.02}\right)$. When $u = 0.1587$, the equation is $-1 = \frac{\ln x - 0.01}{0.02}$ for $x = 0.99005$, and the first year's price is 99.005. For the second year, solve $1.5 = \frac{\ln x - 0.01}{0.02}$ for $x = 1.04081$, and the price is 103.045.

20.13 For this binomial distribution, the probability of no claims is 0.03424, and so if $0 \le u < 0.03424$, the simulated value is 0. The probability of one claim is 0.11751, and so for $0.03424 \le u < 0.15175$, the simulated value is 1. The probability of two 2 claims is 0.19962, and so for $0.15175 \le u < 0.35137$. Because the value of 0.18 is in this interval, the simulated value is 2.

20.14 For claim times, the equation to solve is $u = 1 - \exp(-x/2)$ for $x = -0.5\ln(1-u)$. The simulated times are 0.886, 0.388, and two more we don't need. The first claim is at time 0.886 and the second claim is after time 1, so there is only one claim in the simulated year. For the amount of that claim, the equation to solve is $0.89 = 1 - \left(\frac{1,000}{1,000+x}\right)^2$ for $x = 2,015$. At the time of the first claim, the surplus is $2,000 + 2,200(0.886) - 2,015 = 1,934.2$. Because ruin has not occurred, premiums continue to be collected for an ending surplus of $1,934.2 + 2,200(0.114) = 2,185$.

20.15 The empirical distribution places probability $1/2$ on each of the two points. The mean of this distribution is 2 and the variance of this distribution is 1. There are four possible bootstrap samples: (1,1), (3,1), (1,3), and (3,3). The value of the estimator for each is 0, 1, 1, and 0. The MSE is $(1/4)[(0 - 1)^2 + (1 - 1)^2 + (1 - 1)^2 + (0 - 1)^2] = 0.5$.

20.16 (a) The distribution function is $F(x) = x/10$ and so is 0.2, 0.4, and 0.7 at the three sample value. These are to be compared with the empirical values of 0, 1/3, 2/3, and 1. The maximum difference is 0.7 versus 1 for a test statistic of 0.3.

(b) Simulations by the authors produced an estimated p-value of 0.8882.

20.17 (a) The estimate is $4(7)/3 = 9.33$. The estimated MSE is $(28/3)^2/15 = 5.807$.

(b) There are 27 equally weighted bootstrap samples. For example, the sample 2, 2, 4 produces an estimate of $4(4)/3 = 5.33$ and a contribution to the MSE of $(5.33 - 8.0494)^2 = 7.3769$. Averaging the 27 values produces an estimated MSE of 4.146.

20.18 With $\rho = 0.6$, the matrix $L = \begin{bmatrix} 1 & 0 \\ 0.6 & 0.8 \end{bmatrix}$. For the first simulation, the inverse normals are 2.1201 and -0.1181. The correlated normals are 2.1201 and $0.6(2.1201) + 0.8(-0.1181) = 1.1776$. Next, apply the normal cdf to obtain the correlated uniform values 0.9830 and 0.8805. Finally, apply the Pareto and exponential inverse cdf functions to obtain the simulated loss of 28,891 and expenses of 850. The insured pays 500 of the loss, the insurer pays 10,000, and the reinsurer pays the remaining 18,391. The insurer's share of expenses is $(10,000/28,391)(850) = 299$ and the reinsurer pays 551. For the second simulation, the same calculations lead to a loss of 929 and expenses of 174. The total for the insured is 1,000, for the insurer is $10,000 + 299 + 429 + 174 = 10,902$, and for the reinsurer is $18,391 + 551 = 18,942$.

20.19 The extra step requires a simulated gamma value with $\alpha = 3$ and $\theta = 1/3$. With $u = 0.319$, the simulated value is 0.6613. Dividing its square root into the simulated normals gives $2.1201/0.6613^{1/2} = 2.6070$ and $1.1776/0.6613^{1/2} = 1.4480$. Using the normal cdf to make them uniform and the Pareto and exponential inverse cdfs, respectively, gives a loss of 50,272 and expense of 1,043. For the second simulation, the loss is 710 and the expense is 155. After dividing them up, the insured pays 1,000, the insurer pays $10,000 + 210 + 210 + 155 = 10,575$, and the reinsurer pays $39,772 + 833 = 40,605$.

20.20 The annual charges are simulated from $u = 1 - e^{-x/1,000}$ or $x = -1,000 \ln(1 - u)$. The four simulated values are 356.67, 2,525.73, 1,203.97, and 83.38. The reimbursements are 205.34 (80% of 256.67), 1,000 (the maximum), 883.18 (80% of 1,103.97), and 0. The total is 2,088.52 and the average is 522.13.

20.21 The simulated paid loss is $\exp[0.494\Phi^{-1}(u) + 13.294]$. The four simulated paid losses are 450,161, 330.041, 939,798, and 688,451, for an average of

602,113. The multiplier for unpaid losses is

$$0.801(2006-2005)^{0.851}e^{-0.747(2006-2005)} = 0.3795$$

for an answer of 228,502.

20.22 $0.95 = \Pr(0.95\mu < \bar{X} < 1.05\mu)$ and $\bar{X} \sim N(\mu, \sigma^2/n = 1.44\mu^2/n)$. Then,

$$
\begin{aligned}
0.95 &= \Pr\left(\frac{0.95\mu - \mu}{1.2\mu/\sqrt{n}} < Z < \frac{1.05\mu - \mu}{1.2\mu/\sqrt{n}}\right) \\
&= \Pr(-0.05\sqrt{n}/1.2 < Z < 0.05\sqrt{n}/1.2,
\end{aligned}
$$

and therefore $0.05\sqrt{n}/1.2 = 1.96$ for $n = 2{,}212.76$.

20.23 $F(300) = 1 - e^{-300/100} = 0.9502$. The variance of the estimate is $0.9502(0.0498)/n$. The equation to solve is

$$0.9502(0.01) = 2.576\sqrt{\frac{0.9502(0.0498)}{n}}.$$

The solution is $n = 3{,}477.81$.

20.24 There are 4 possible bootstrap samples for the 2 fire losses and 4 for the wind losses, making 16 equally likely outcomes. There are 9 unique cases, as follows. The losses are presented as the first fire loss, second fire loss, first wind loss, second wind loss.

Case 1: loss is $(3,3,0,0)$; total is 6; eliminated is 0; fraction is 0; square error is $(0 - 0.2)^2 = 0.04$; probability 1/16.

Case 2: loss is $(3,3,0,3)$; total 9; eliminated 2; fraction 0.22; error 0.0005; probability 2/16 [includes $(3,3,3,0)$].

Case 3: loss is $(3,3,3,3)$; total 12; eliminated 4; fraction 0.33; error 0.0178; probability 1/16.

Case 4: loss is $(3,4,0,0)$; total 7; eliminated 0; fraction 0; error 0.04; probability 2/16.

Case 5: loss is $(3,4,0,3)$; total 10; eliminated 2; fraction 0.2; error 0; probability 4/16.

Case 6: loss is $(3,4,3,3)$; total 13; eliminated 4; fraction 0.3077; error 0.0116; probability 2/16.

Case 7: loss is $(4,4,0,0)$; total 8; eliminated 0; fraction 0; error 0.04; probability 1/16.

Case 8: loss is $(4,4,0,3)$; total 11; eliminated 2; fraction 0.1818; error 0.0003; probability 2/16.

Case 9: loss is $(4,4,3,3)$; total 14, eliminated 4; fraction 0.2857; error 0.0073; probability 1.16.

The MSE is $[1(0.04) + 2(0.0005) + \cdots + 1(0.0073)]/16 = 0.0131$.

WILEY SERIES IN PROBABILITY AND STATISTICS
ESTABLISHED BY WALTER A. SHEWHART AND SAMUEL S. WILKS

Editors: *David J. Balding, Noel A. C. Cressie, Garrett M. Fitzmaurice, Harvey Goldstein, Iain M. Johnstone, Geert Molenberghs, David W. Scott, Adrian F. M. Smith, Ruey S. Tsay, Sanford Weisberg*
Editors Emeriti: *Vic Barnett, J. Stuart Hunter, Joseph B. Kadane, Jozef L. Teugels*

The *Wiley Series in Probability and Statistics* is well established and authoritative. It covers many topics of current research interest in both pure and applied statistics and probability theory. Written by leading statisticians and institutions, the titles span both state-of-the-art developments in the field and classical methods.

Reflecting the wide range of current research in statistics, the series encompasses applied, methodological and theoretical statistics, ranging from applications and new techniques made possible by advances in computerized practice to rigorous treatment of theoretical approaches.

This series provides essential and invaluable reading for all statisticians, whether in academia, industry, government, or research.

*Now available in a lower priced paperback edition in the Wiley Classics Library.
†Now available in a lower priced paperback edition in the Wiley–Interscience Paperback Series.

BEIRLANT, GOEGEBEUR, SEGERS, TEUGELS, and DE WAAL · Statistics of Extremes: Theory and Applications

BELSLEY · Conditioning Diagnostics: Collinearity and Weak Data in Regression

† BELSLEY, KUH, and WELSCH · Regression Diagnostics: Identifying Influential Data and Sources of Collinearity

BENDAT and PIERSOL · Random Data: Analysis and Measurement Procedures, *Fourth Edition*

BERNARDO and SMITH · Bayesian Theory

BERZUINI, DAWID, and BERNARDINELL · Causality: Statistical Perspectives and Applications

BHAT and MILLER · Elements of Applied Stochastic Processes, *Third Edition*

BHATTACHARYA and WAYMIRE · Stochastic Processes with Applications

BIEMER, GROVES, LYBERG, MATHIOWETZ, and SUDMAN · Measurement Errors in Surveys

BILLINGSLEY · Convergence of Probability Measures, *Second Edition*

BILLINGSLEY · Probability and Measure, *Anniversary Edition*

BIRKES and DODGE · Alternative Methods of Regression

BISGAARD and KULAHCI · Time Series Analysis and Forecasting by Example

BISWAS, DATTA, FINE, and SEGAL · Statistical Advances in the Biomedical Sciences: Clinical Trials, Epidemiology, Survival Analysis, and Bioinformatics

BLISCHKE and MURTHY (editors) · Case Studies in Reliability and Maintenance

BLISCHKE and MURTHY · Reliability: Modeling, Prediction, and Optimization

BLOOMFIELD · Fourier Analysis of Time Series: An Introduction, *Second Edition*

BOLLEN · Structural Equations with Latent Variables

BOLLEN and CURRAN · Latent Curve Models: A Structural Equation Perspective

BOROVKOV · Ergodicity and Stability of Stochastic Processes

BOSQ and BLANKE · Inference and Prediction in Large Dimensions

BOULEAU · Numerical Methods for Stochastic Processes

* BOX and TIAO · Bayesian Inference in Statistical Analysis

BOX · Improving Almost Anything, *Revised Edition*

* BOX and DRAPER · Evolutionary Operation: A Statistical Method for Process Improvement

BOX and DRAPER · Response Surfaces, Mixtures, and Ridge Analyses, *Second Edition*

BOX, HUNTER, and HUNTER · Statistics for Experimenters: Design, Innovation, and Discovery, *Second Editon*

BOX, JENKINS, and REINSEL · Time Series Analysis: Forcasting and Control, *Fourth Edition*

BOX, LUCEÑO, and PANIAGUA-QUIÑONES · Statistical Control by Monitoring and Adjustment, *Second Edition*

* BROWN and HOLLANDER · Statistics: A Biomedical Introduction

CAIROLI and DALANG · Sequential Stochastic Optimization

CASTILLO, HADI, BALAKRISHNAN, and SARABIA · Extreme Value and Related Models with Applications in Engineering and Science

CHAN · Time Series: Applications to Finance with R and S-Plus®, *Second Edition*

CHARALAMBIDES · Combinatorial Methods in Discrete Distributions

CHATTERJEE and HADI · Regression Analysis by Example, *Fifth Edition*

CHATTERJEE and HADI · Sensitivity Analysis in Linear Regression

CHERNICK · Bootstrap Methods: A Guide for Practitioners and Researchers, *Second Edition*

CHERNICK and FRIIS · Introductory Biostatistics for the Health Sciences

CHILÈS and DELFINER · Geostatistics: Modeling Spatial Uncertainty, *Second Edition*

CHOW and LIU · Design and Analysis of Clinical Trials: Concepts and Methodologies, *Second Edition*

CLARKE · Linear Models: The Theory and Application of Analysis of Variance

*Now available in a lower priced paperback edition in the Wiley Classics Library.

†Now available in a lower priced paperback edition in the Wiley–Interscience Paperback Series.

---

*Now available in a lower priced paperback edition in the Wiley Classics Library.

†Now available in a lower priced paperback edition in the Wiley–Interscience Paperback Series.

---

*Now available in a lower priced paperback edition in the Wiley Classics Library.

†Now available in a lower priced paperback edition in the Wiley–Interscience Paperback Series.

* HOAGLIN, MOSTELLER, and TUKEY · Understanding Robust and Exploratory Data Analysis

HOCHBERG and TAMHANE · Multiple Comparison Procedures

HOCKING · Methods and Applications of Linear Models: Regression and the Analysis of Variance, *Second Edition*

HOEL · Introduction to Mathematical Statistics, *Fifth Edition*

HOGG and KLUGMAN · Loss Distributions

HOLLANDER and WOLFE · Nonparametric Statistical Methods, *Second Edition*

HOSMER and LEMESHOW · Applied Logistic Regression, *Second Edition*

HOSMER, LEMESHOW, and MAY · Applied Survival Analysis: Regression Modeling of Time-to-Event Data, *Second Edition*

HUBER · Data Analysis: What Can Be Learned From the Past 50 Years

HUBER · Robust Statistics

† HUBER and RONCHETTI · Robust Statistics, *Second Edition*

HUBERTY · Applied Discriminant Analysis, *Second Edition*

HUBERTY and OLEJNIK · Applied MANOVA and Discriminant Analysis, *Second Edition*

HUITEMA · The Analysis of Covariance and Alternatives: Statistical Methods for Experiments, Quasi-Experiments, and Single-Case Studies, *Second Edition*

HUNT and KENNEDY · Financial Derivatives in Theory and Practice, *Revised Edition*

HURD and MIAMEE · Periodically Correlated Random Sequences: Spectral Theory and Practice

HUSKOVA, BERAN, and DUPAC · Collected Works of Jaroslav Hajek—with Commentary

HUZURBAZAR , Flowgraph Models for Multistate Time-to-Event Data

JACKMAN · Bayesian Analysis for the Social Sciences

† JACKSON · A User's Guide to Principle Components

JOHN · Statistical Methods in Engineering and Quality Assurance

JOHNSON · Multivariate Statistical Simulation

JOHNSON and BALAKRISHNAN · Advances in the Theory and Practice of Statistics: A Volume in Honor of Samuel Kotz

JOHNSON, KEMP, and KOTZ · Univariate Discrete Distributions, *Third Edition*

JOHNSON and KOTZ (editors) · Leading Personalities in Statistical Sciences: From the Seventeenth Century to the Present

JOHNSON, KOTZ, and BALAKRISHNAN · Continuous Univariate Distributions, Volume 1, *Second Edition*

JOHNSON, KOTZ, and BALAKRISHNAN · Continuous Univariate Distributions, Volume 2, *Second Edition*

JOHNSON, KOTZ, and BALAKRISHNAN · Discrete Multivariate Distributions

JUDGE, GRIFFITHS, HILL, LÜTKEPOHL, and LEE · The Theory and Practice of Econometrics, *Second Edition*

JUREK and MASON · Operator-Limit Distributions in Probability Theory

KADANE · Bayesian Methods and Ethics in a Clinical Trial Design

KADANE AND SCHUM · A Probabilistic Analysis of the Sacco and Vanzetti Evidence

KALBFLEISCH and PRENTICE · The Statistical Analysis of Failure Time Data, *Second Edition*

KARIYA and KURATA · Generalized Least Squares

KASS and VOS · Geometrical Foundations of Asymptotic Inference

† KAUFMAN and ROUSSEEUW · Finding Groups in Data: An Introduction to Cluster Analysis

KEDEM and FOKIANOS · Regression Models for Time Series Analysis

KENDALL, BARDEN, CARNE, and LE · Shape and Shape Theory

KHURI · Advanced Calculus with Applications in Statistics, *Second Edition*

KHURI, MATHEW, and SINHA · Statistical Tests for Mixed Linear Models

---

*Now available in a lower priced paperback edition in the Wiley Classics Library.

†Now available in a lower priced paperback edition in the Wiley–Interscience Paperback Series.

*Now available in a lower priced paperback edition in the Wiley Classics Library.

†Now available in a lower priced paperback edition in the Wiley–Interscience Paperback Series.

MARKOVICH · Nonparametric Analysis of Univariate Heavy-Tailed Data: Research and Practice

MARONNA, MARTIN and YOHAI · Robust Statistics: Theory and Methods

MASON, GUNST, and HESS · Statistical Design and Analysis of Experiments with Applications to Engineering and Science, *Second Edition*

McCOOL · Using the Weibull Distribution: Reliability, Modeling, and Inference

McCULLOCH, SEARLE, and NEUHAUS · Generalized, Linear, and Mixed Models, *Second Edition*

McFADDEN · Management of Data in Clinical Trials, *Second Edition*

* McLACHLAN · Discriminant Analysis and Statistical Pattern Recognition

McLACHLAN, DO, and AMBROISE · Analyzing Microarray Gene Expression Data

McLACHLAN and KRISHNAN · The EM Algorithm and Extensions, *Second Edition*

McLACHLAN and PEEL · Finite Mixture Models

McNEIL · Epidemiological Research Methods

MEEKER and ESCOBAR · Statistical Methods for Reliability Data

MEERSCHAERT and SCHEFFLER · Limit Distributions for Sums of Independent Random Vectors: Heavy Tails in Theory and Practice

MENGERSEN, ROBERT, and TITTERINGTON · Mixtures: Estimation and Applications

MICKEY, DUNN, and CLARK · Applied Statistics: Analysis of Variance and Regression, *Third Edition*

* MILLER · Survival Analysis, *Second Edition*

MONTGOMERY, JENNINGS, and KULAHCI · Introduction to Time Series Analysis and Forecasting

MONTGOMERY, PECK, and VINING · Introduction to Linear Regression Analysis, *Fifth Edition*

MORGENTHALER and TUKEY · Configural Polysampling: A Route to Practical Robustness

MUIRHEAD · Aspects of Multivariate Statistical Theory

MULLER and STOYAN · Comparison Methods for Stochastic Models and Risks

MURTHY, XIE, and JIANG · Weibull Models

MYERS, MONTGOMERY, and ANDERSON-COOK · Response Surface Methodology: Process and Product Optimization Using Designed Experiments, *Third Edition*

MYERS, MONTGOMERY, VINING, and ROBINSON · Generalized Linear Models. With Applications in Engineering and the Sciences, *Second Edition*

NATVIG · Multistate Systems Reliability Theory With Applications

† NELSON · Accelerated Testing, Statistical Models, Test Plans, and Data Analyses

† NELSON · Applied Life Data Analysis

NEWMAN · Biostatistical Methods in Epidemiology

NG, TAIN, and TANG · Dirichlet Theory: Theory, Methods and Applications

OKABE, BOOTS, SUGIHARA, and CHIU · Spatial Tesselations: Concepts and Applications of Voronoi Diagrams, *Second Edition*

OLIVER and SMITH · Influence Diagrams, Belief Nets and Decision Analysis

PALTA · Quantitative Methods in Population Health: Extensions of Ordinary Regressions

PANJER · Operational Risk: Modeling and Analytics

PANKRATZ · Forecasting with Dynamic Regression Models

PANKRATZ · Forecasting with Univariate Box-Jenkins Models: Concepts and Cases

PARDOUX · Markov Processes and Applications: Algorithms, Networks, Genome and Finance

PARMIGIANI and INOUE · Decision Theory: Principles and Approaches

* PARZEN · Modern Probability Theory and Its Applications

PEÑA, TIAO, and TSAY · A Course in Time Series Analysis

PESARIN and SALMASO · Permutation Tests for Complex Data: Applications and Software

PIANTADOSI · Clinical Trials: A Methodologic Perspective, *Second Edition*
POURAHMADI · Foundations of Time Series Analysis and Prediction Theory
POWELL · Approximate Dynamic Programming: Solving the Curses of Dimensionality, *Second Edition*
POWELL and RYZHOV · Optimal Learning
PRESS · Subjective and Objective Bayesian Statistics, *Second Edition*
PRESS and TANUR · The Subjectivity of Scientists and the Bayesian Approach
PURI, VILAPLANA, and WERTZ · New Perspectives in Theoretical and Applied Statistics
† PUTERMAN · Markov Decision Processes: Discrete Stochastic Dynamic Programming
QIU · Image Processing and Jump Regression Analysis
* RAO · Linear Statistical Inference and Its Applications, *Second Edition*
RAO · Statistical Inference for Fractional Diffusion Processes
RAUSAND and HØYLAND · System Reliability Theory: Models, Statistical Methods, and Applications, *Second Edition*
RAYNER, THAS, and BEST · Smooth Tests of Goodnes of Fit: Using R, *Second Edition*
RENCHER and SCHAALJE · Linear Models in Statistics, *Second Edition*
RENCHER and CHRISTENSEN · Methods of Multivariate Analysis, *Third Edition*
RENCHER · Multivariate Statistical Inference with Applications
RIGDON and BASU · Statistical Methods for the Reliability of Repairable Systems
* RIPLEY · Spatial Statistics
* RIPLEY · Stochastic Simulation
ROHATGI and SALEH · An Introduction to Probability and Statistics, *Second Edition*
ROLSKI, SCHMIDLI, SCHMIDT, and TEUGELS · Stochastic Processes for Insurance and Finance
ROSENBERGER and LACHIN · Randomization in Clinical Trials: Theory and Practice
ROSSI, ALLENBY, and McCULLOCH · Bayesian Statistics and Marketing
† ROUSSEEUW and LEROY · Robust Regression and Outlier Detection
ROYSTON and SAUERBREI · Multivariate Model Building: A Pragmatic Approach to Regression Analysis Based on Fractional Polynomials for Modeling Continuous Variables
* RUBIN · Multiple Imputation for Nonresponse in Surveys
RUBINSTEIN and KROESE · Simulation and the Monte Carlo Method, *Second Edition*
RUBINSTEIN and MELAMED · Modern Simulation and Modeling
RYAN · Modern Engineering Statistics
RYAN · Modern Experimental Design
RYAN · Modern Regression Methods, *Second Edition*
RYAN · Statistical Methods for Quality Improvement, *Third Edition*
SALEH · Theory of Preliminary Test and Stein-Type Estimation with Applications
SALTELLI, CHAN, and SCOTT (editors) · Sensitivity Analysis
SCHERER · Batch Effects and Noise in Microarray Experiments: Sources and Solutions
* SCHEFFE · The Analysis of Variance
SCHIMEK · Smoothing and Regression: Approaches, Computation, and Application
SCHOTT · Matrix Analysis for Statistics, *Second Edition*
SCHOUTENS · Levy Processes in Finance: Pricing Financial Derivatives
SCOTT · Multivariate Density Estimation: Theory, Practice, and Visualization
* SEARLE · Linear Models
† SEARLE · Linear Models for Unbalanced Data
† SEARLE · Matrix Algebra Useful for Statistics
† SEARLE, CASELLA, and McCULLOCH · Variance Components
SEARLE and WILLETT · Matrix Algebra for Applied Economics
SEBER · A Matrix Handbook For Statisticians
† SEBER · Multivariate Observations
SEBER and LEE · Linear Regression Analysis, *Second Edition*

*Now available in a lower priced paperback edition in the Wiley Classics Library.
†Now available in a lower priced paperback edition in the Wiley–Interscience Paperback Series.

† SEBER and WILD · Nonlinear Regression

SENNOTT · Stochastic Dynamic Programming and the Control of Queueing Systems

* SERFLING · Approximation Theorems of Mathematical Statistics

SHAFER and VOVK · Probability and Finance: It's Only a Game!

SHERMAN · Spatial Statistics and Spatio-Temporal Data: Covariance Functions and Directional Properties

SILVAPULLE and SEN · Constrained Statistical Inference: Inequality, Order, and Shape Restrictions

SINGPURWALLA · Reliability and Risk: A Bayesian Perspective

SMALL and McLEISH · Hilbert Space Methods in Probability and Statistical Inference

SRIVASTAVA · Methods of Multivariate Statistics

STAPLETON · Linear Statistical Models, *Second Edition*

STAPLETON · Models for Probability and Statistical Inference: Theory and Applications

STAUDTE and SHEATHER · Robust Estimation and Testing

STOYAN · Counterexamples in Probability, *Second Edition*

STOYAN, KENDALL, and MECKE · Stochastic Geometry and Its Applications, *Second Edition*

STOYAN and STOYAN · Fractals, Random Shapes and Point Fields: Methods of Geometrical Statistics

STREET and BURGESS · The Construction of Optimal Stated Choice Experiments: Theory and Methods

STYAN · The Collected Papers of T. W. Anderson: 1943–1985

SUTTON, ABRAMS, JONES, SHELDON, and SONG · Methods for Meta-Analysis in Medical Research

TAKEZAWA · Introduction to Nonparametric Regression

TAMHANE · Statistical Analysis of Designed Experiments: Theory and Applications

TANAKA · Time Series Analysis: Nonstationary and Noninvertible Distribution Theory

THOMPSON · Empirical Model Building: Data, Models, and Reality, *Second Edition*

THOMPSON · Sampling, *Third Edition*

THOMPSON · Simulation: A Modeler's Approach

THOMPSON and SEBER · Adaptive Sampling

THOMPSON, WILLIAMS, and FINDLAY · Models for Investors in Real World Markets

TIERNEY · LISP-STAT: An Object-Oriented Environment for Statistical Computing and Dynamic Graphics

TSAY · Analysis of Financial Time Series, *Third Edition*

TSAY · An Introduction to Analysis of Financial Data with R

UPTON and FINGLETON · Spatial Data Analysis by Example, Volume II: Categorical and Directional Data

† VAN BELLE · Statistical Rules of Thumb, *Second Edition*

VAN BELLE, FISHER, HEAGERTY, and LUMLEY · Biostatistics: A Methodology for the Health Sciences, *Second Edition*

VESTRUP · The Theory of Measures and Integration

VIDAKOVIC · Statistical Modeling by Wavelets

VIERTL · Statistical Methods for Fuzzy Data

VINOD and REAGLE · Preparing for the Worst: Incorporating Downside Risk in Stock Market Investments

WALLER and GOTWAY · Applied Spatial Statistics for Public Health Data

WEISBERG · Applied Linear Regression, *Third Edition*

WEISBERG · Bias and Causation: Models and Judgment for Valid Comparisons

WELSH · Aspects of Statistical Inference

WESTFALL and YOUNG · Resampling-Based Multiple Testing: Examples and Methods for p-Value Adjustment

*Now available in a lower priced paperback edition in the Wiley Classics Library.

†Now available in a lower priced paperback edition in the Wiley–Interscience Paperback Series.

*Now available in a lower priced paperback edition in the Wiley Classics Library.

†Now available in a lower priced paperback edition in the Wiley–Interscience Paperback Series.

Printed in the United States of America
ED-09-12-12